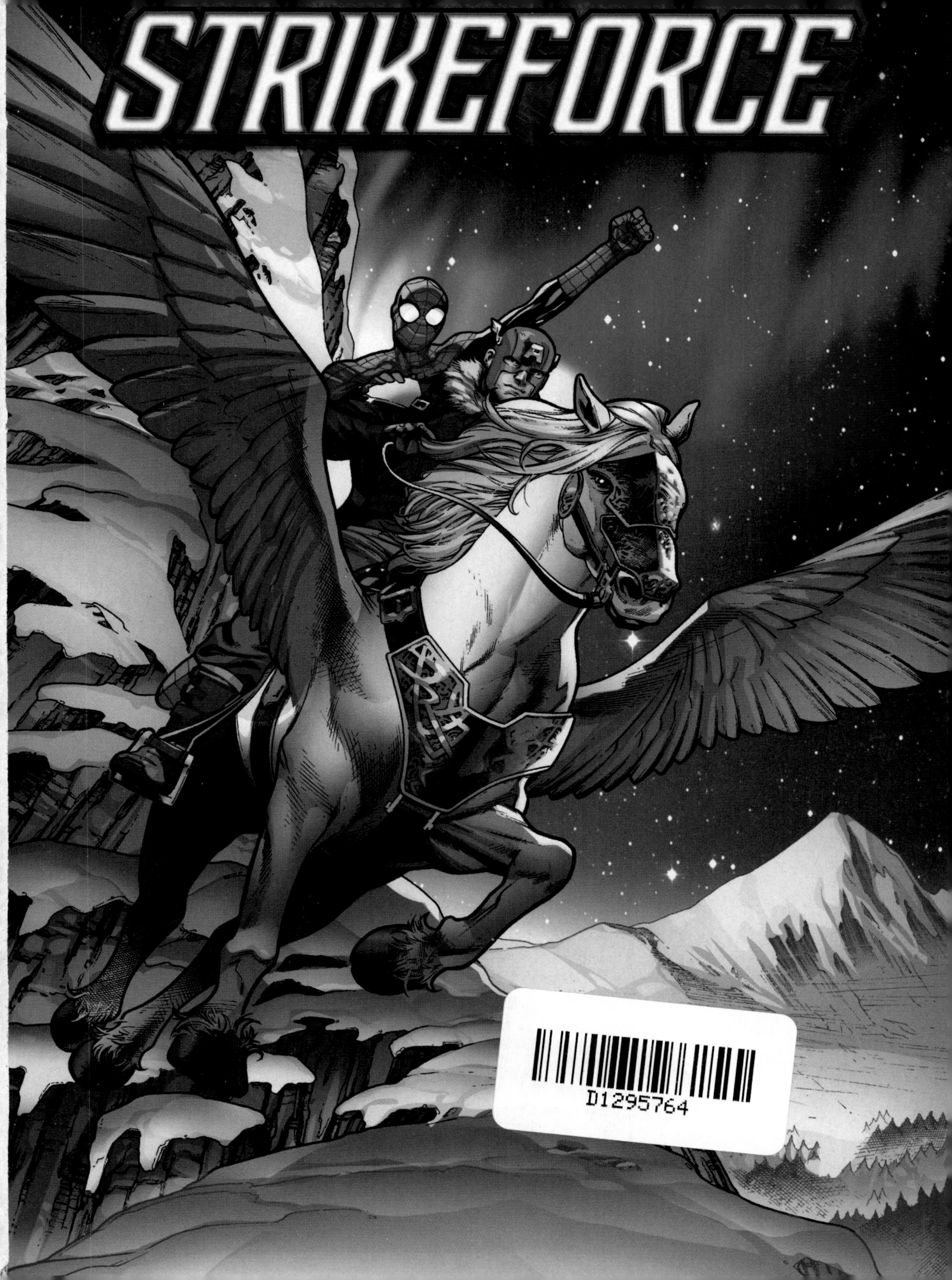
STRIKEFORCE

THE WAR OF THE REALMS

After laying waste to nine of the Ten Realms, the Dark Elf
King Malekith and his powerful allies have finally brought the
War of the Realms to Midgard — the last realm standing!

Earth's heroes assembled to fight back against
Malekith's invasion, but they were quickly overpowered
and retreated to Avengers Mountain.

COLLECTION EDITOR **JENNIFER GRÜNWALD**   **CAITLIN O'CONNELL** ASSISTANT EDITOR
ASSOCIATE MANAGING EDITOR **KATERI WOODY**   **MARK D. BEAZLEY** EDITOR, SPECIAL PROJECTS
VP PRODUCTION & SPECIAL PROJECTS **JEFF YOUNGQUIST**   **JAY BOWEN** BOOK DESIGNER

SVP PRINT, SALES & MARKETING **DAVID GABRIEL**   **SVEN LARSEN** DIRECTOR, LICENSED PUBLISHING
EDITOR IN CHIEF **C.B. CEBULSKI**   **JOE QUESADA** CHIEF CREATIVE OFFICER
PRESIDENT **DAN BUCKLEY**   **ALAN FINE** EXECUTIVE PRODUCER

WAR OF THE REALMS STRIKEFORCE. Contains material originally published in magazine form as WAR OF THE REALMS STRIKEFORCE: THE LAND OF THE GIANTS #1, WAR OF THE REALMS STRIKEFORCE: THE DARK ELF REALM #1 and WAR OF THE REALMS STRIKEFORCE: THE WAR AVENGERS #1. First printing 2019. ISBN 978-1-302-91855-2. Published by MARVEL WORLDWIDE, INC., a subsidiary of MARVEL ENTERTAINMENT, LLC. OFFICE OF PUBLICATION: 135 West 50th Street, New York, NY 10020. © 2019 MARVEL No similarity between any of the names, characters, persons, and/or institutions in this magazine with those of any living or dead person or institution is intended, and any such similarity which may exist is purely coincidental. **Printed in the U.S.A.** DAN BUCKLEY, President, Marvel Entertainment; JOHN NEE, Publisher; JOE QUESADA, Chief Creative Officer; TOM BREVOORT, SVP of Publishing; DAVID BOGART, Associate Publisher & SVP of Talent Affairs; DAVID GABRIEL, SVP of Sales & Marketing, Publishing; JEFF YOUNGQUIST, VP of Production & Special Projects; DAN CARR, Executive Director of Publishing Technology; ALEX MORALES, Director of Publishing Operations; DAN EDINGTON, Managing Editor; SUSAN CRESPI, Production Manager; STAN LEE, Chairman Emeritus. For information regarding advertising in Marvel Comics or on Marvel.com, please contact Vit DeBellis, Custom Solutions & Integrated Advertising Manager, at vdebellis@marvel.com. For Marvel subscription inquiries, please call 888-511-5480. Manufactured between 6/28/2019 and 7/29/2019 by LSC COMMUNICATIONS INC., KENDALLVILLE, IN, USA.

STRIKEFORCE

**Bryan Hill, Tom Taylor
& Dennis "Hopeless" Hallum**
WRITERS

**Leinil Francis Yu, Jorge Molina,
Kim Jacinto & Ario Anindito**
PENCILERS

**Gerry Alanguilan, Adriano Di Benedetto,
Kim Jacinto & Ario Anindito**
INKERS

**Matt Hollingsworth, David Curiel,
Java Tartaglia & Felipe Sobreiro**
COLORISTS

VC's Joe Sabino
LETTERER

Leinil Francis Yu & Matt Hollingsworth;
Cully Hamner & Morry Hollowell;
AND Kim Jacinto & Matt Hollingsworth
COVER ART

Sarah Brunstad
ASSOCIATE EDITOR

Wil Moss
EDITOR

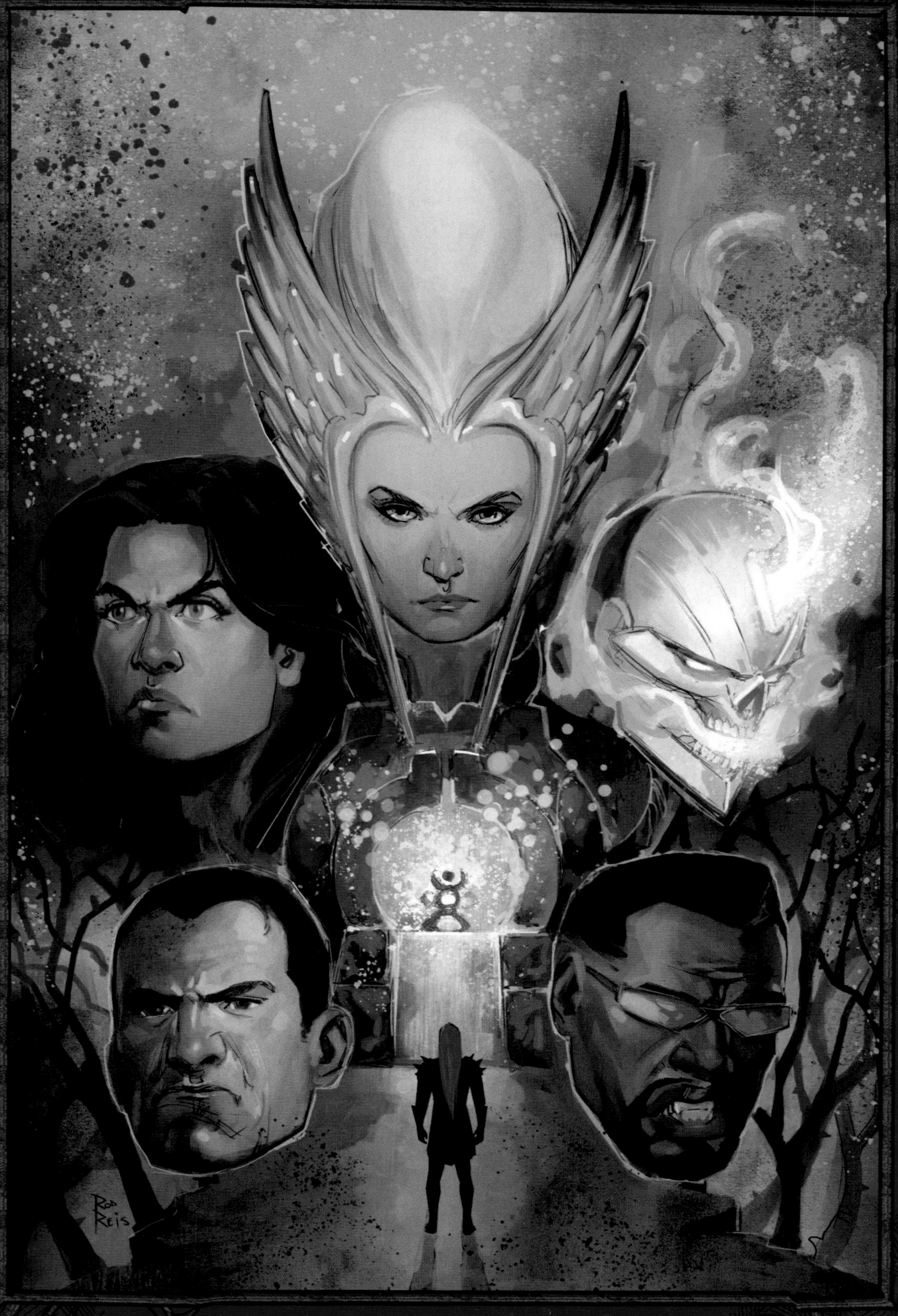
ROD REIS
THE DARK ELF REALM VARIANT BY Rod Reis

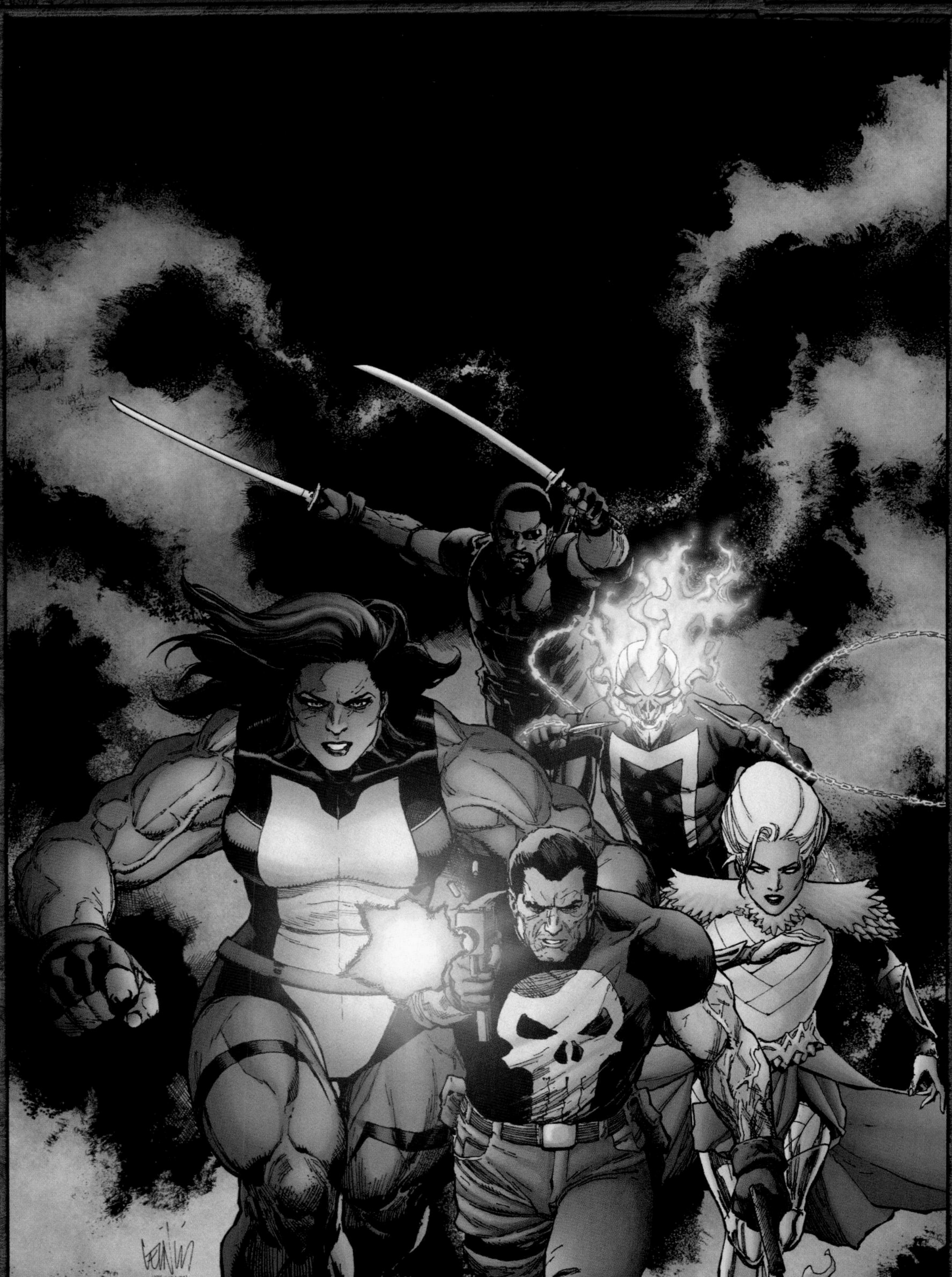

The Dark Elf Realm

The war has already spread across the globe thanks to the Black Bifrost, Malekith's corrupted version of the Rainbow Bridge, located in his home realm of Svartalfheim.

If the heroes and Asgardians are going to reclaim Earth, the Black Bifrost must fall. With Thor trapped in Jotunheim and Odin grievously injured, it is up to Thor's mother, Lady Freyja, to take on the mission. But she will not go alone...

THE WAR OF THE REALMS

STRIKEFORCE

THE DARK ELF REALM

written by
BRYAN HILL

penciled by
LEINIL FRANCIS YU

inked by
GERRY ALANGUILAN

colored by
MATT HOLLINGSWORTH

lettered by
VC's JOE SABINO

cover artists
LEINIL FRANCIS YU & MATT HOLLINGSWORTH

variant cover artist
ROD REIS

SARAH BRUNSTAD
associate editor

WIL MOSS
editor

Note: Read WAR OF THE REALMS #1-3 before this issue.

TOM BREVOORT   C.B. CEBULSKI   JOE QUESADA   DAN BUCKLEY   ALAN FINE
executive editor   editor in chief   chief creative officer   president   executive producer

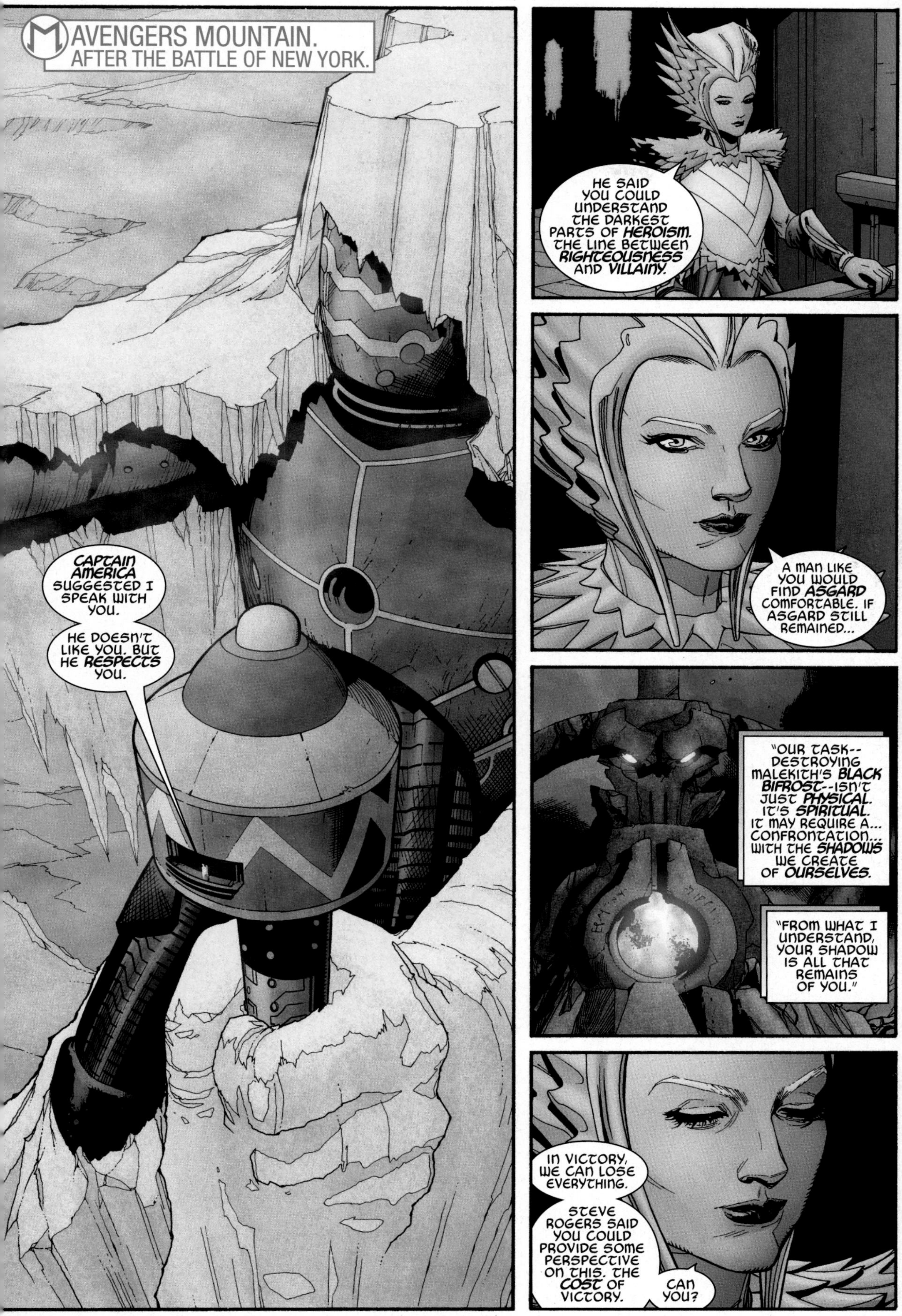
AVENGERS MOUNTAIN.
AFTER THE BATTLE OF NEW YORK.
CAPTAIN AMERICA SUGGESTED I SPEAK WITH YOU.
HE DOESN'T LIKE YOU. BUT HE RESPECTS YOU.
HE SAID YOU COULD UNDERSTAND THE DARKEST PARTS OF HEROISM. THE LINE BETWEEN RIGHTEOUSNESS AND VILLAINY.
A MAN LIKE YOU WOULD FIND ASGARD COMFORTABLE. IF ASGARD STILL REMAINED...
"OUR TASK--DESTROYING MALEKITH'S BLACK BIFROST--ISN'T JUST PHYSICAL. IT'S SPIRITUAL. IT MAY REQUIRE A... CONFRONTATION... WITH THE SHADOWS WE CREATE OF OURSELVES.
"FROM WHAT I UNDERSTAND, YOUR SHADOW IS ALL THAT REMAINS OF YOU."
IN VICTORY, WE CAN LOSE EVERYTHING.
STEVE ROGERS SAID YOU COULD PROVIDE SOME PERSPECTIVE ON THIS. THE COST OF VICTORY.
CAN YOU?

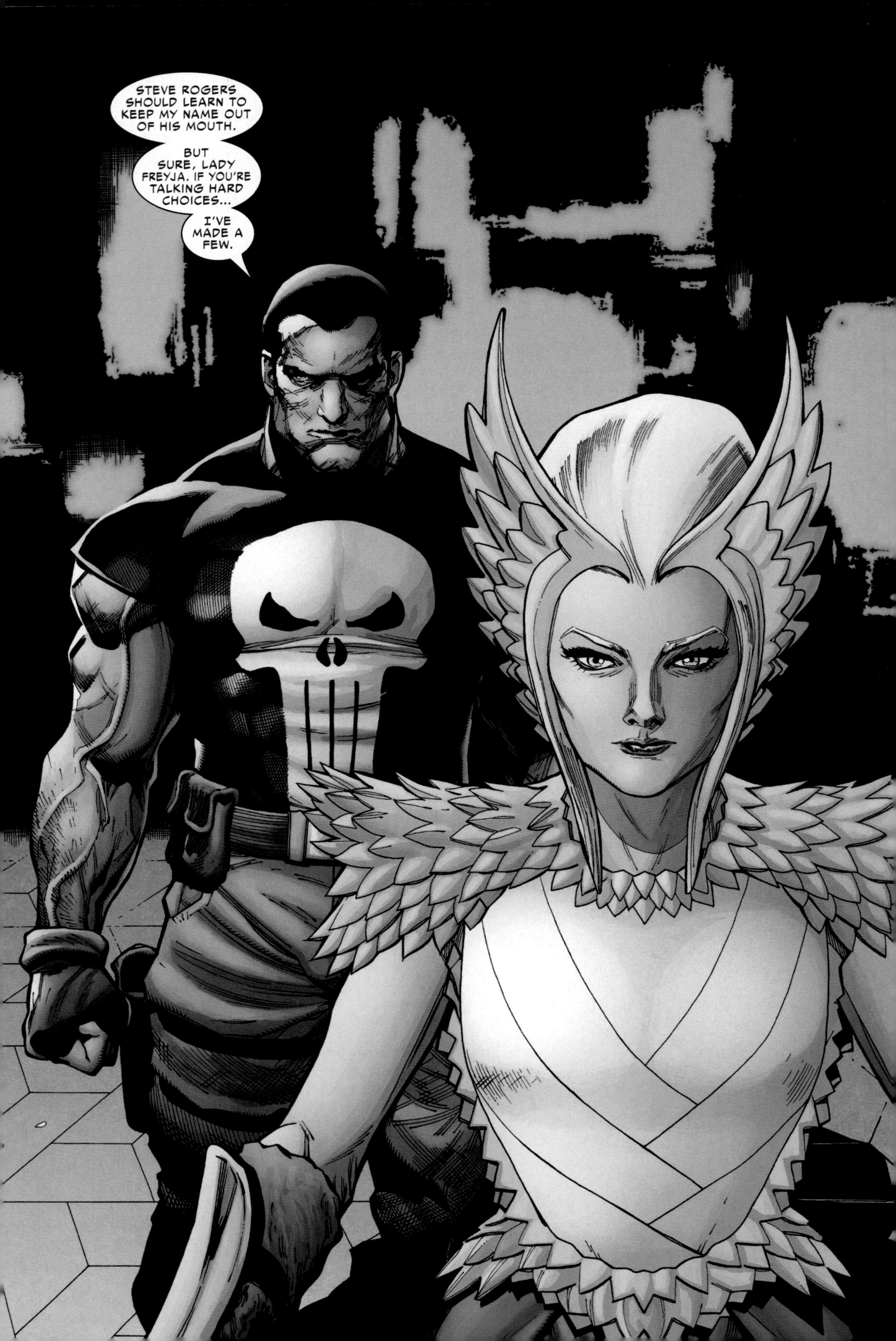

STEVE ROGERS SHOULD LEARN TO KEEP MY NAME OUT OF HIS MOUTH.
BUT SURE, LADY FREYJA. IF YOU'RE TALKING HARD CHOICES...
I'VE MADE A FEW.

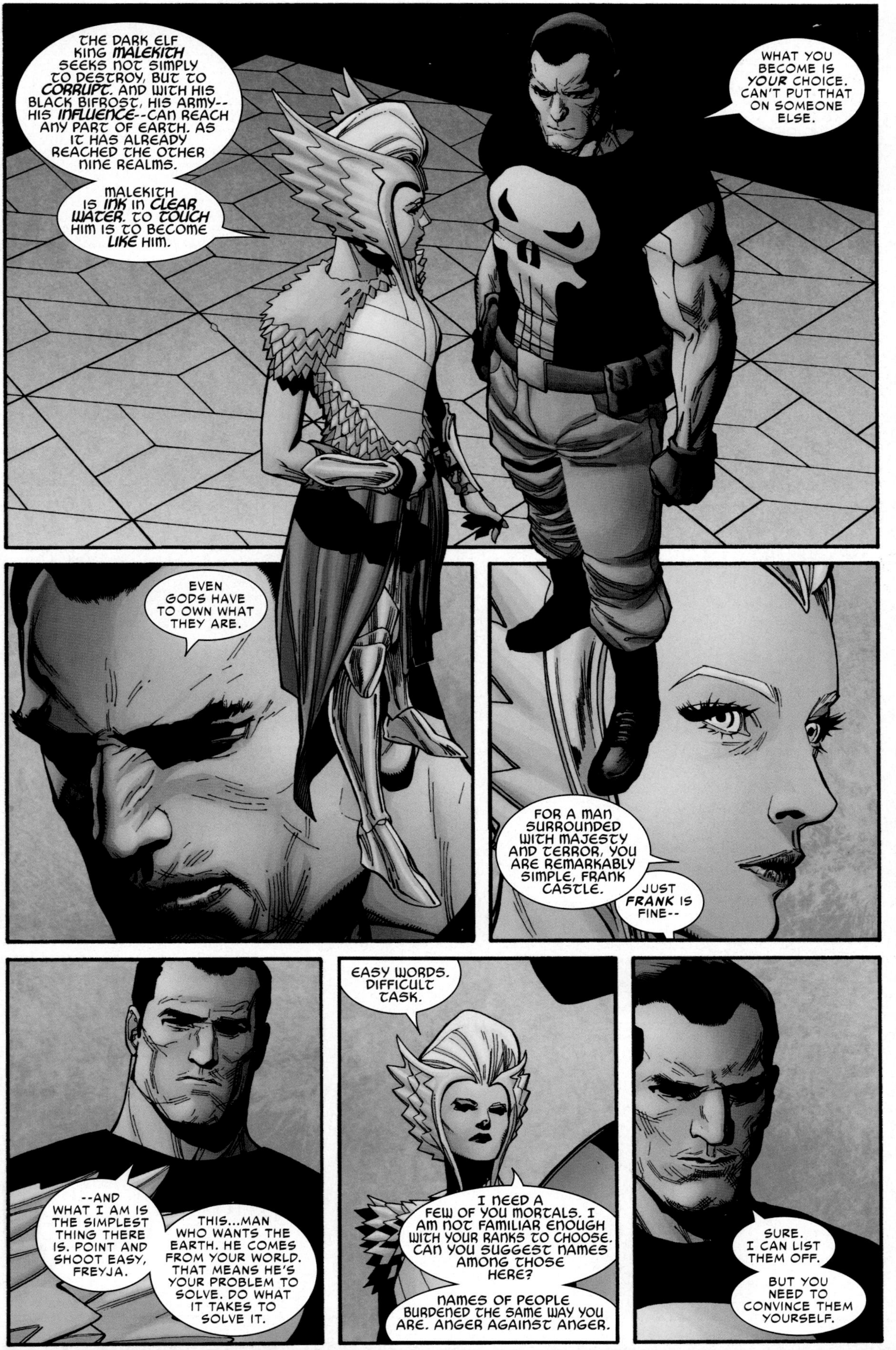
THE DARK ELF KING MALEKITH SEEKS NOT SIMPLY TO DESTROY, BUT TO CORRUPT. AND WITH HIS BLACK BIFROST, HIS ARMY--HIS INFLUENCE--CAN REACH ANY PART OF EARTH. AS IT HAS ALREADY REACHED THE OTHER NINE REALMS.
MALEKITH IS INK IN CLEAR WATER. TO TOUCH HIM IS TO BECOME LIKE HIM.
WHAT YOU BECOME IS YOUR CHOICE. CAN'T PUT THAT ON SOMEONE ELSE.
EVEN GODS HAVE TO OWN WHAT THEY ARE.
FOR A MAN SURROUNDED WITH MAJESTY AND TERROR, YOU ARE REMARKABLY SIMPLE, FRANK CASTLE.
JUST FRANK IS FINE--
--AND WHAT I AM IS THE SIMPLEST THING THERE IS. POINT AND SHOOT EASY, FREYJA.
THIS...MAN WHO WANTS THE EARTH. HE COMES FROM YOUR WORLD. THAT MEANS HE'S YOUR PROBLEM TO SOLVE. DO WHAT IT TAKES TO SOLVE IT.
EASY WORDS. DIFFICULT TASK.
I NEED A FEW OF YOU MORTALS. I AM NOT FAMILIAR ENOUGH WITH YOUR RANKS TO CHOOSE. CAN YOU SUGGEST NAMES AMONG THOSE HERE?
NAMES OF PEOPLE BURDENED THE SAME WAY YOU ARE. ANGER AGAINST ANGER.
SURE. I CAN LIST THEM OFF.
BUT YOU NEED TO CONVINCE THEM YOURSELF.

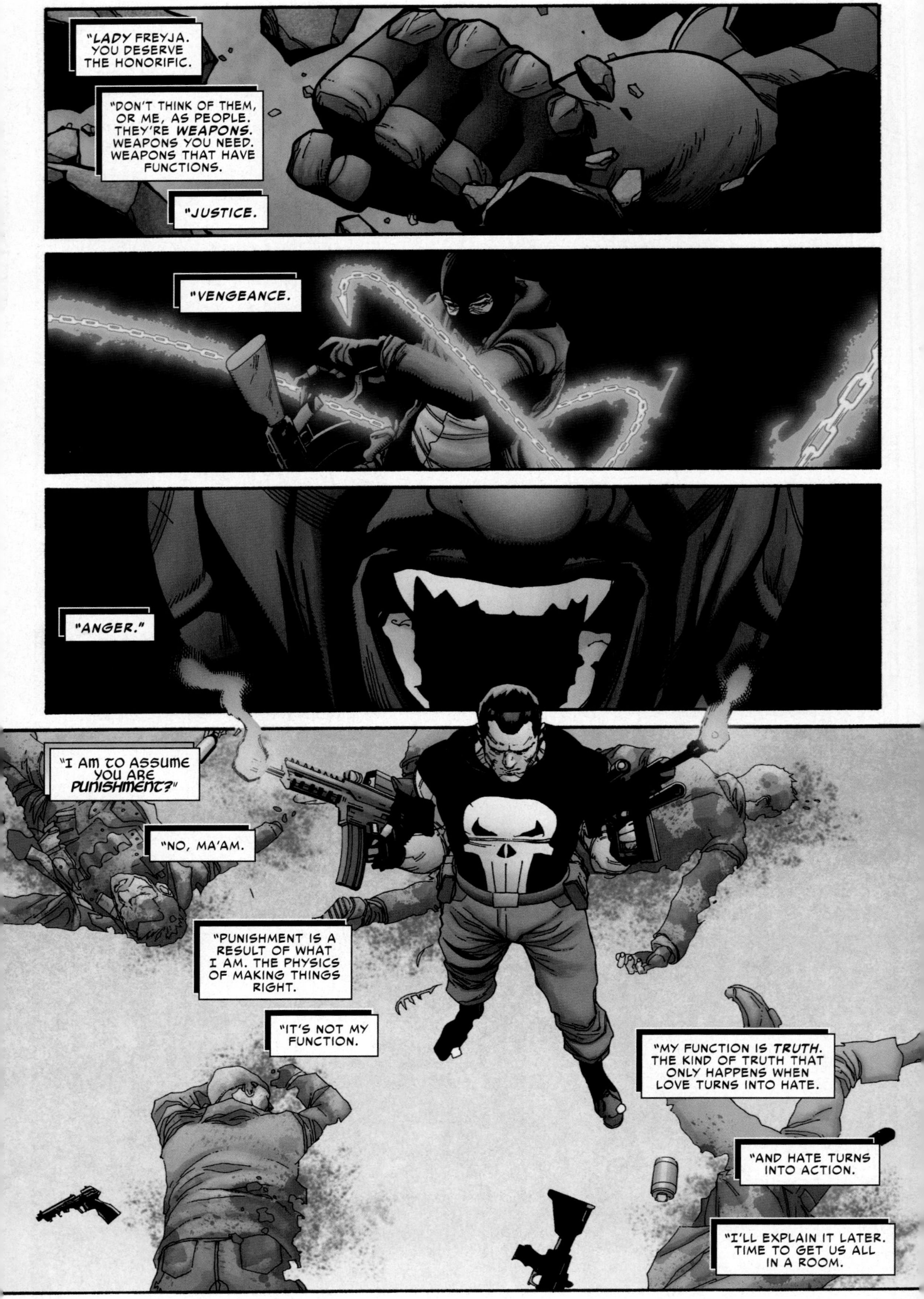
"LADY FREYJA. YOU DESERVE THE HONORIFIC.
"DON'T THINK OF THEM, OR ME, AS PEOPLE. THEY'RE WEAPONS. WEAPONS YOU NEED. WEAPONS THAT HAVE FUNCTIONS.
"JUSTICE.
"VENGEANCE.
"ANGER."
"I AM TO ASSUME YOU ARE PUNISHMENT?"
"NO, MA'AM.
"PUNISHMENT IS A RESULT OF WHAT I AM. THE PHYSICS OF MAKING THINGS RIGHT.
"IT'S NOT MY FUNCTION.
"MY FUNCTION IS TRUTH. THE KIND OF TRUTH THAT ONLY HAPPENS WHEN LOVE TURNS INTO HATE.
"AND HATE TURNS INTO ACTION.
"I'LL EXPLAIN IT LATER. TIME TO GET US ALL IN A ROOM.

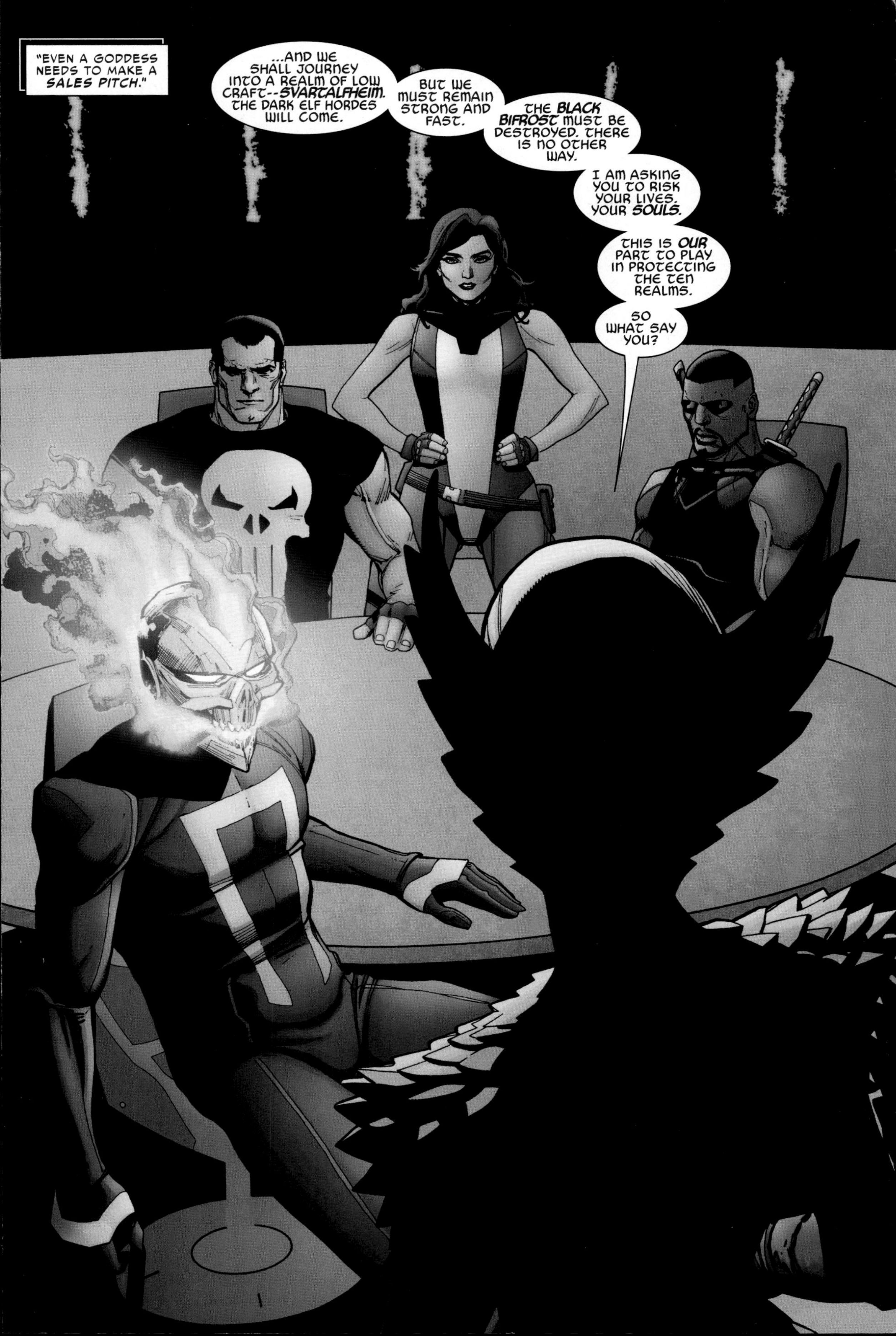
"EVEN A GODDESS NEEDS TO MAKE A SALES PITCH."
...AND WE SHALL JOURNEY INTO A REALM OF LOW CRAFT--SVARTALFHEIM. THE DARK ELF HORDES WILL COME.
BUT WE MUST REMAIN STRONG AND FAST.
THE BLACK BIFROST MUST BE DESTROYED. THERE IS NO OTHER WAY.
I AM ASKING YOU TO RISK YOUR LIVES. YOUR SOULS.
THIS IS OUR PART TO PLAY IN PROTECTING THE TEN REALMS.
SO WHAT SAY YOU?

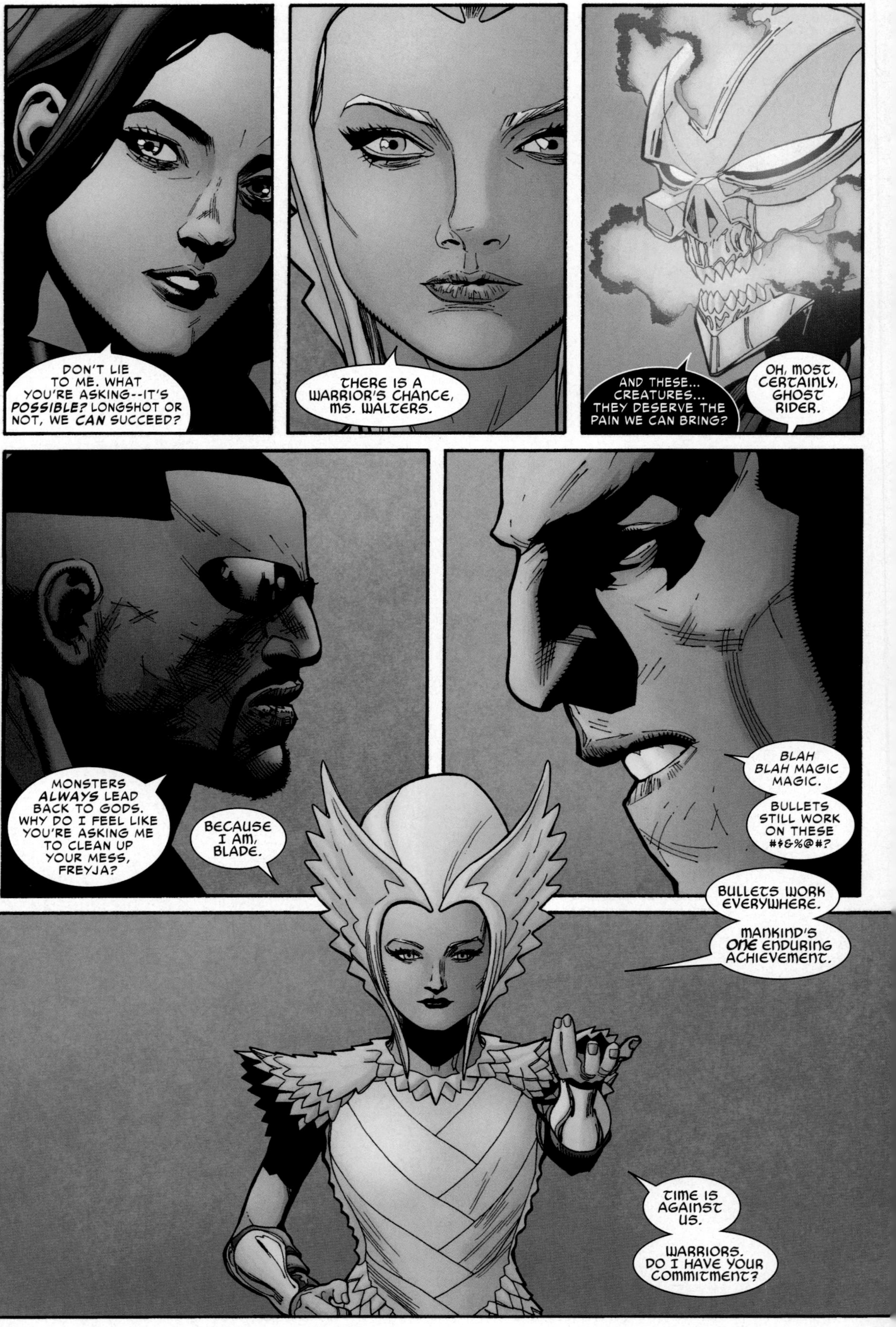
DON'T LIE TO ME. WHAT YOU'RE ASKING--IT'S *POSSIBLE?* LONGSHOT OR NOT, WE *CAN* SUCCEED?
THERE IS A WARRIOR'S CHANCE, MS. WALTERS.
AND THESE... CREATURES... THEY DESERVE THE PAIN WE CAN BRING?
OH, MOST CERTAINLY, GHOST RIDER.
MONSTERS *ALWAYS* LEAD BACK TO GODS. WHY DO I FEEL LIKE YOU'RE ASKING ME TO CLEAN UP YOUR MESS, FREYJA?
BECAUSE I AM, BLADE.
BLAH BLAH MAGIC MAGIC.
BULLETS STILL WORK ON THESE #$&%@#?
BULLETS WORK EVERYWHERE.
MANKIND'S *ONE* ENDURING ACHIEVEMENT.
TIME IS AGAINST US.
WARRIORS. DO I HAVE YOUR COMMITMENT?

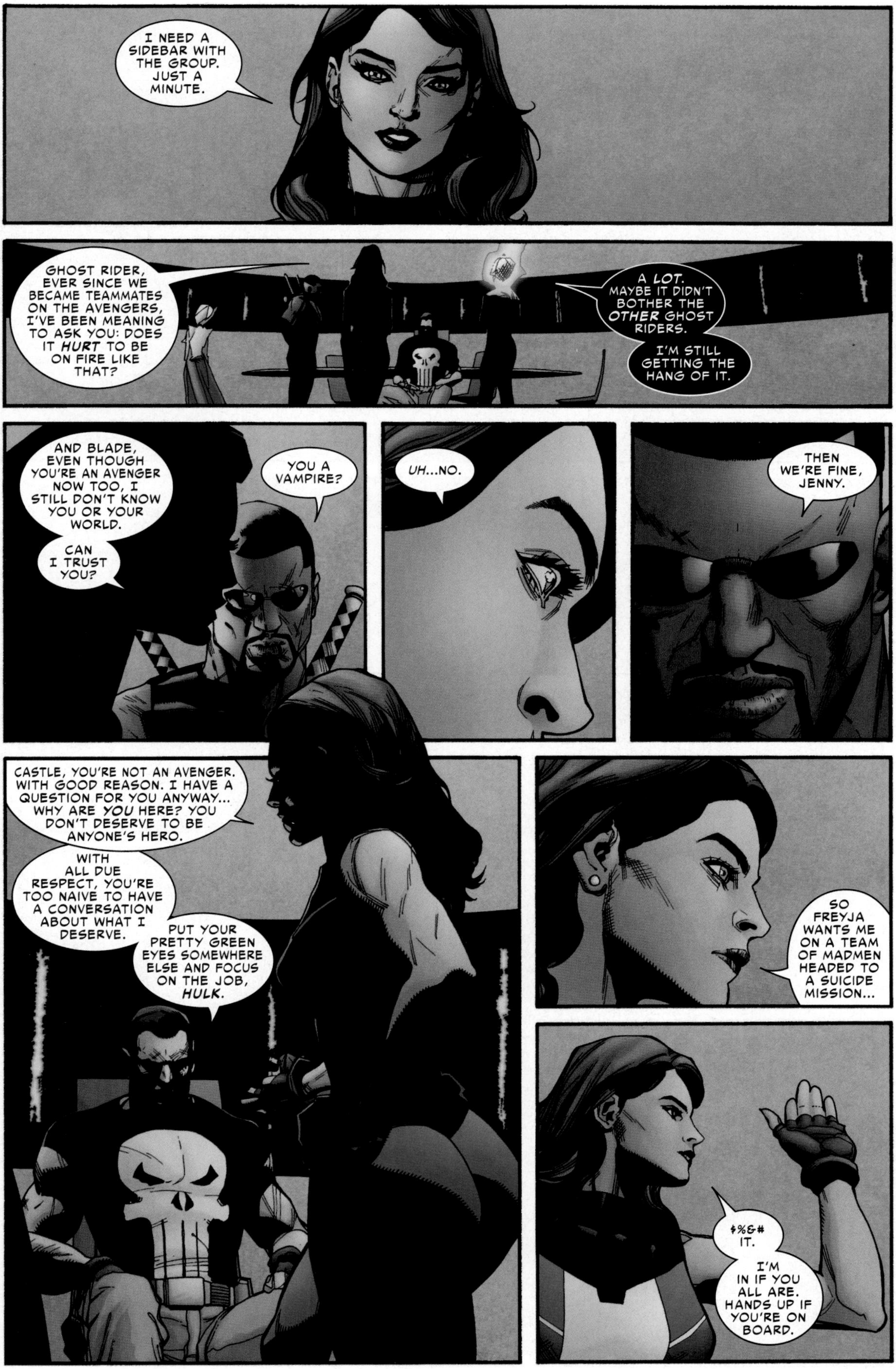
I NEED A SIDEBAR WITH THE GROUP. JUST A MINUTE.
GHOST RIDER, EVER SINCE WE BECAME TEAMMATES ON THE AVENGERS, I'VE BEEN MEANING TO ASK YOU: DOES IT *HURT* TO BE ON FIRE LIKE THAT?
A *LOT*. MAYBE IT DIDN'T BOTHER THE *OTHER* GHOST RIDERS.
I'M STILL GETTING THE HANG OF IT.
AND BLADE, EVEN THOUGH YOU'RE AN AVENGER NOW TOO, I STILL DON'T KNOW YOU OR YOUR WORLD.
CAN I TRUST YOU?
YOU A VAMPIRE?
UH...NO.
THEN WE'RE FINE, JENNY.
CASTLE, YOU'RE NOT AN AVENGER. WITH GOOD REASON. I HAVE A QUESTION FOR YOU ANYWAY... WHY ARE *YOU* HERE? YOU DON'T DESERVE TO BE ANYONE'S HERO.
WITH ALL DUE RESPECT, YOU'RE TOO NAIVE TO HAVE A CONVERSATION ABOUT WHAT I DESERVE.
PUT YOUR PRETTY GREEN EYES SOMEWHERE ELSE AND FOCUS ON THE JOB, *HULK*.
SO FREYJA WANTS ME ON A TEAM OF MADMEN HEADED TO A SUICIDE MISSION...
$%&# IT.
I'M IN IF YOU ALL ARE. HANDS UP IF YOU'RE ON BOARD.

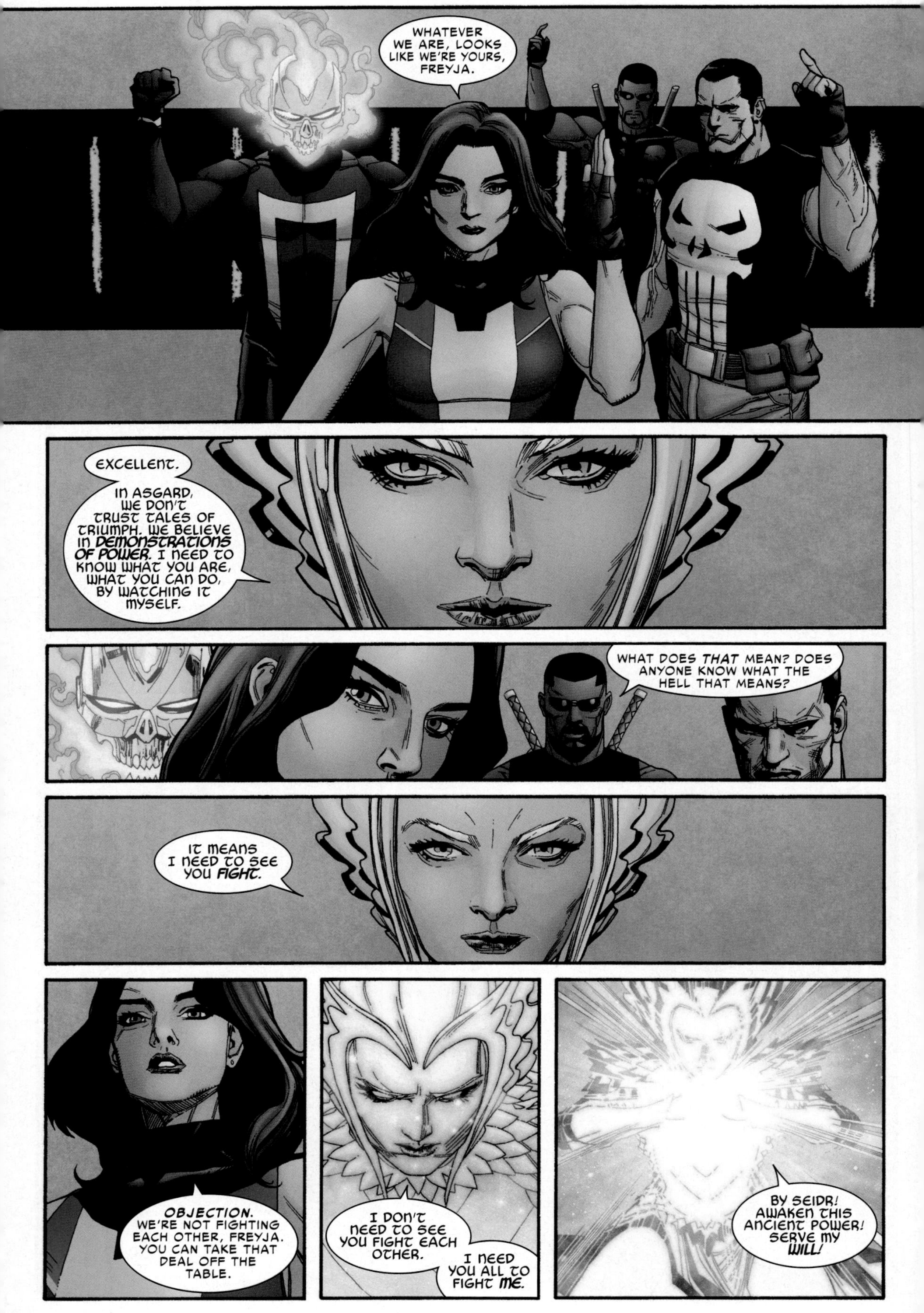
WHATEVER WE ARE, LOOKS LIKE WE'RE YOURS, FREYJA.
EXCELLENT.
IN ASGARD, WE DON'T TRUST TALES OF TRIUMPH. WE BELIEVE IN *DEMONSTRATIONS OF POWER*. I NEED TO KNOW WHAT YOU ARE, WHAT YOU CAN DO, BY WATCHING IT MYSELF.
WHAT DOES *THAT* MEAN? DOES ANYONE KNOW WHAT THE HELL THAT MEANS?
IT MEANS I NEED TO SEE YOU *FIGHT*.
OBJECTION. WE'RE NOT FIGHTING EACH OTHER, FREYJA. YOU CAN TAKE THAT DEAL OFF THE TABLE.
I DON'T NEED TO SEE YOU FIGHT EACH OTHER.
I NEED YOU ALL TO FIGHT *ME*.
BY SEIDR! AWAKEN THIS ANCIENT POWER! SERVE MY *WILL*!

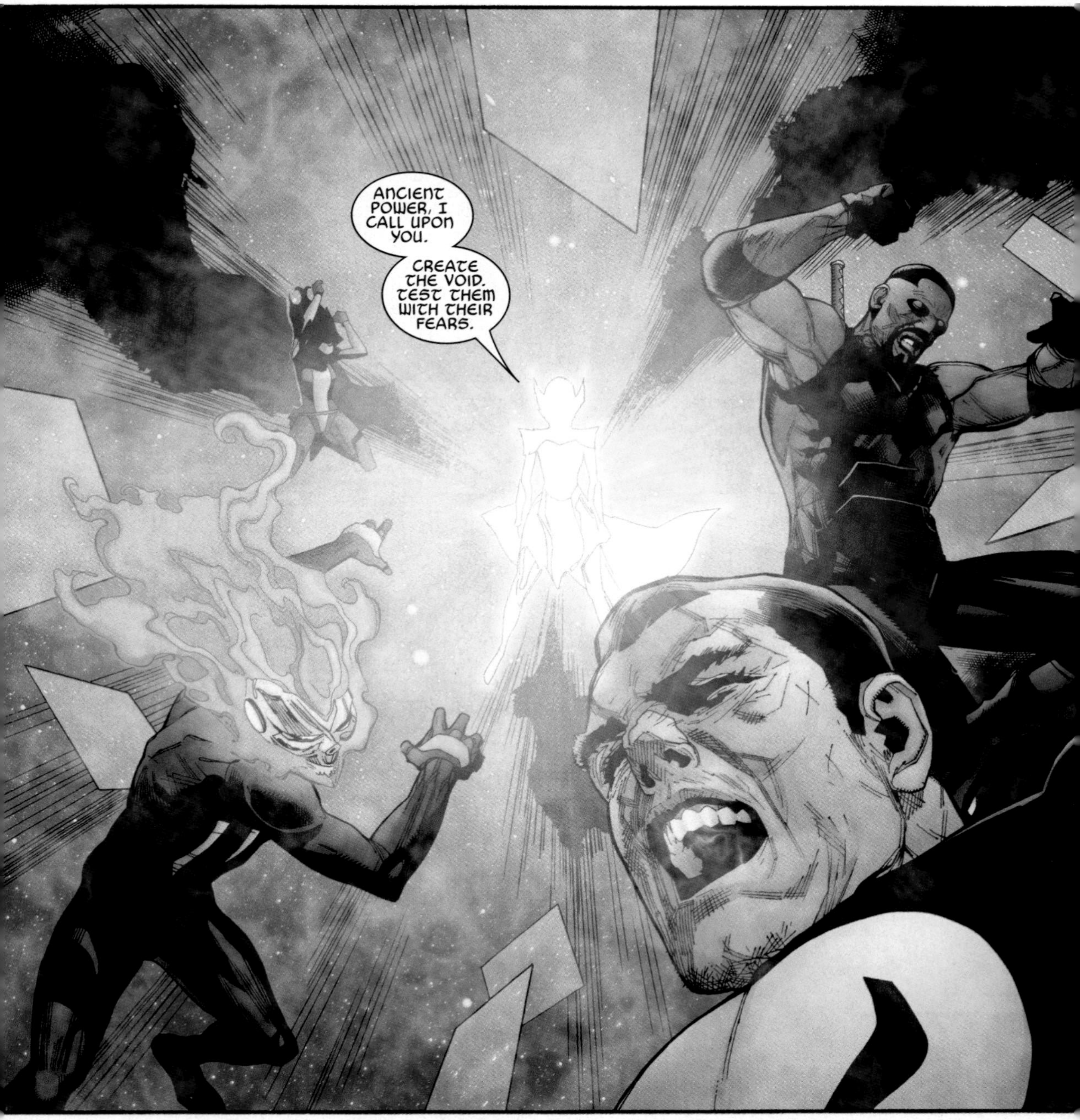
ANCIENT POWER, I CALL UPON YOU.
CREATE THE VOID. TEST THEM WITH THEIR FEARS.

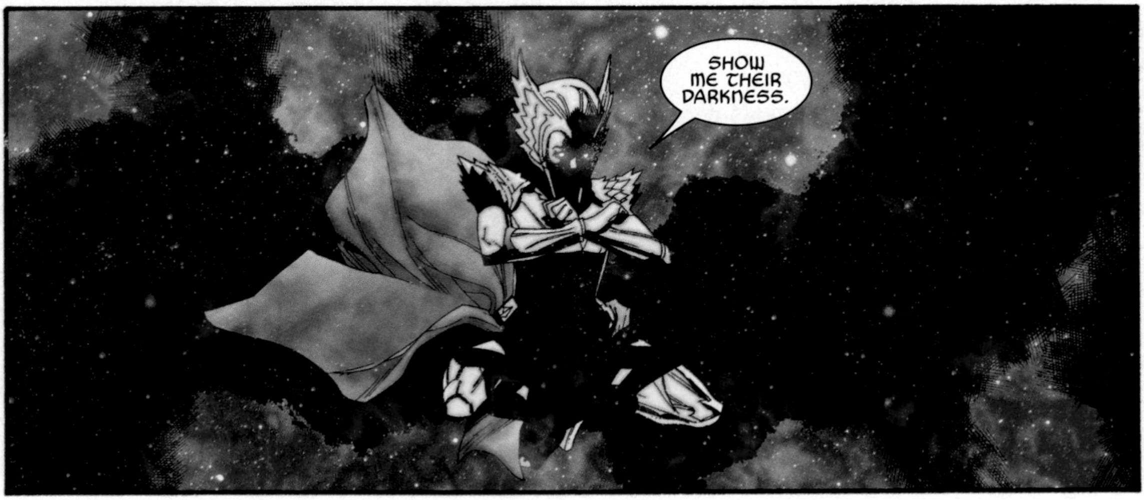
SHOW ME THEIR DARKNESS.

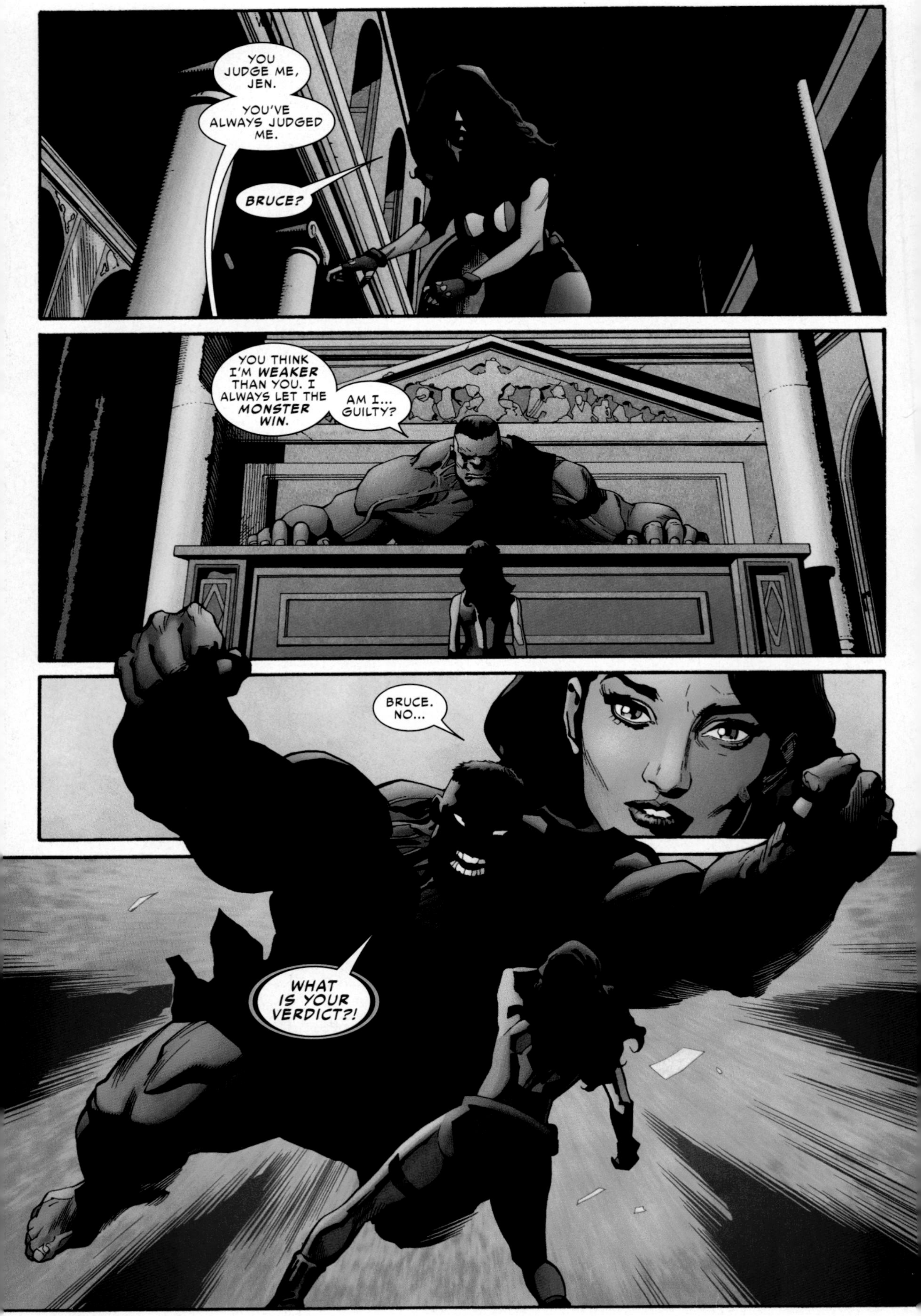
YOU JUDGE ME, JEN.
YOU'VE ALWAYS JUDGED ME.
BRUCE?
YOU THINK I'M WEAKER THAN YOU. I ALWAYS LET THE MONSTER WIN.
AM I... GUILTY?
BRUCE. NO...
WHAT IS YOUR VERDICT?!

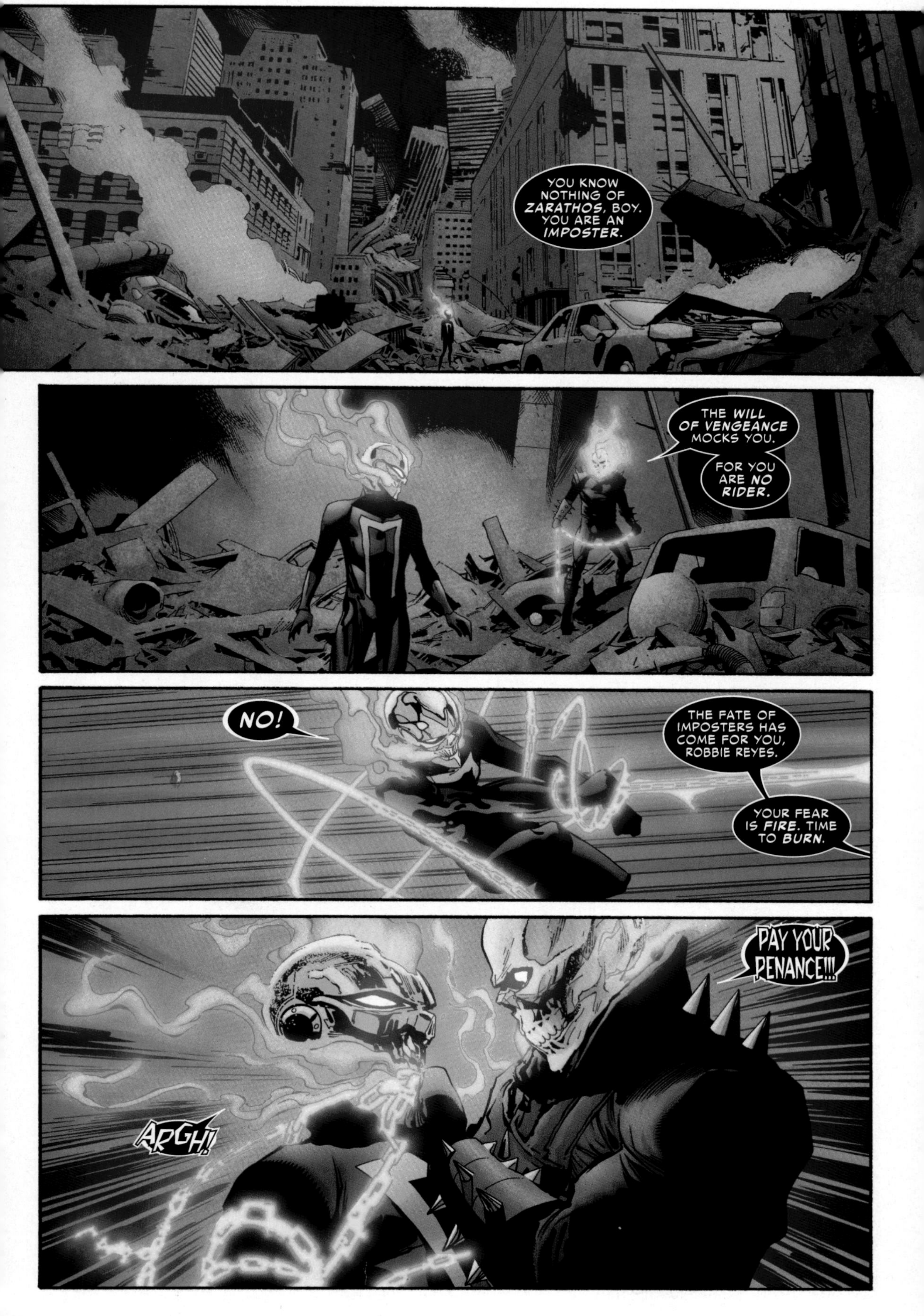
YOU KNOW NOTHING OF ZARATHOS, BOY. YOU ARE AN IMPOSTER.
THE WILL OF VENGEANCE MOCKS YOU.
FOR YOU ARE NO RIDER.
NO!
THE FATE OF IMPOSTERS HAS COME FOR YOU, ROBBIE REYES.
YOUR FEAR IS FIRE. TIME TO BURN.
PAY YOUR PENANCE!!!
ARGH!

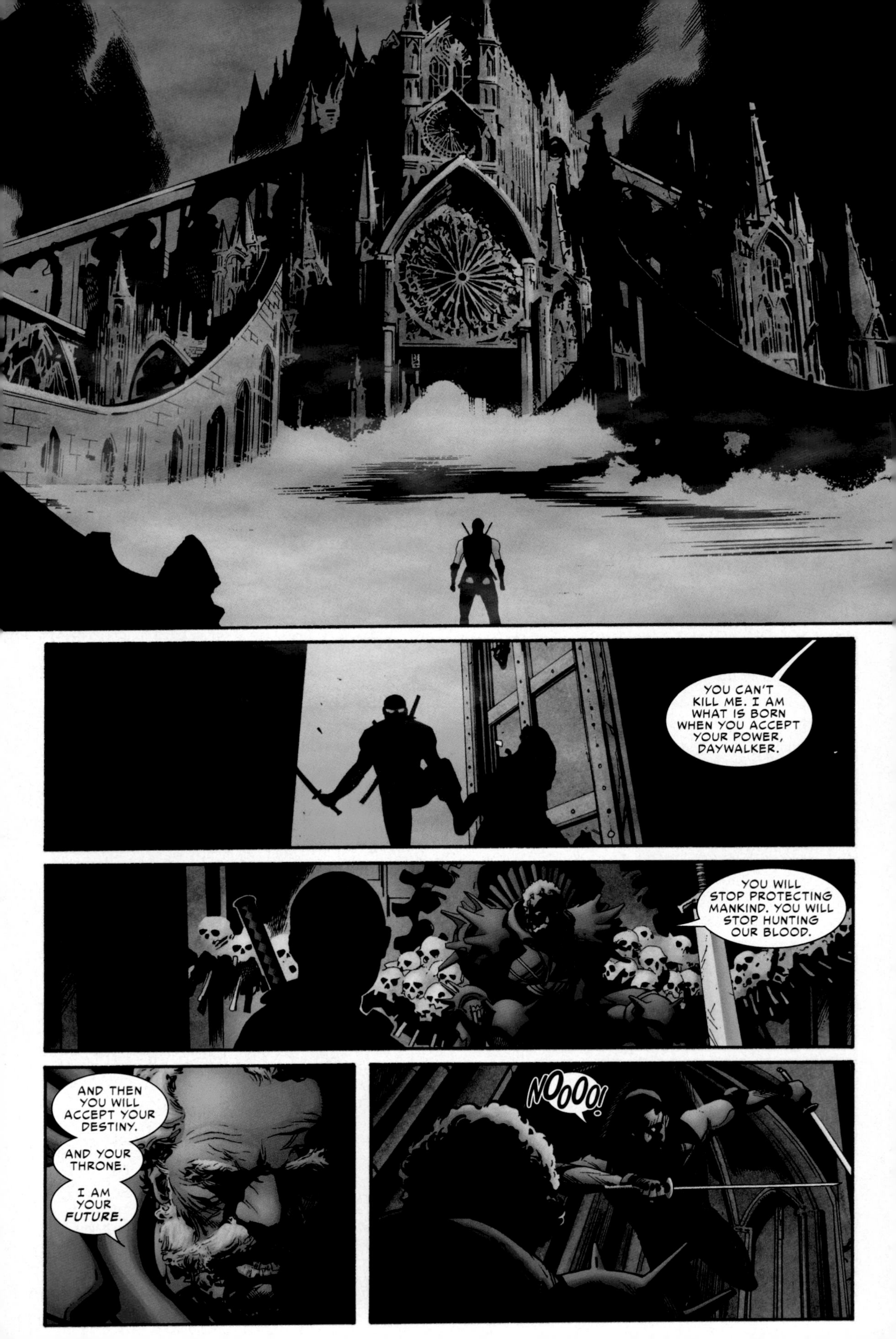
YOU CAN'T KILL ME. I AM WHAT IS BORN WHEN YOU ACCEPT YOUR POWER, DAYWALKER.
YOU WILL STOP PROTECTING MANKIND. YOU WILL STOP HUNTING OUR BLOOD.
AND THEN YOU WILL ACCEPT YOUR DESTINY.
AND YOUR THRONE.
I AM YOUR FUTURE.
NOOOO!

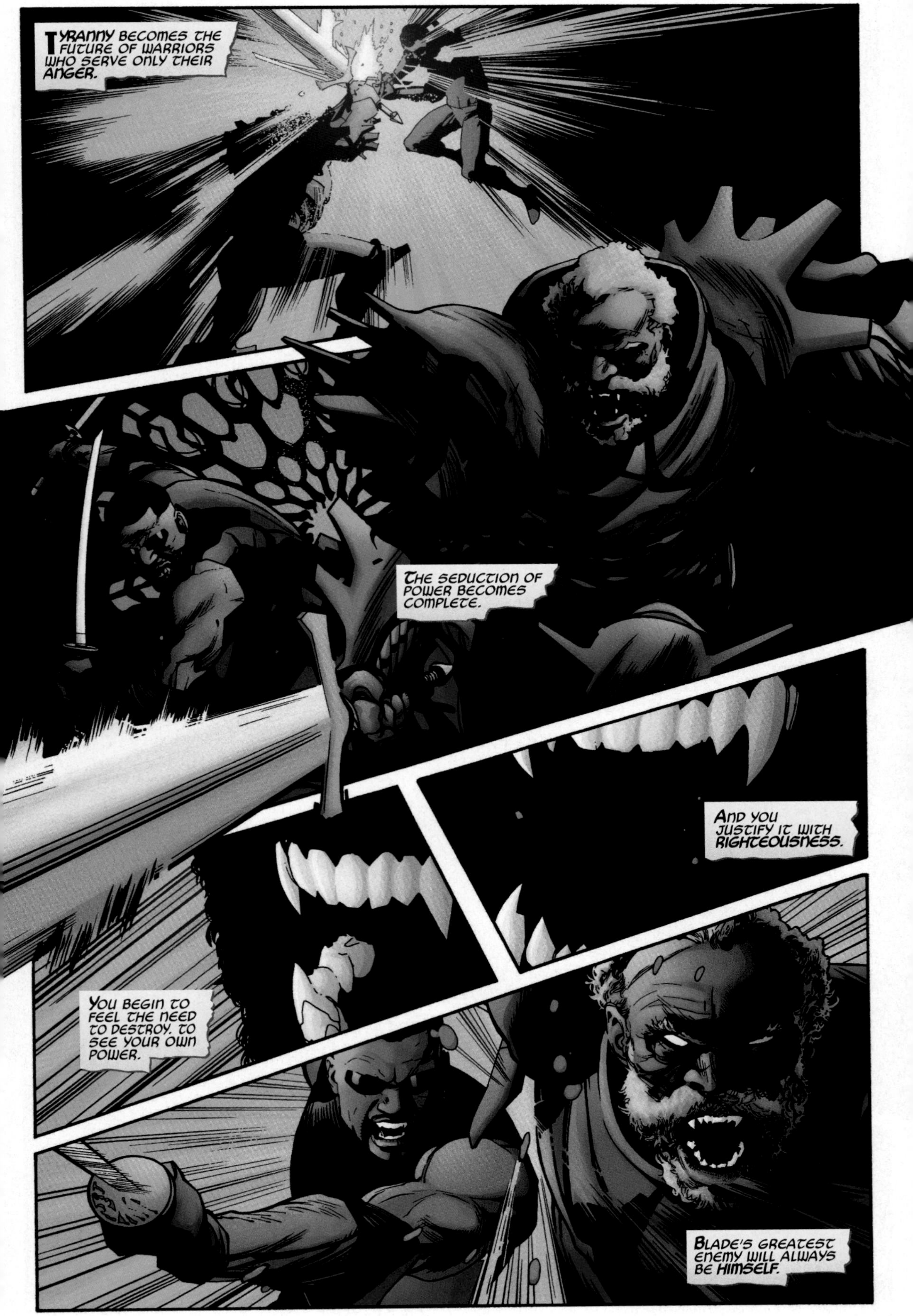

TYRANNY BECOMES THE FUTURE OF WARRIORS WHO SERVE ONLY THEIR ANGER.
THE SEDUCTION OF POWER BECOMES COMPLETE.
AND YOU JUSTIFY IT WITH RIGHTEOUSNESS.
YOU BEGIN TO FEEL THE NEED TO DESTROY. TO SEE YOUR OWN POWER.
BLADE'S GREATEST ENEMY WILL ALWAYS BE HIMSELF.

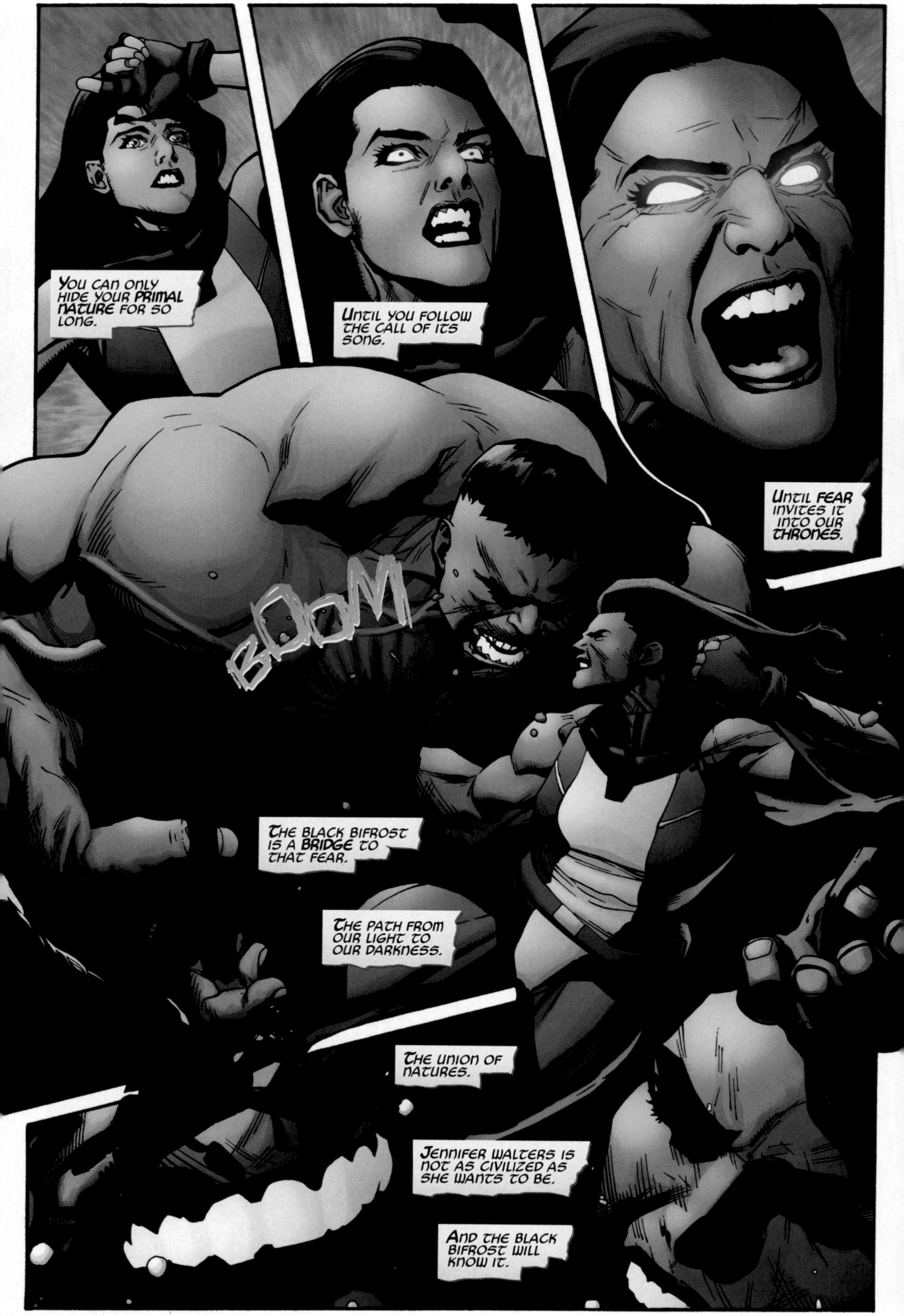

You can only hide your PRIMAL NATURE for so long.
Until you follow the call of its song.
Until FEAR invites it into our THRONES.
BOOM
The black Bifrost is a BRIDGE to that fear.
The path from our light to our darkness.
The union of natures.
Jennifer Walters is not as civilized as she wants to be.
And the Black Bifrost will know it.

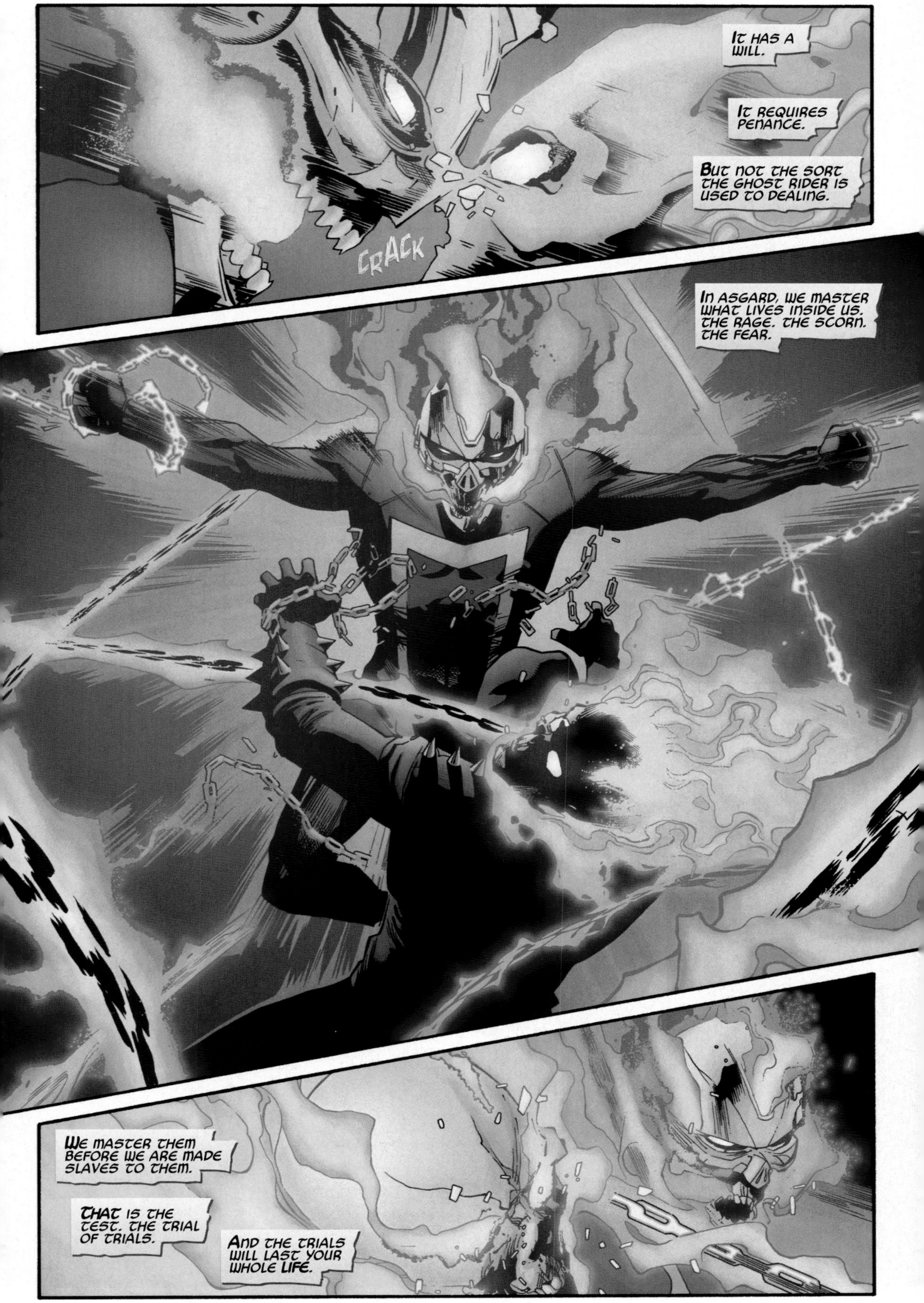
IT HAS A WILL.
IT REQUIRES PENANCE.
BUT NOT THE SORT THE GHOST RIDER IS USED TO DEALING.
CRACK
IN ASGARD, WE MASTER WHAT LIVES INSIDE US. THE RAGE. THE SCORN. THE FEAR.
WE MASTER THEM BEFORE WE ARE MADE SLAVES TO THEM.
THAT IS THE TEST. THE TRIAL OF TRIALS.
AND THE TRIALS WILL LAST YOUR WHOLE LIFE.

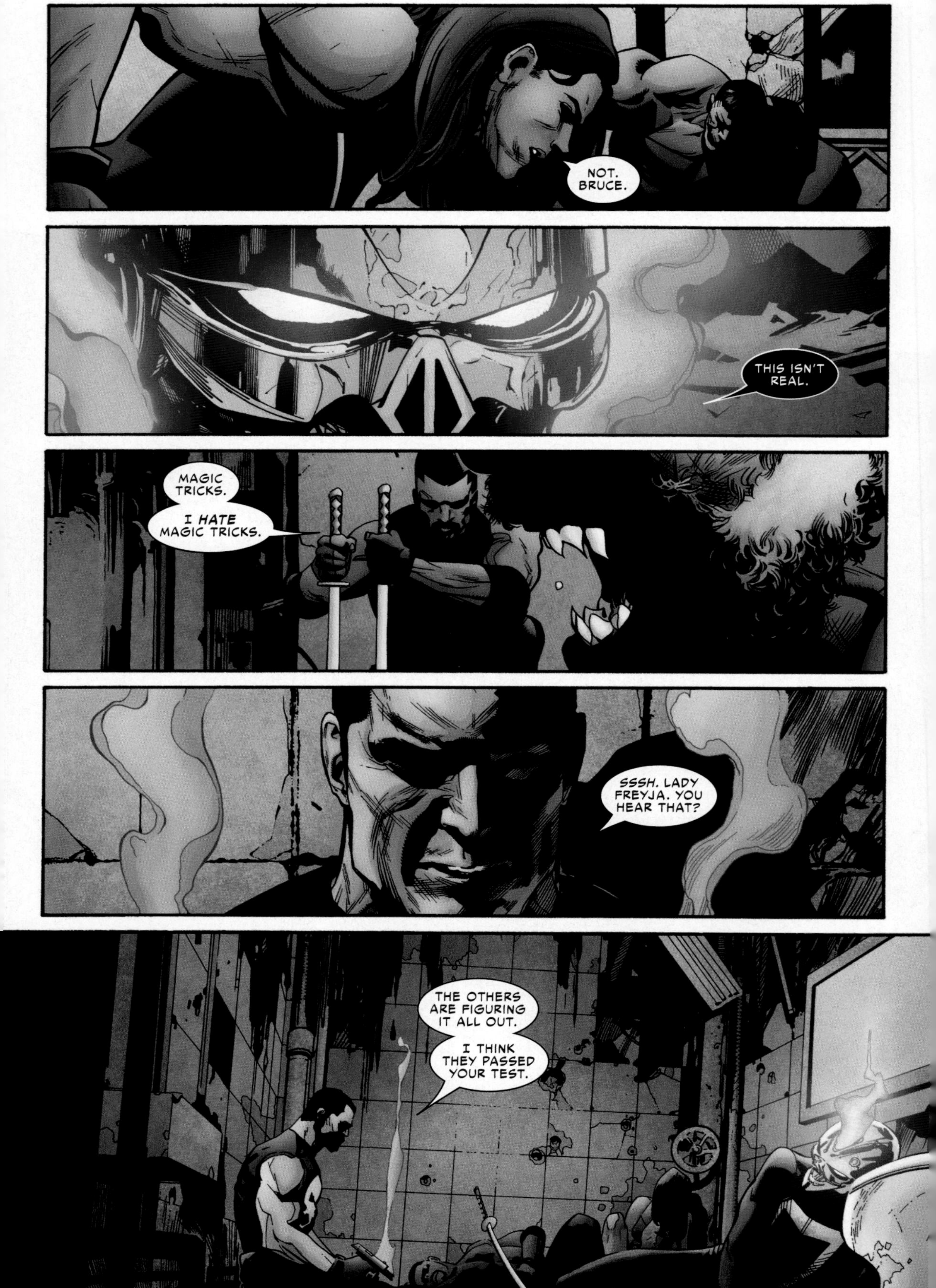
NOT. BRUCE.
THIS ISN'T REAL.
MAGIC TRICKS.
I *HATE* MAGIC TRICKS.
SSSH. LADY FREYJA. YOU HEAR THAT?
THE OTHERS ARE FIGURING IT ALL OUT.
I THINK THEY PASSED YOUR TEST.

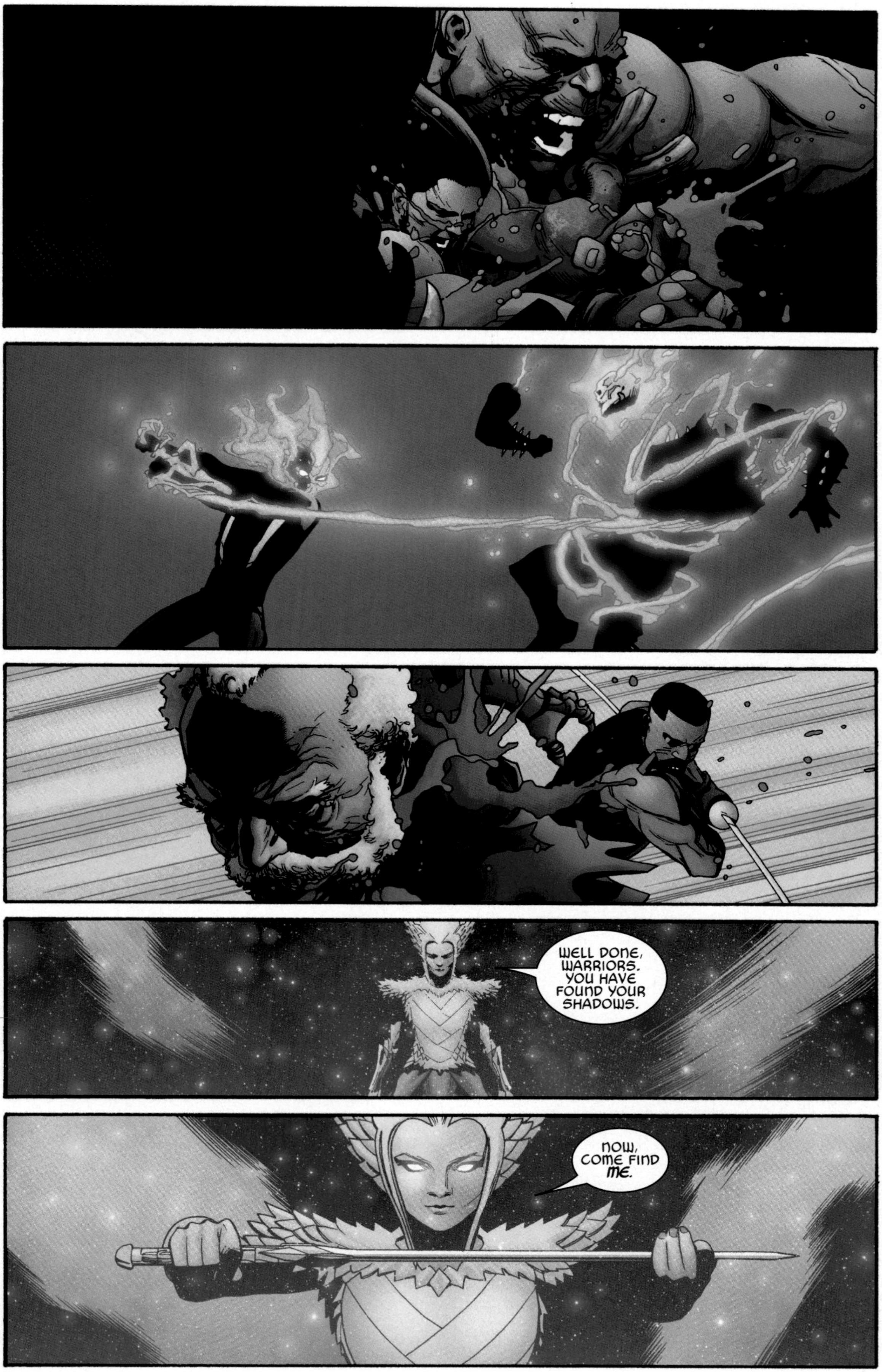
WELL DONE, WARRIORS. YOU HAVE FOUND YOUR SHADOWS.
NOW, COME FIND ME.

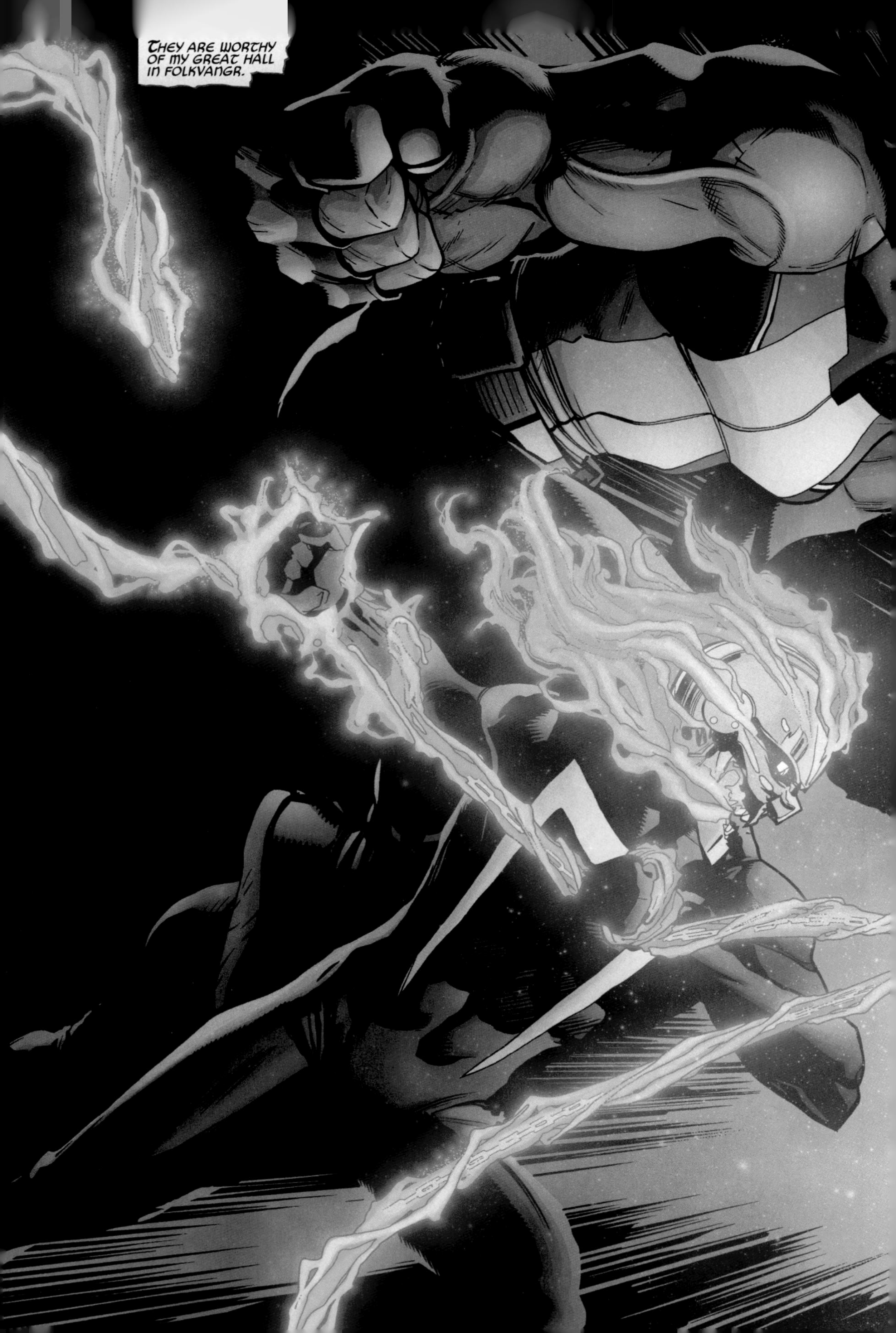
THEY ARE WORTHY OF MY GREAT HALL IN FOLKVANGR.

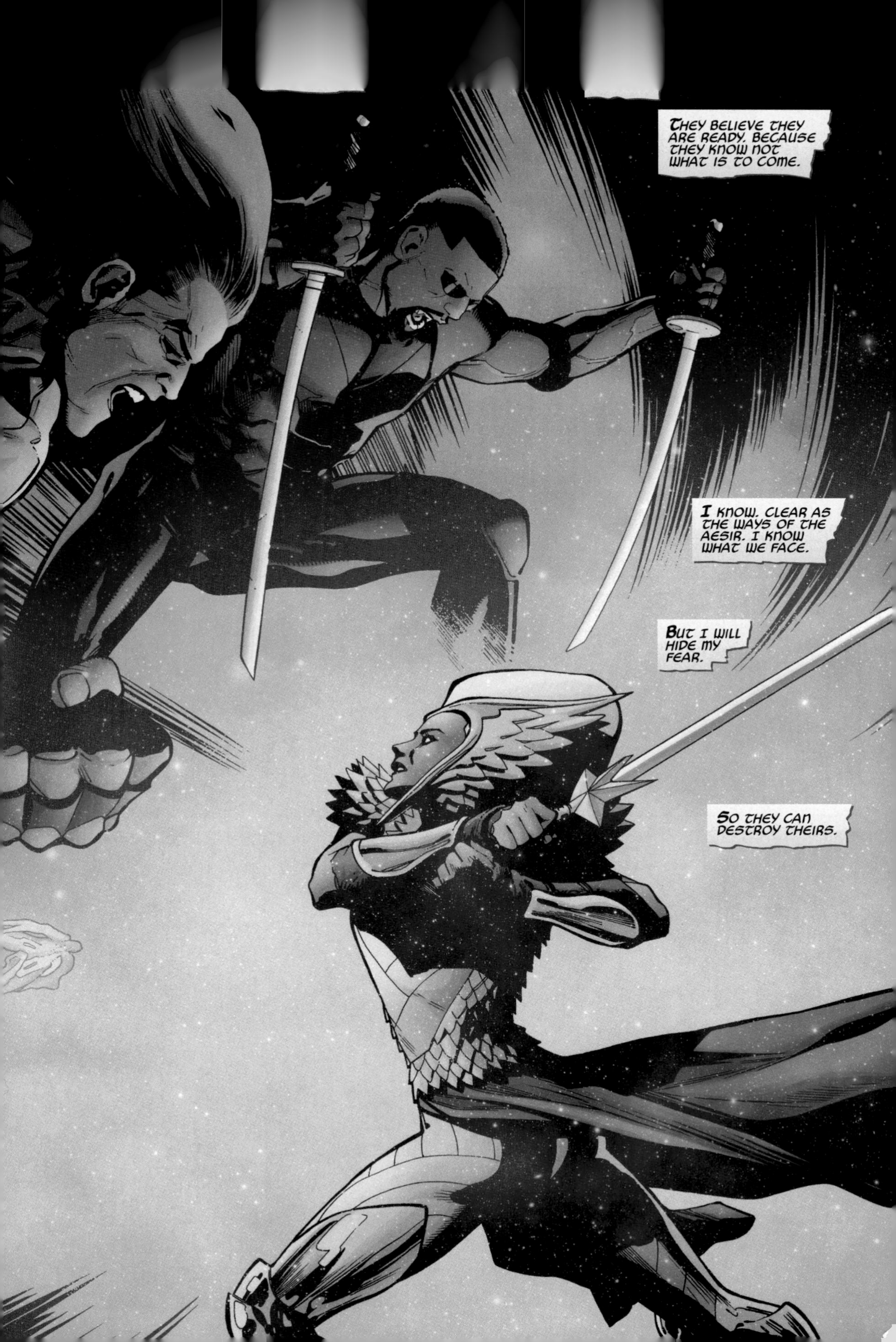
THEY BELIEVE THEY ARE READY. BECAUSE THEY KNOW NOT WHAT IS TO COME.
I KNOW. CLEAR AS THE WAYS OF THE AESIR. I KNOW WHAT WE FACE.
BUT I WILL HIDE MY FEAR.
SO THEY CAN DESTROY THEIRS.

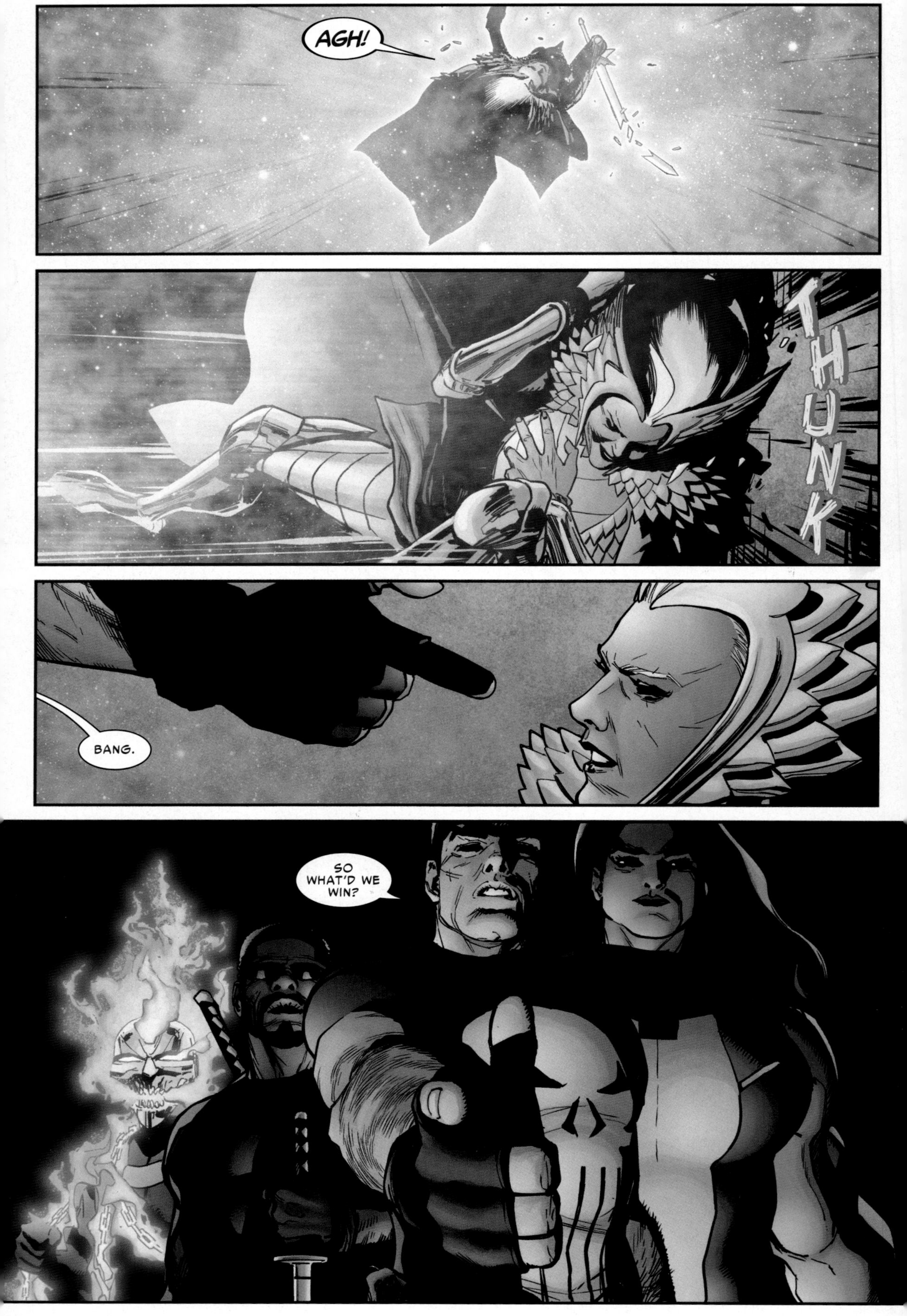
AGH!
THUNK
BANG.
SO WHAT'D WE WIN?

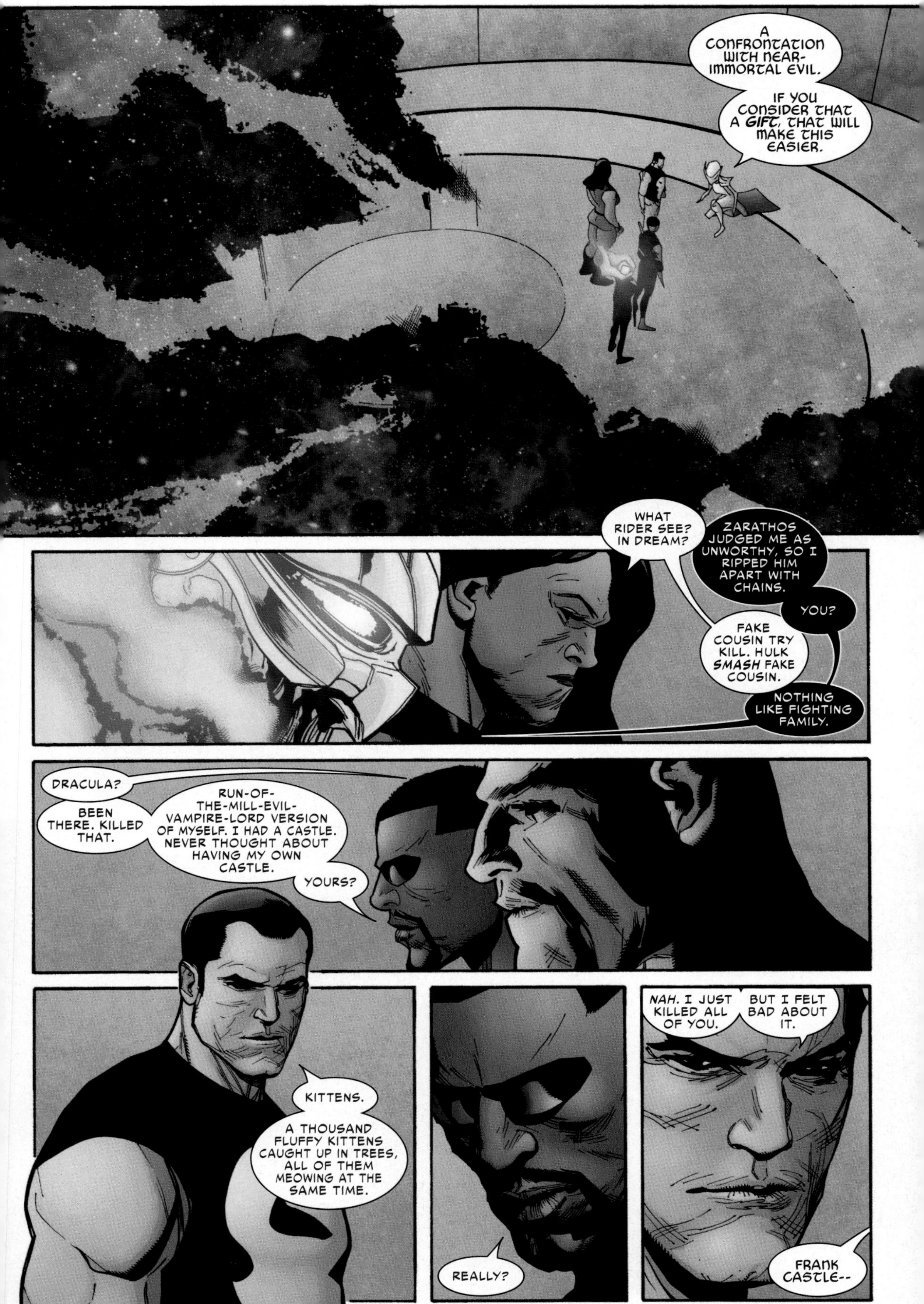
A CONFRONTATION WITH NEAR-IMMORTAL EVIL.
IF YOU CONSIDER THAT A GIFT, THAT WILL MAKE THIS EASIER.
WHAT RIDER SEE? IN DREAM?
ZARATHOS JUDGED ME AS UNWORTHY, SO I RIPPED HIM APART WITH CHAINS.
YOU?
FAKE COUSIN TRY KILL. HULK SMASH FAKE COUSIN.
NOTHING LIKE FIGHTING FAMILY.
DRACULA?
BEEN THERE. KILLED THAT.
RUN-OF-THE-MILL-EVIL-VAMPIRE-LORD VERSION OF MYSELF. I HAD A CASTLE. NEVER THOUGHT ABOUT HAVING MY OWN CASTLE.
YOURS?
KITTENS.
A THOUSAND FLUFFY KITTENS CAUGHT UP IN TREES, ALL OF THEM MEOWING AT THE SAME TIME.
REALLY?
NAH. I JUST KILLED ALL OF YOU.
BUT I FELT BAD ABOUT IT.
FRANK CASTLE--

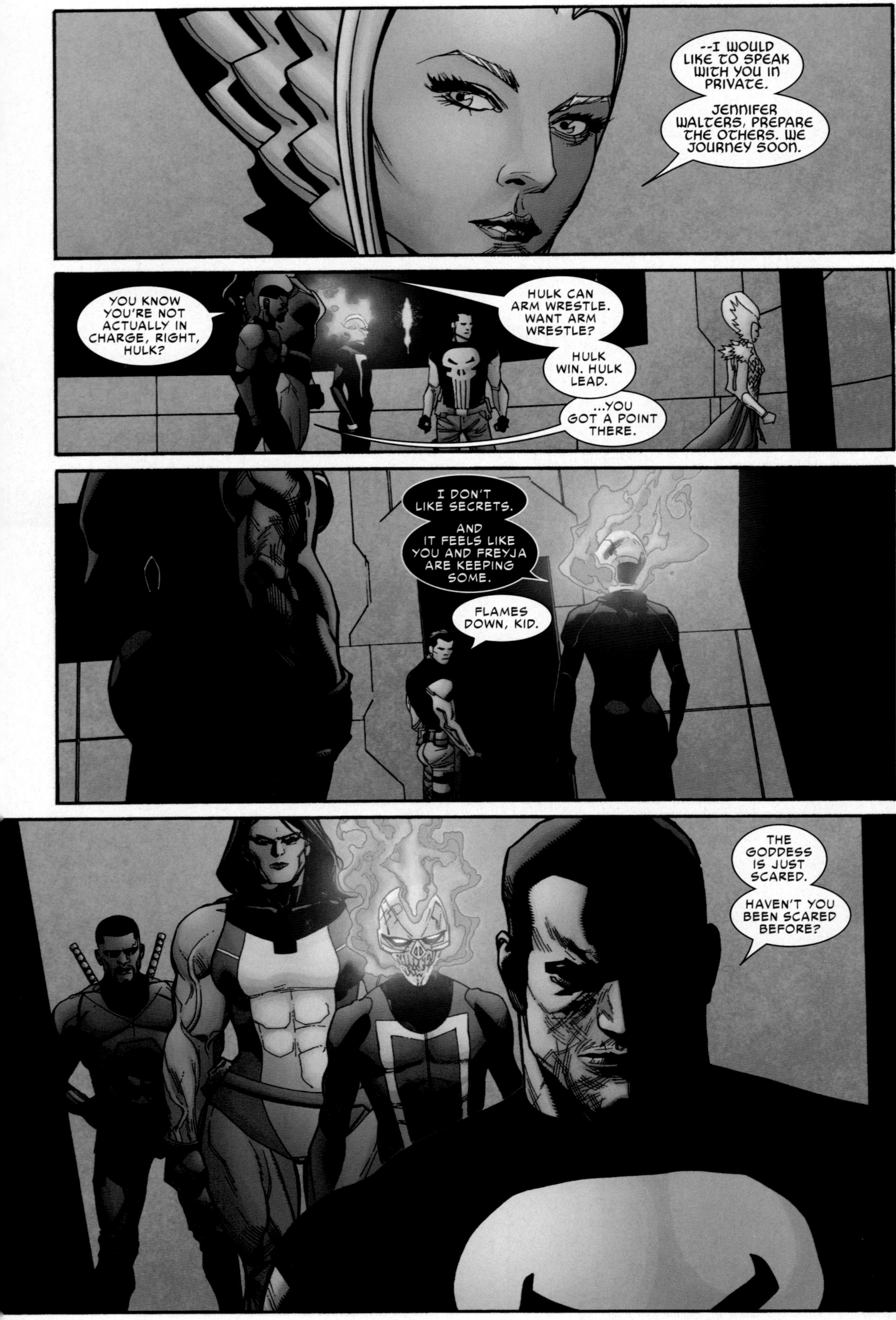
--I WOULD LIKE TO SPEAK WITH YOU IN PRIVATE.
JENNIFER WALTERS, PREPARE THE OTHERS. WE JOURNEY SOON.
YOU KNOW YOU'RE NOT ACTUALLY IN CHARGE, RIGHT, HULK?
HULK CAN ARM WRESTLE. WANT ARM WRESTLE?
HULK WIN. HULK LEAD.
...YOU GOT A POINT THERE.
I DON'T LIKE SECRETS.
AND IT FEELS LIKE YOU AND FREYJA ARE KEEPING SOME.
FLAMES DOWN, KID.
THE GODDESS IS JUST SCARED.
HAVEN'T YOU BEEN SCARED BEFORE?

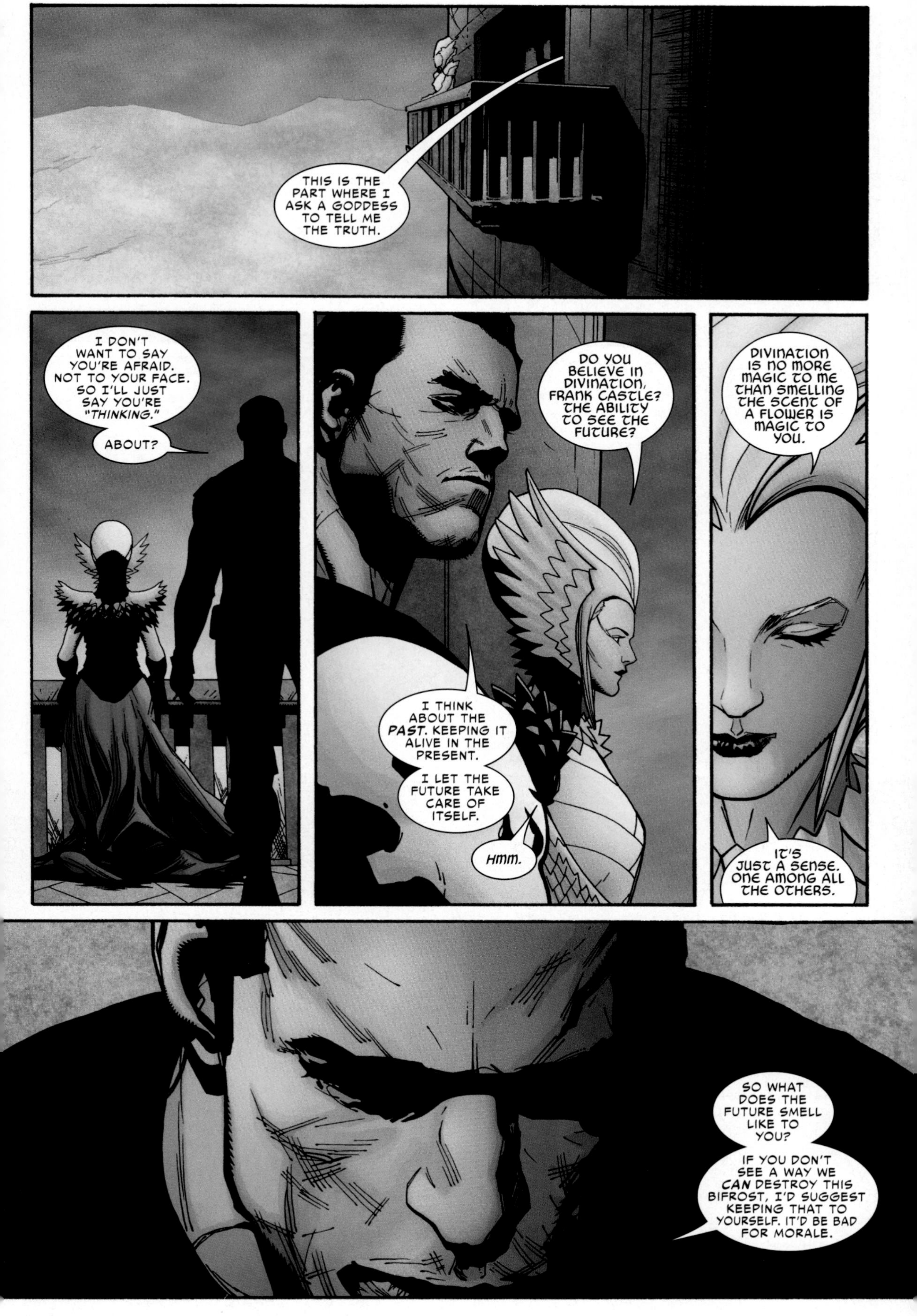
THIS IS THE PART WHERE I ASK A GODDESS TO TELL ME THE TRUTH.
I DON'T WANT TO SAY YOU'RE AFRAID. NOT TO YOUR FACE. SO I'LL JUST SAY YOU'RE "THINKING."
ABOUT?
DO YOU BELIEVE IN DIVINATION, FRANK CASTLE? THE ABILITY TO SEE THE FUTURE?
I THINK ABOUT THE PAST. KEEPING IT ALIVE IN THE PRESENT.
I LET THE FUTURE TAKE CARE OF ITSELF.
HMM.
DIVINATION IS NO MORE MAGIC TO ME THAN SMELLING THE SCENT OF A FLOWER IS MAGIC TO YOU.
IT'S JUST A SENSE. ONE AMONG ALL THE OTHERS.
SO WHAT DOES THE FUTURE SMELL LIKE TO YOU?
IF YOU DON'T SEE A WAY WE CAN DESTROY THIS BIFROST, I'D SUGGEST KEEPING THAT TO YOURSELF. IT'D BE BAD FOR MORALE.

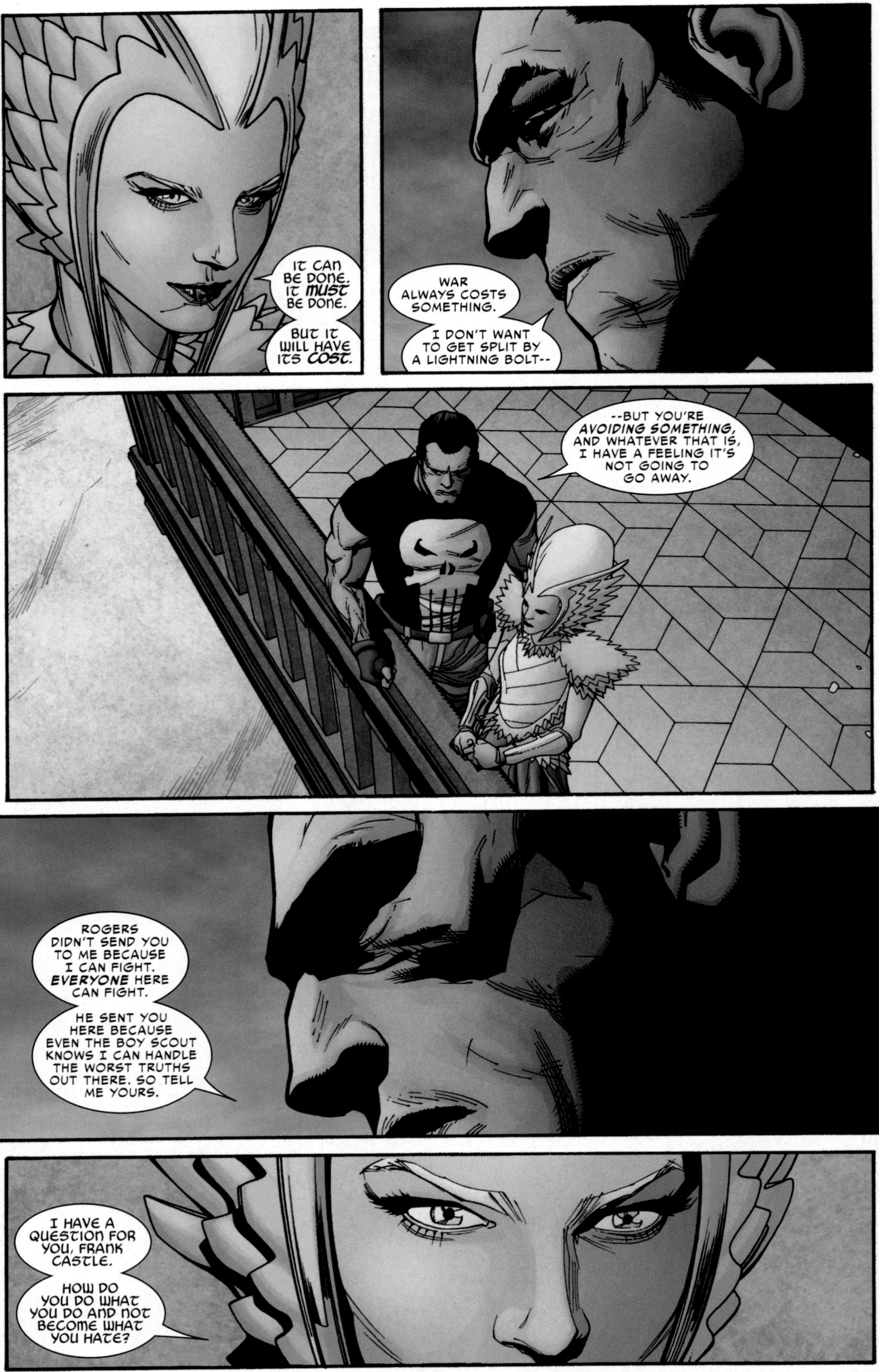
IT CAN BE DONE. IT MUST BE DONE.
BUT IT WILL HAVE ITS COST.
WAR ALWAYS COSTS SOMETHING.
I DON'T WANT TO GET SPLIT BY A LIGHTNING BOLT--
--BUT YOU'RE AVOIDING SOMETHING, AND WHATEVER THAT IS, I HAVE A FEELING IT'S NOT GOING TO GO AWAY.
ROGERS DIDN'T SEND YOU TO ME BECAUSE I CAN FIGHT. EVERYONE HERE CAN FIGHT.
HE SENT YOU HERE BECAUSE EVEN THE BOY SCOUT KNOWS I CAN HANDLE THE WORST TRUTHS OUT THERE. SO TELL ME YOURS.
I HAVE A QUESTION FOR YOU, FRANK CASTLE.
HOW DO YOU DO WHAT YOU DO AND NOT BECOME WHAT YOU HATE?

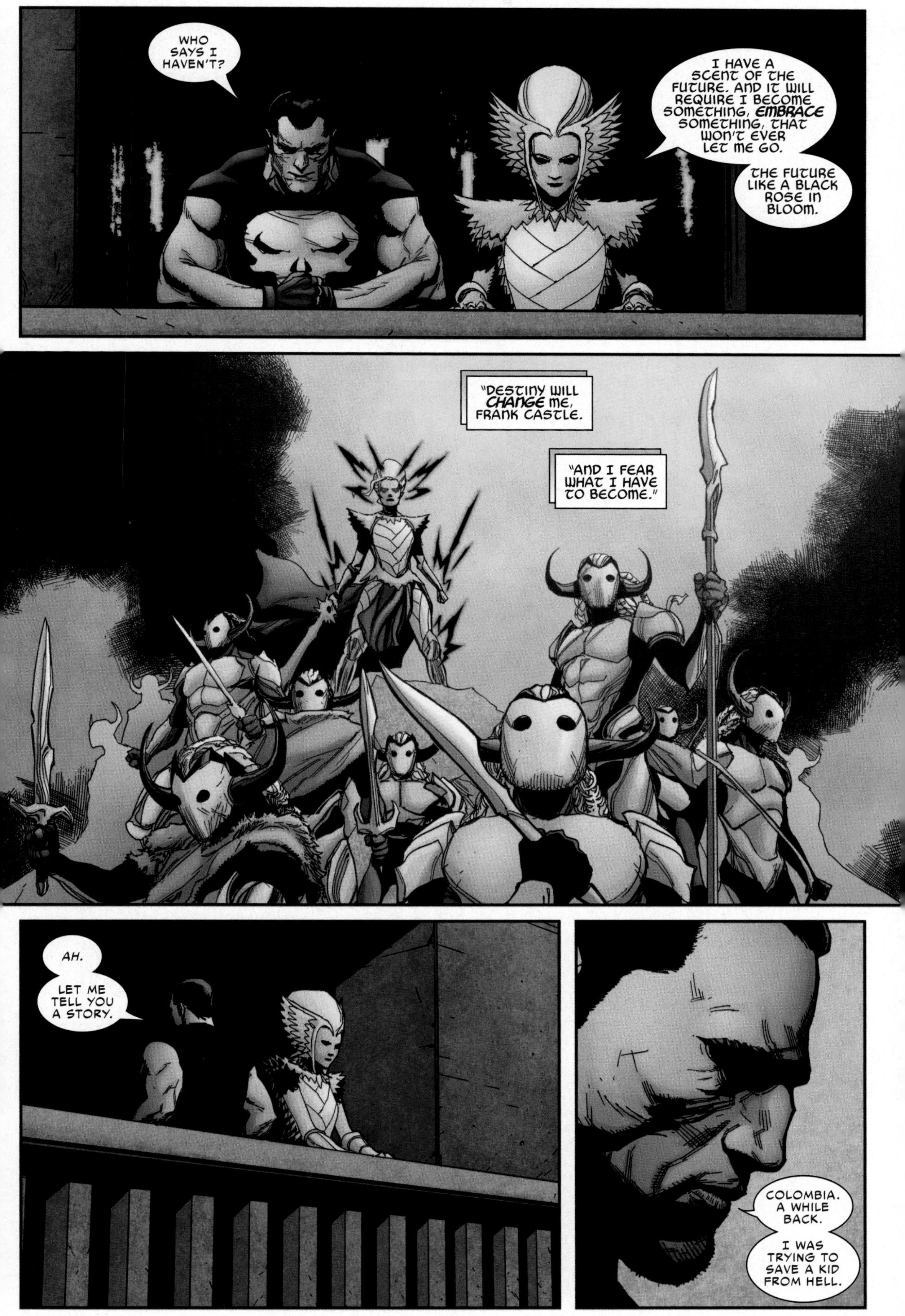

WHO SAYS I HAVEN'T?
I HAVE A SCENT OF THE FUTURE. AND IT WILL REQUIRE I BECOME SOMETHING, EMBRACE SOMETHING, THAT WON'T EVER LET ME GO.
THE FUTURE LIKE A BLACK ROSE IN BLOOM.
"DESTINY WILL CHANGE ME, FRANK CASTLE.
"AND I FEAR WHAT I HAVE TO BECOME."
AH.
LET ME TELL YOU A STORY.
COLOMBIA. A WHILE BACK.
I WAS TRYING TO SAVE A KID FROM HELL.

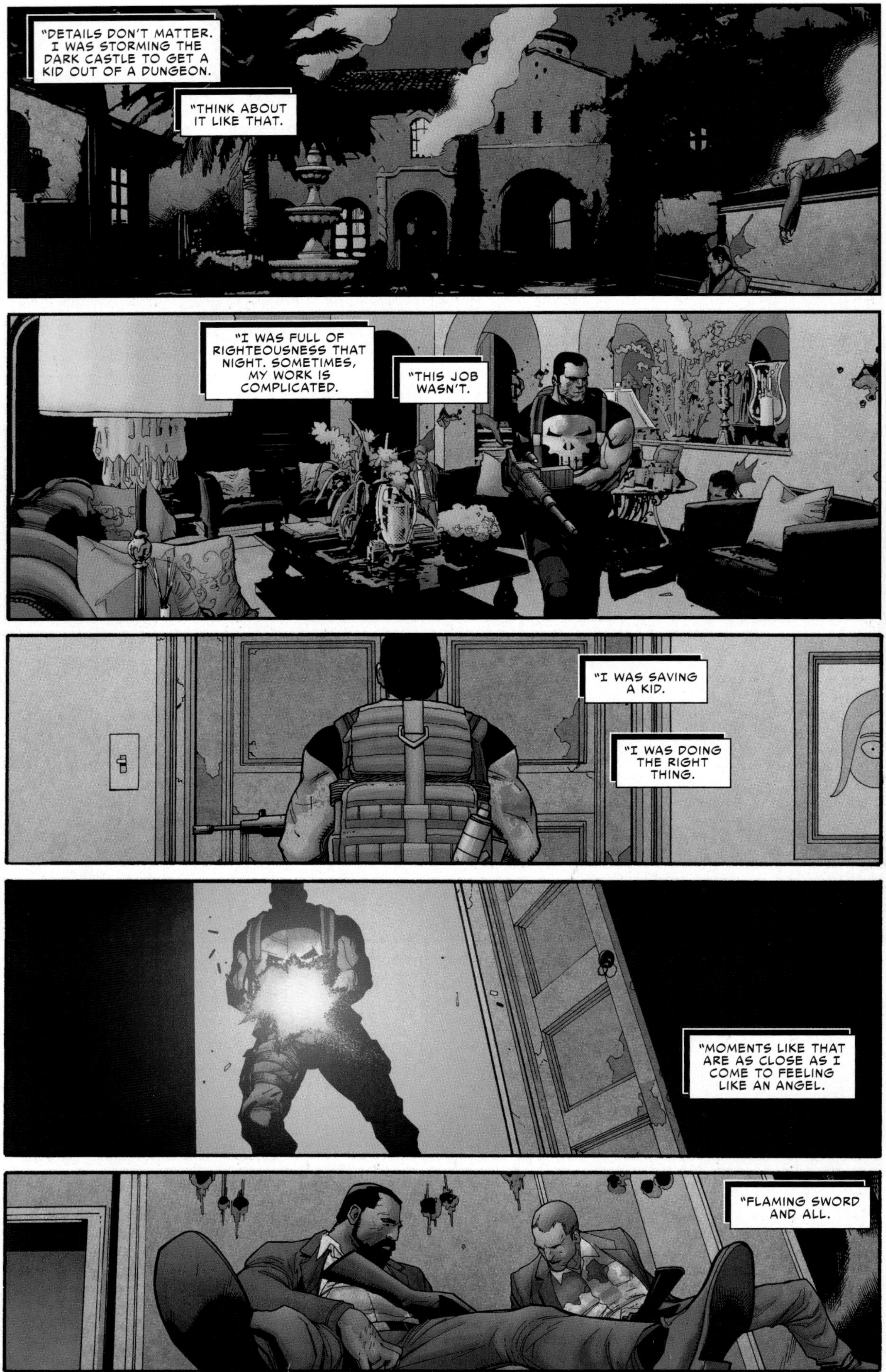
"DETAILS DON'T MATTER. I WAS STORMING THE DARK CASTLE TO GET A KID OUT OF A DUNGEON.
"THINK ABOUT IT LIKE THAT.
"I WAS FULL OF RIGHTEOUSNESS THAT NIGHT. SOMETIMES, MY WORK IS COMPLICATED.
"THIS JOB WASN'T.
"I WAS SAVING A KID.
"I WAS DOING THE RIGHT THING.
"MOMENTS LIKE THAT ARE AS CLOSE AS I COME TO FEELING LIKE AN ANGEL.
"FLAMING SWORD AND ALL.

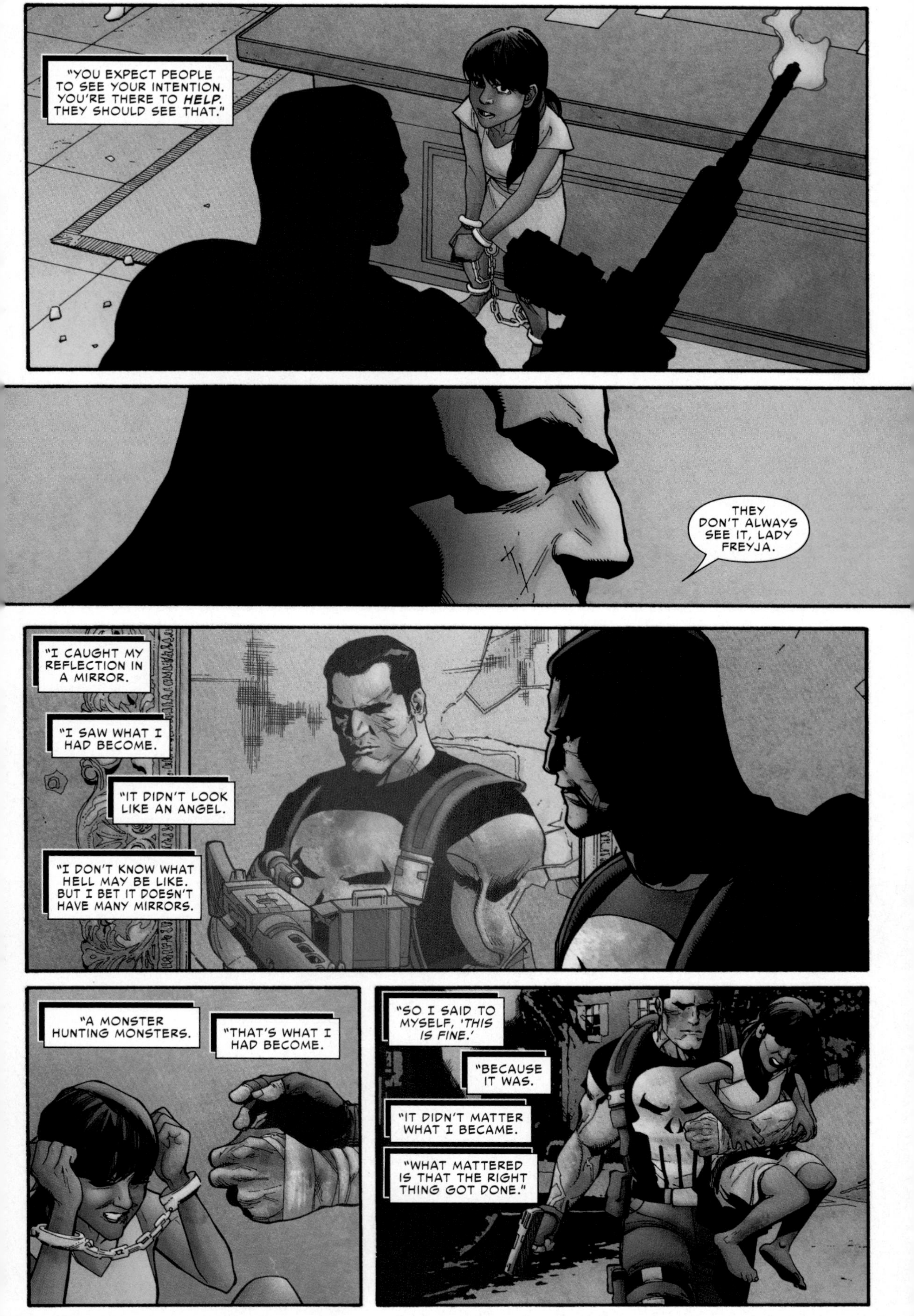
"YOU EXPECT PEOPLE TO SEE YOUR INTENTION. YOU'RE THERE TO *HELP*. THEY SHOULD SEE THAT."
THEY DON'T ALWAYS SEE IT, LADY FREYJA.
"I CAUGHT MY REFLECTION IN A MIRROR.
"I SAW WHAT I HAD BECOME.
"IT DIDN'T LOOK LIKE AN ANGEL.
"I DON'T KNOW WHAT HELL MAY BE LIKE. BUT I BET IT DOESN'T HAVE MANY MIRRORS.
"A MONSTER HUNTING MONSTERS.
"THAT'S WHAT I HAD BECOME.
"SO I SAID TO MYSELF, '*THIS IS FINE.*'
"BECAUSE IT WAS.
"IT DIDN'T MATTER WHAT I BECAME.
"WHAT MATTERED IS THAT THE RIGHT THING GOT DONE."

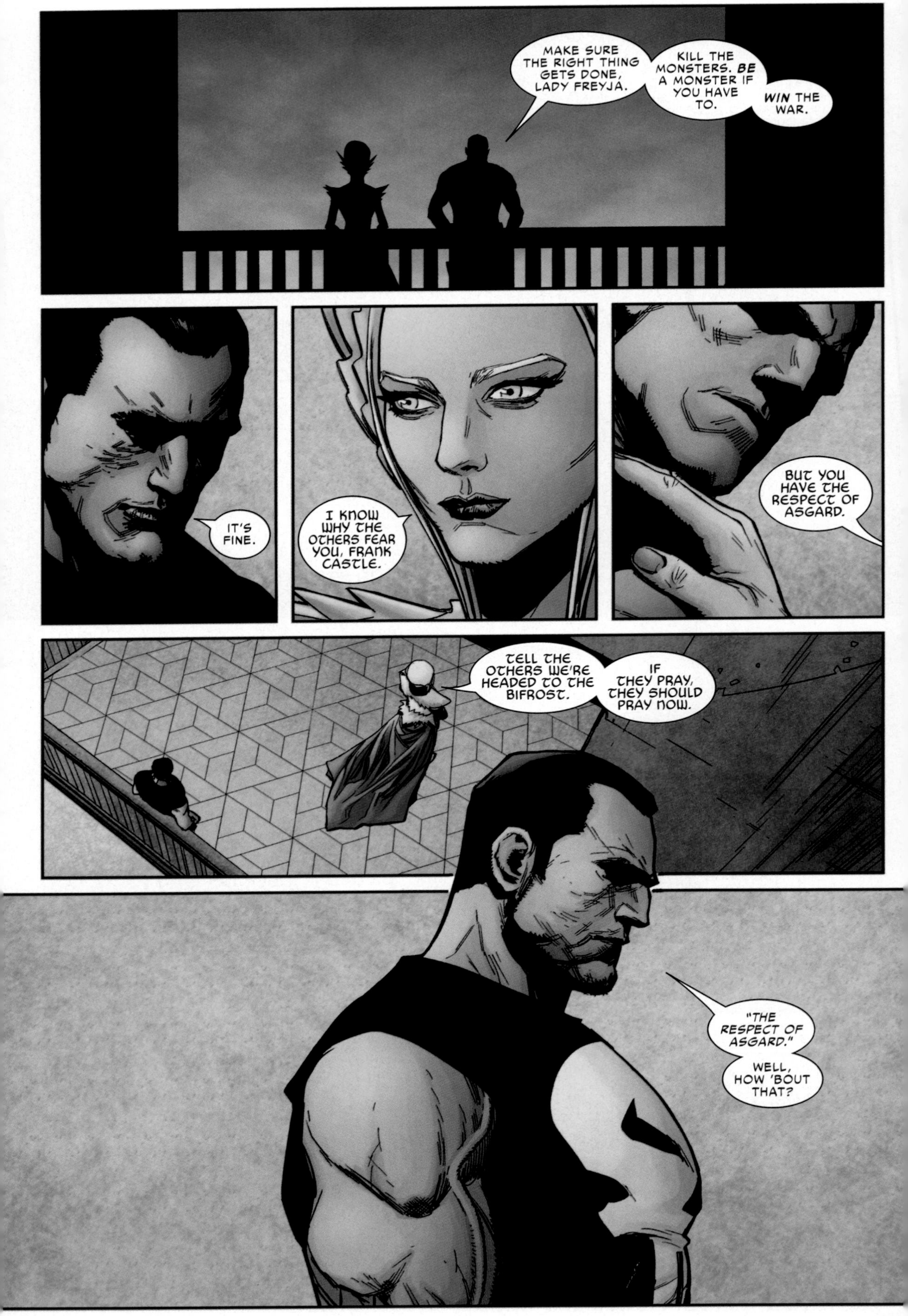
MAKE SURE THE RIGHT THING GETS DONE, LADY FREYJA.
KILL THE MONSTERS. BE A MONSTER IF YOU HAVE TO.
WIN THE WAR.
IT'S FINE.
I KNOW WHY THE OTHERS FEAR YOU, FRANK CASTLE.
BUT YOU HAVE THE RESPECT OF ASGARD.
TELL THE OTHERS WE'RE HEADED TO THE BIFROST.
IF THEY PRAY, THEY SHOULD PRAY NOW.
"THE RESPECT OF ASGARD."
WELL, HOW 'BOUT THAT?

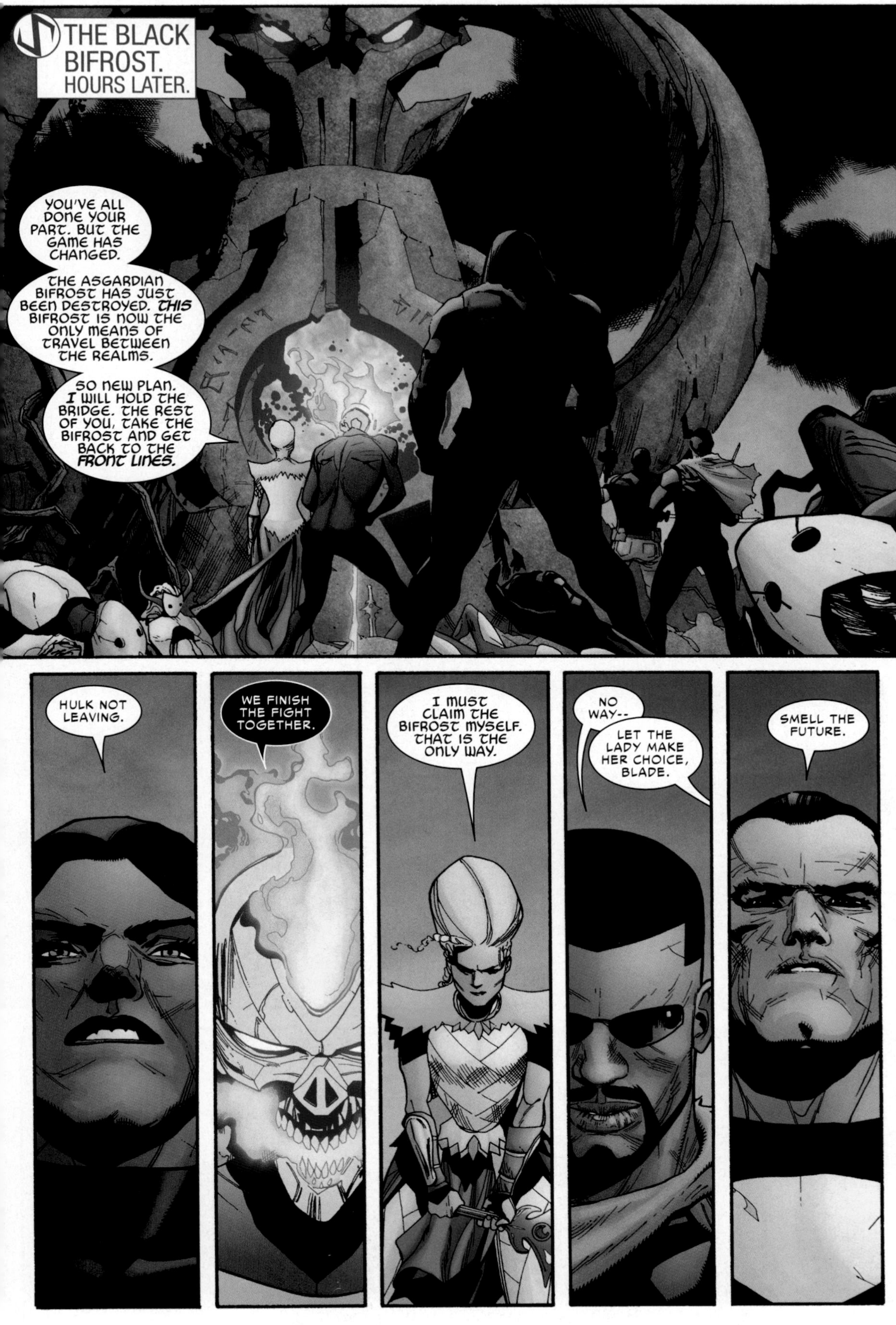
THE BLACK BIFROST. HOURS LATER.
YOU'VE ALL DONE YOUR PART. BUT THE GAME HAS CHANGED.
THE ASGARDIAN BIFROST HAS JUST BEEN DESTROYED. THIS BIFROST IS NOW THE ONLY MEANS OF TRAVEL BETWEEN THE REALMS.
SO NEW PLAN. I WILL HOLD THE BRIDGE. THE REST OF YOU, TAKE THE BIFROST AND GET BACK TO THE FRONT LINES.
HULK NOT LEAVING.
WE FINISH THE FIGHT TOGETHER.
I MUST CLAIM THE BIFROST MYSELF. THAT IS THE ONLY WAY.
NO WAY--
LET THE LADY MAKE HER CHOICE, BLADE.
SMELL THE FUTURE.

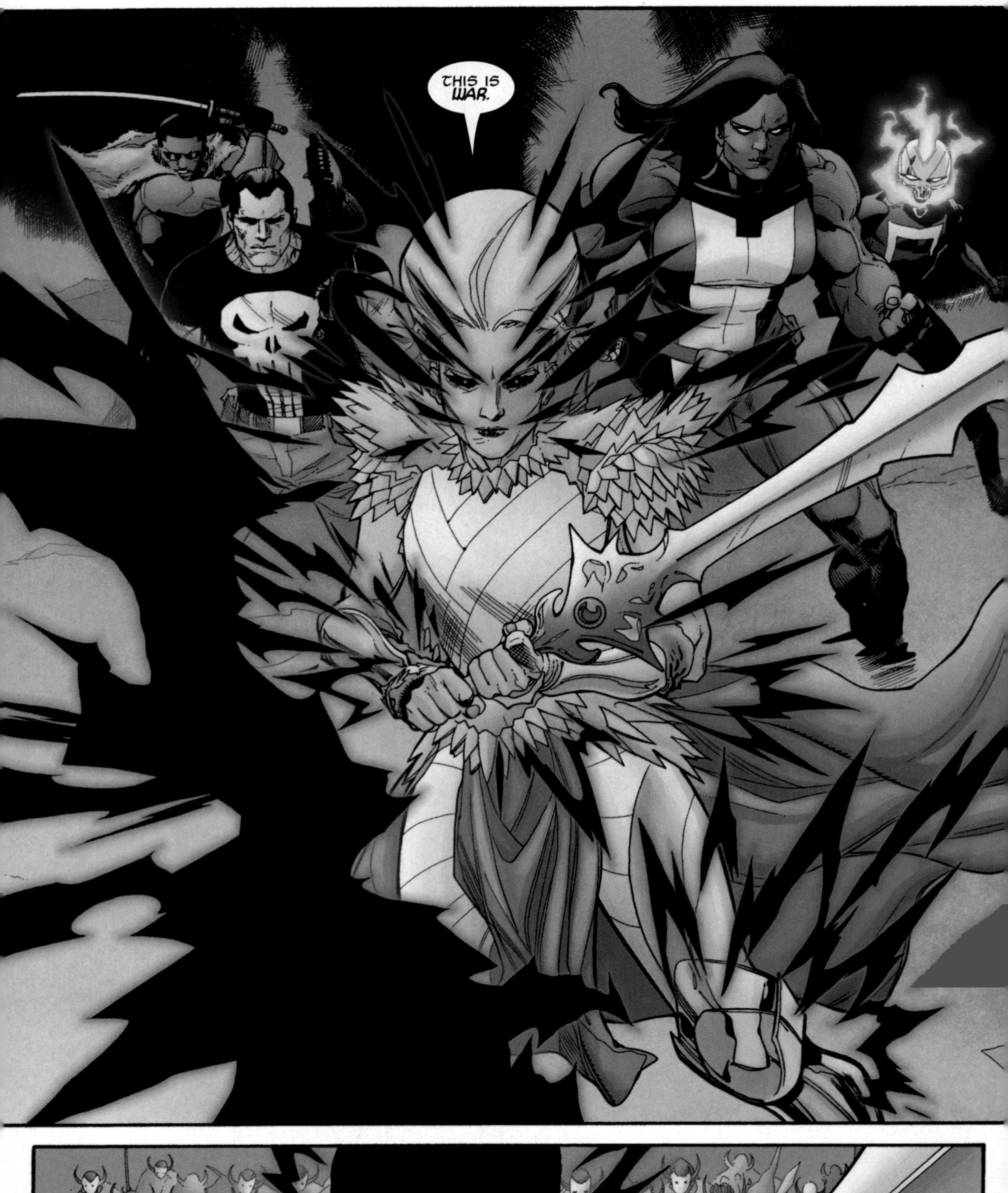
THIS IS WAR.

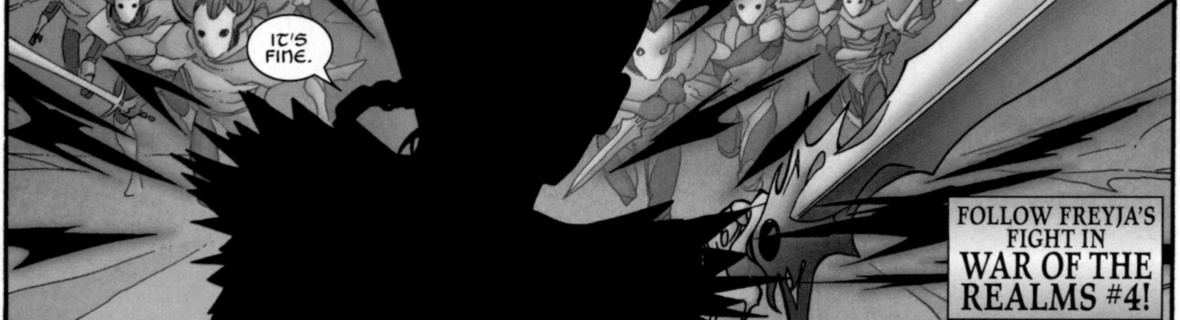
IT'S FINE.
FOLLOW FREYJA'S FIGHT IN WAR OF THE REALMS #4!

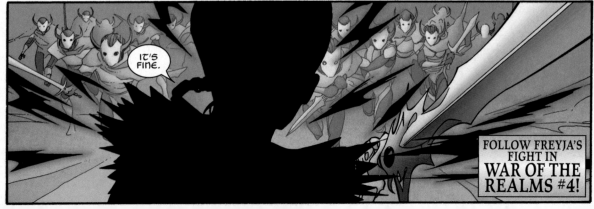

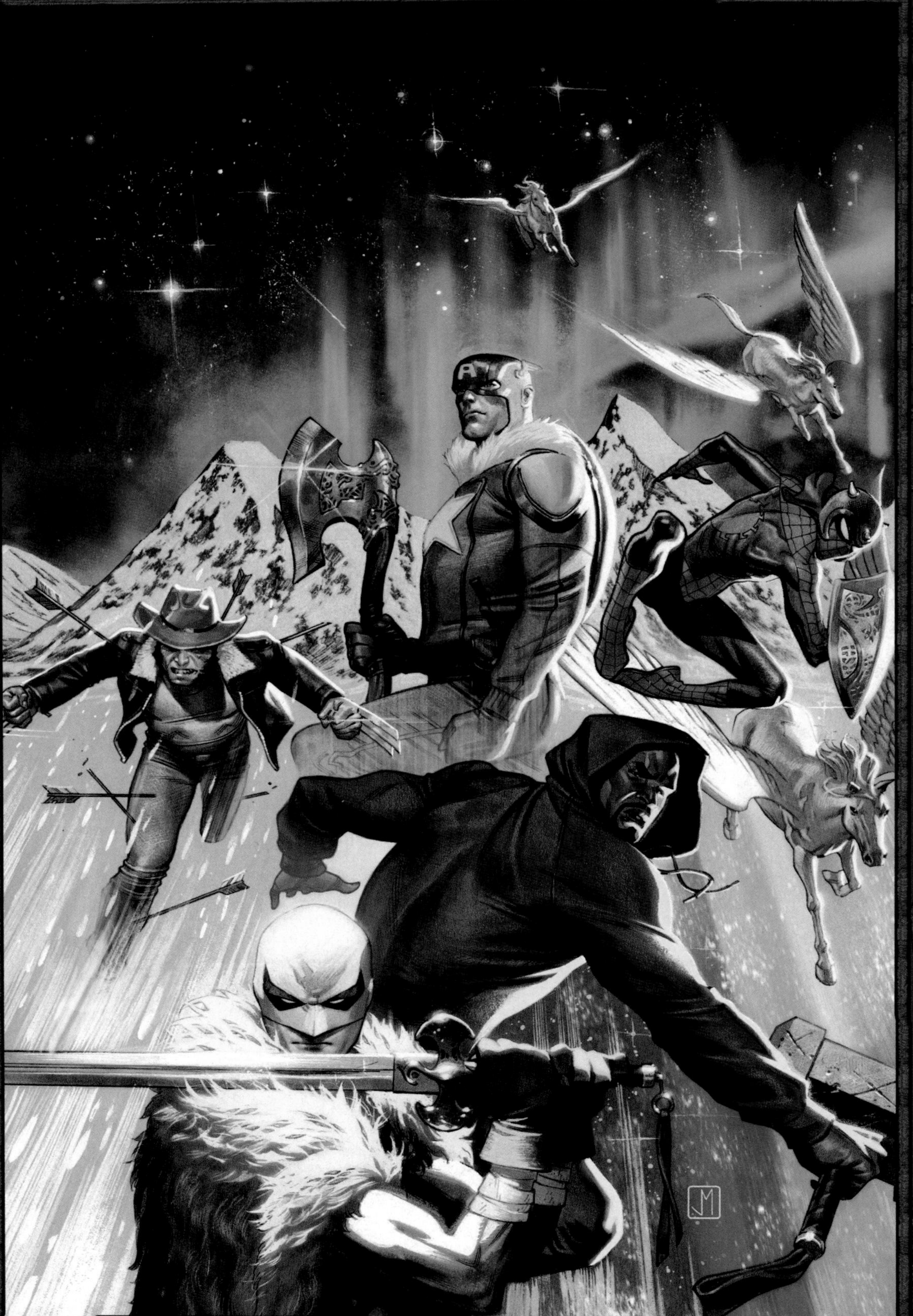

The Land of Giants

Malekith's first move was to trap his greatest enemy—Thor—in the Frost Giant realm of Jotunheim, leaving Midgard ripe for the taking. If they have any hope of retaking Earth, they'll have to find and rescue the God of Thunder.

And Lady Freyja knows just the man for the job: Captain America.

THE WAR OF THE REALMS
STRIKEFORCE
THE LAND OF GIANTS

written by
TOM TAYLOR

penciled by
JORGE MOLINA

inked by
ADRIANO DI BENEDETTO

colored by
DAVID CURIEL

lettered by
VC's JOE SABINO

cover artist
JORGE MOLINA

variant cover artists
CULLY HAMNER & MORRY HOLLOWELL

SARAH BRUNSTAD   WIL MOSS
associate editor   editor

Note: Read WAR OF THE REALMS #1-3 before this issue.

TOM BREVOORT   C.B. CEBULSKI   JOE QUESADA   DAN BUCKLEY   ALAN FINE
executive editor   editor in chief   chief creative officer   president   executive producer

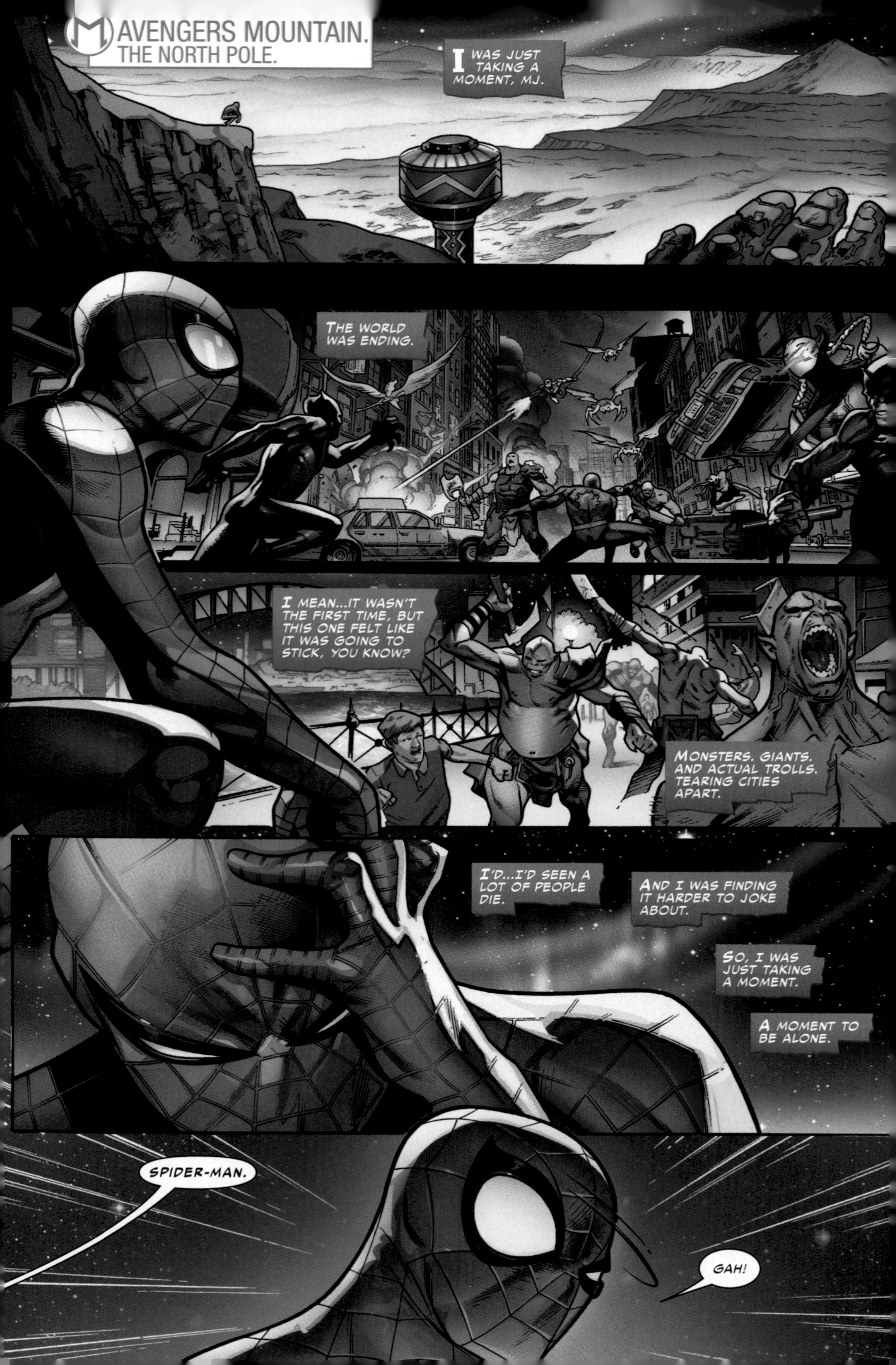
AVENGERS MOUNTAIN.
THE NORTH POLE.
I WAS JUST TAKING A MOMENT, MJ.
THE WORLD WAS ENDING.
I MEAN...IT WASN'T THE FIRST TIME, BUT THIS ONE FELT LIKE IT WAS GOING TO STICK, YOU KNOW?
MONSTERS. GIANTS. AND ACTUAL TROLLS. TEARING CITIES APART.
I'D...I'D SEEN A LOT OF PEOPLE DIE.
AND I WAS FINDING IT HARDER TO JOKE ABOUT.
SO, I WAS JUST TAKING A MOMENT.
A MOMENT TO BE ALONE.
SPIDER-MAN.
GAH!

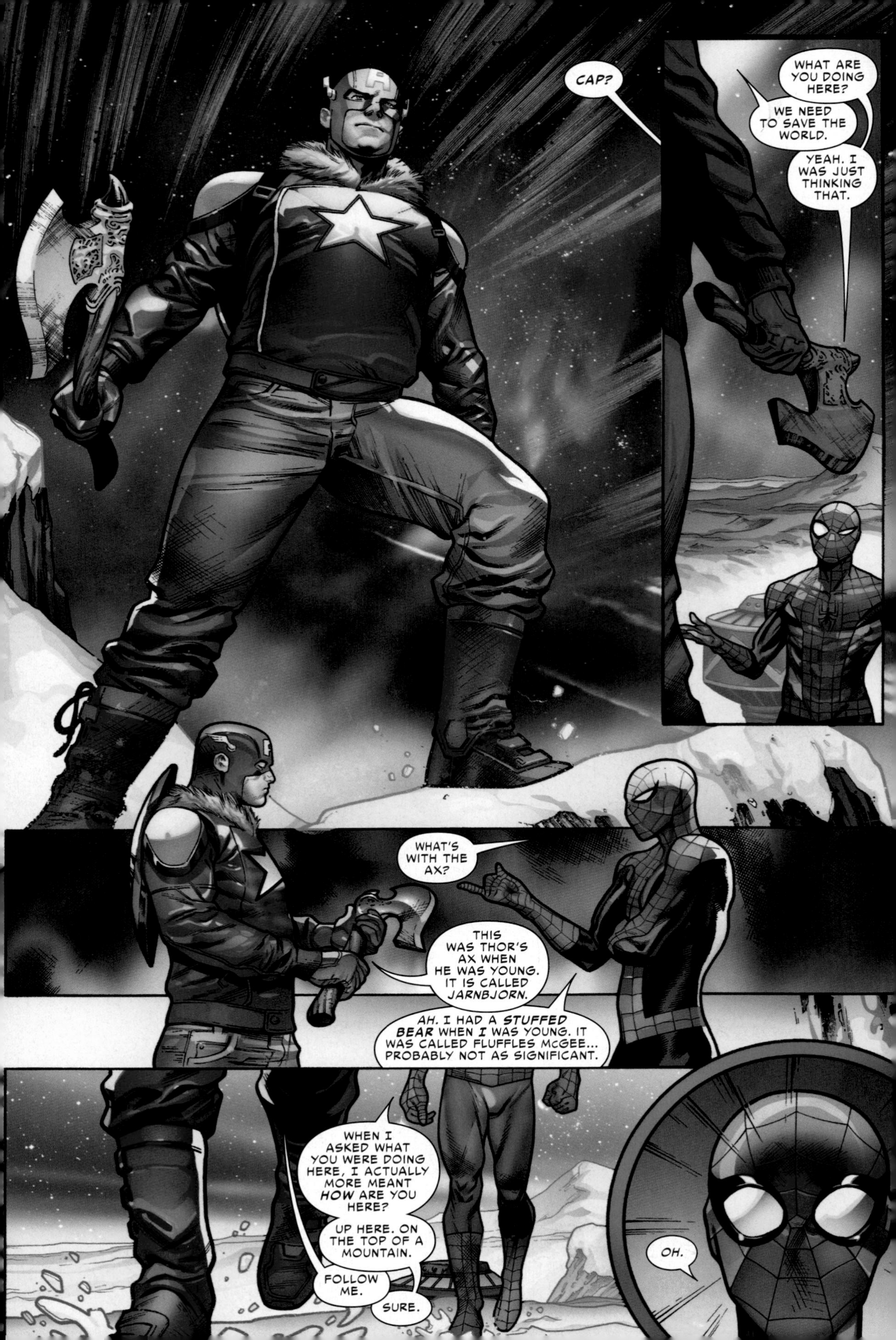
CAP?
WHAT ARE YOU DOING HERE?
WE NEED TO SAVE THE WORLD.
YEAH. I WAS JUST THINKING THAT.
WHAT'S WITH THE AX?
THIS WAS THOR'S AX WHEN HE WAS YOUNG. IT IS CALLED JARNBJORN.
AH. I HAD A STUFFED BEAR WHEN I WAS YOUNG. IT WAS CALLED FLUFFLES McGEE... PROBABLY NOT AS SIGNIFICANT.
WHEN I ASKED WHAT YOU WERE DOING HERE, I ACTUALLY MORE MEANT HOW ARE YOU HERE?
UP HERE. ON THE TOP OF A MOUNTAIN.
FOLLOW ME.
SURE.
OH.

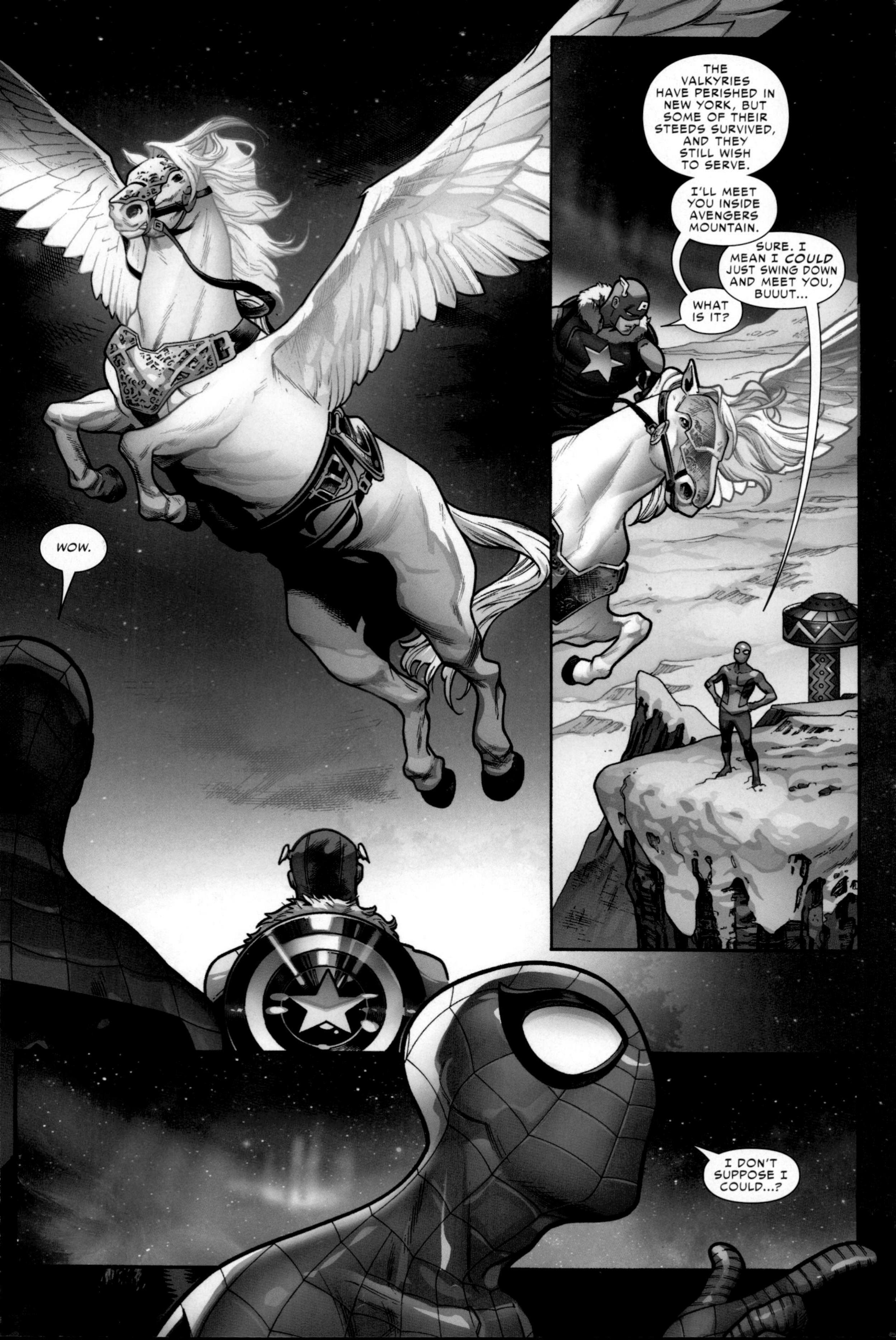
THE VALKYRIES HAVE PERISHED IN NEW YORK, BUT SOME OF THEIR STEEDS SURVIVED, AND THEY STILL WISH TO SERVE.
I'LL MEET YOU INSIDE AVENGERS MOUNTAIN.
SURE. I MEAN I *COULD* JUST SWING DOWN AND MEET YOU, BUUUT...
WHAT IS IT?
WOW.
I DON'T SUPPOSE I COULD...?

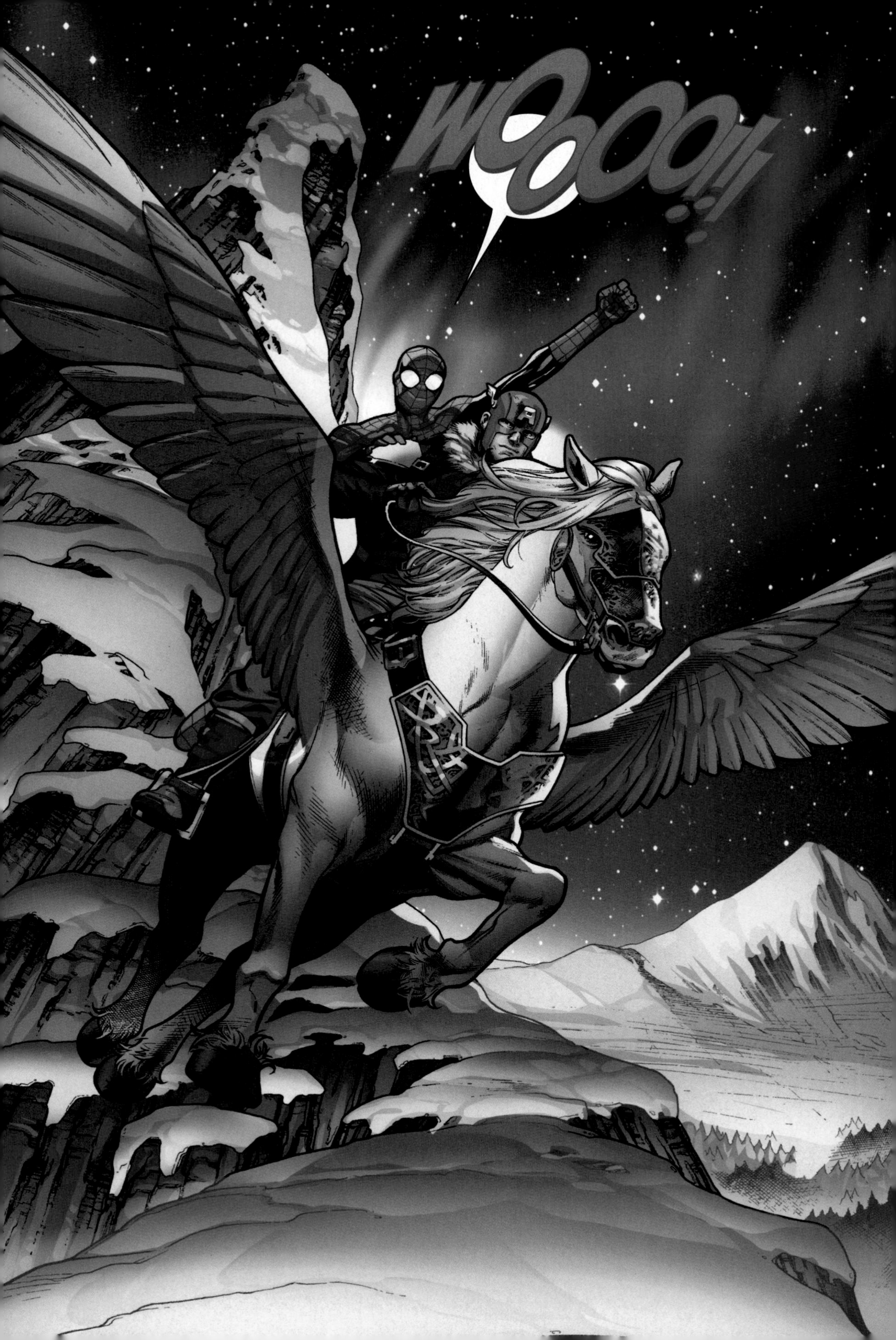

WOOOO!!

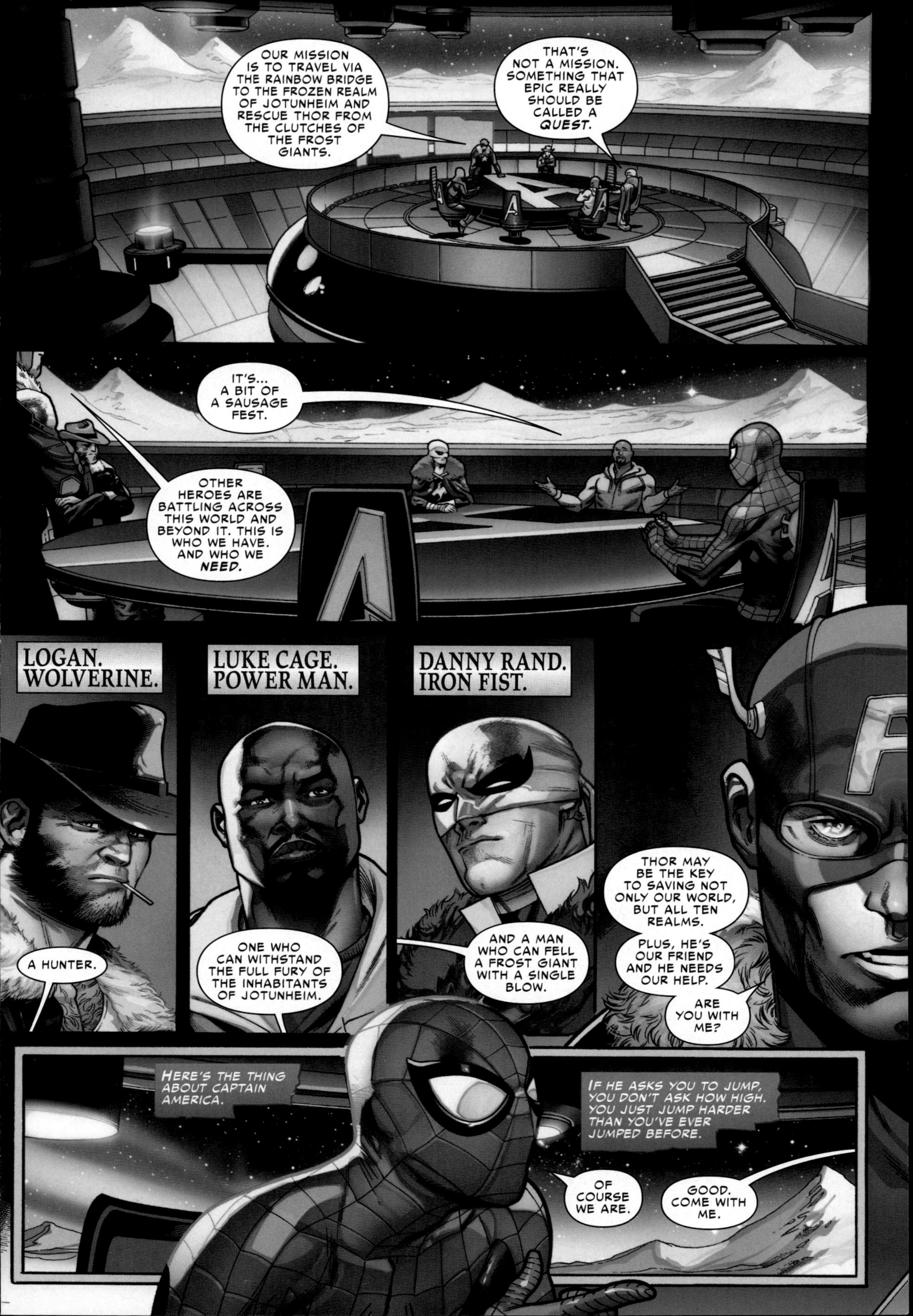
OUR MISSION IS TO TRAVEL VIA THE RAINBOW BRIDGE TO THE FROZEN REALM OF JOTUNHEIM AND RESCUE THOR FROM THE CLUTCHES OF THE FROST GIANTS.
THAT'S NOT A MISSION. SOMETHING THAT EPIC REALLY SHOULD BE CALLED A *QUEST*.
IT'S... A BIT OF A SAUSAGE FEST.
OTHER HEROES ARE BATTLING ACROSS THIS WORLD AND BEYOND IT. THIS IS WHO WE HAVE. AND WHO WE *NEED*.
LOGAN. WOLVERINE.
LUKE CAGE. POWER MAN.
DANNY RAND. IRON FIST.
A HUNTER.
ONE WHO CAN WITHSTAND THE FULL FURY OF THE INHABITANTS OF JOTUNHEIM.
AND A MAN WHO CAN FELL A FROST GIANT WITH A SINGLE BLOW.
THOR MAY BE THE KEY TO SAVING NOT ONLY OUR WORLD, BUT ALL TEN REALMS.
PLUS, HE'S OUR FRIEND AND HE NEEDS OUR HELP.
ARE YOU WITH ME?
HERE'S THE THING ABOUT CAPTAIN AMERICA.
IF HE ASKS YOU TO JUMP, YOU DON'T ASK HOW HIGH. YOU JUST JUMP HARDER THAN YOU'VE EVER JUMPED BEFORE.
OF COURSE WE ARE.
GOOD. COME WITH ME.

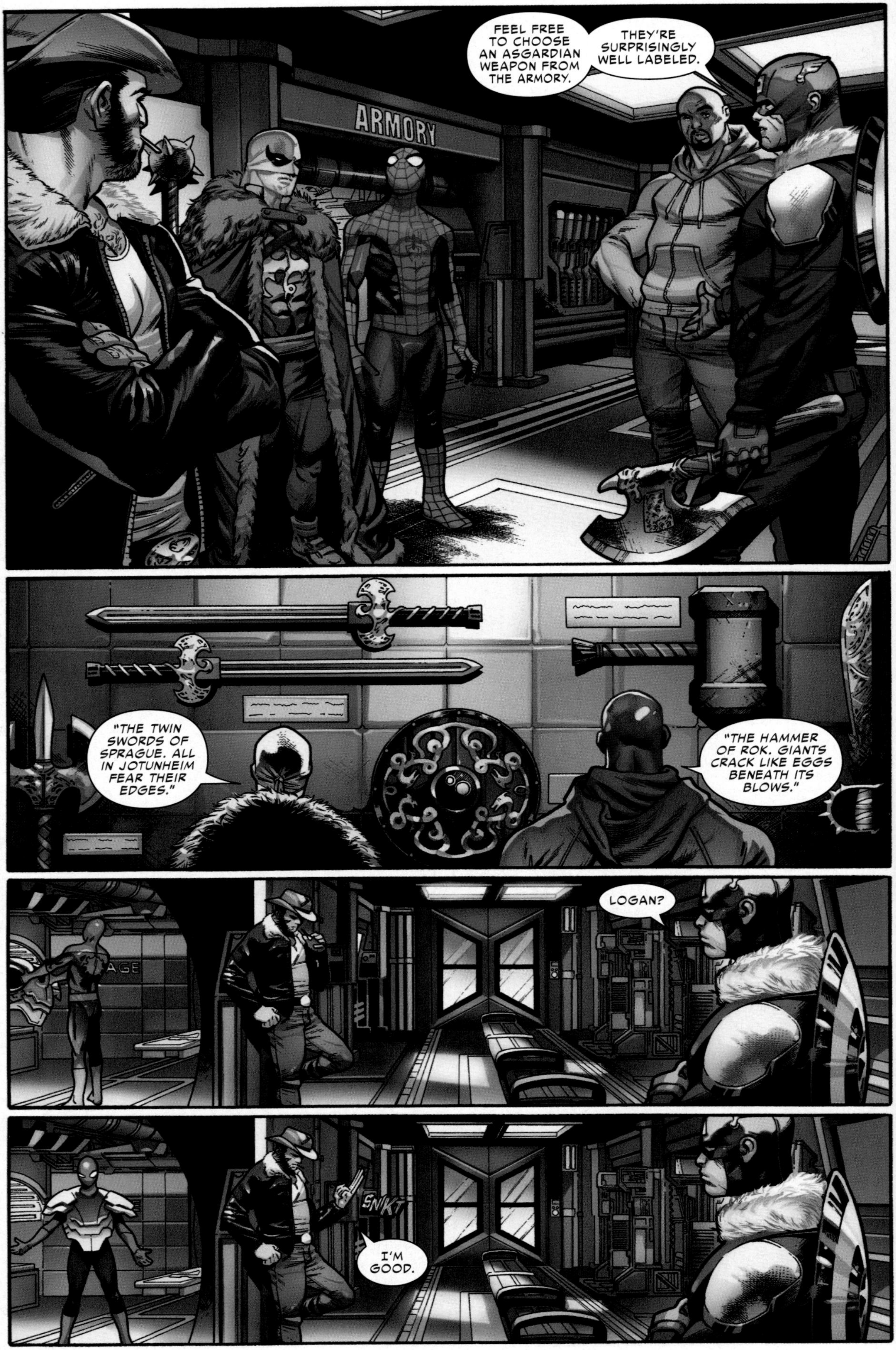
FEEL FREE TO CHOOSE AN ASGARDIAN WEAPON FROM THE ARMORY.
THEY'RE SURPRISINGLY WELL LABELED.
ARMORY
"THE TWIN SWORDS OF SPRAGUE. ALL IN JOTUNHEIM FEAR THEIR EDGES."
"THE HAMMER OF ROK. GIANTS CRACK LIKE EGGS BENEATH ITS BLOWS."
LOGAN?
SNIKT
I'M GOOD.

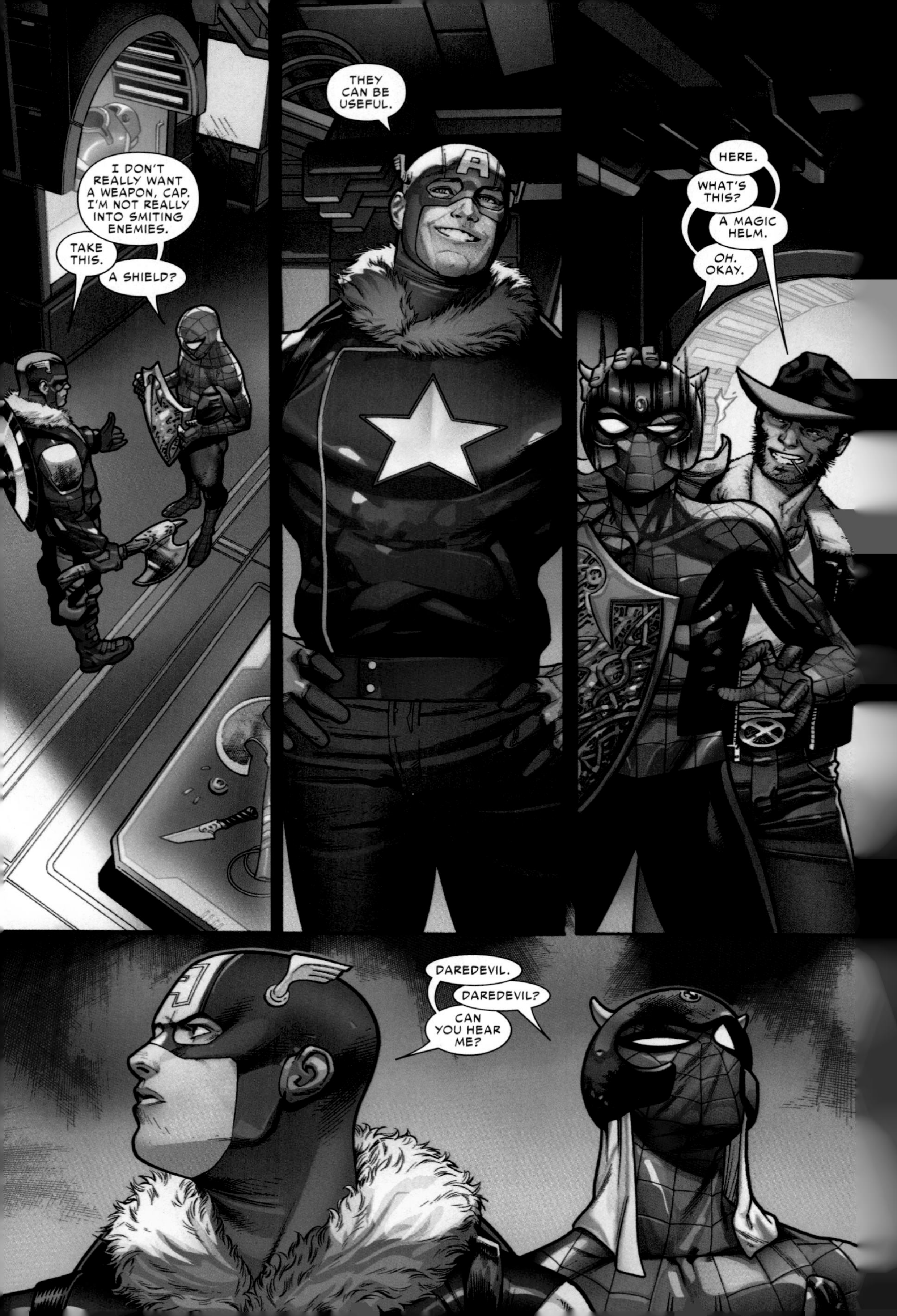
I DON'T REALLY WANT A WEAPON, CAP. I'M NOT REALLY INTO SMITING ENEMIES.
TAKE THIS.
A SHIELD?
THEY CAN BE USEFUL.
HERE.
WHAT'S THIS?
A MAGIC HELM.
OH. OKAY.
DAREDEVIL.
DAREDEVIL?
CAN YOU HEAR ME?

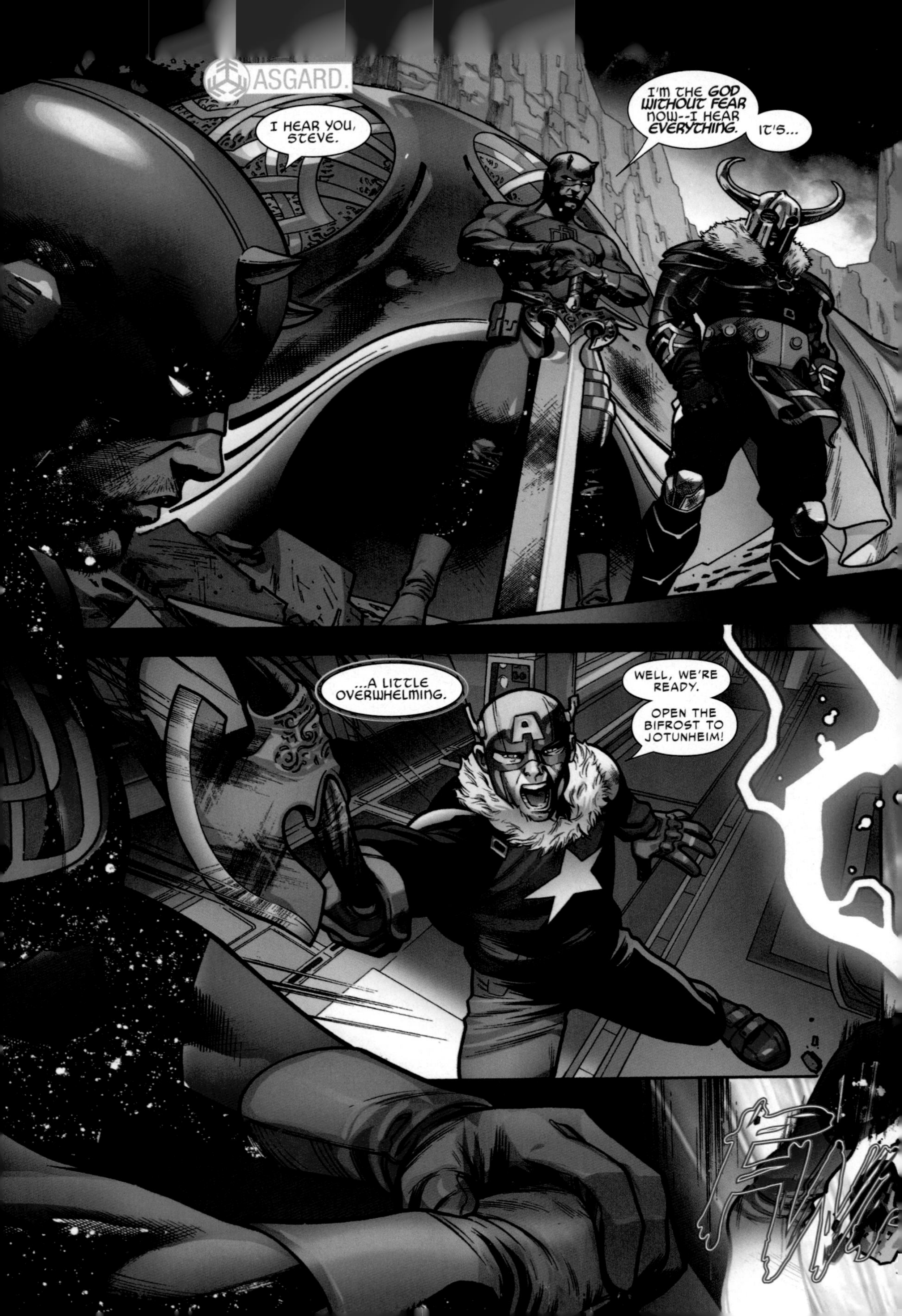
ASGARD.
I HEAR YOU, STEVE.
I'M THE GOD WITHOUT FEAR NOW--I HEAR EVERYTHING.
IT'S...
...A LITTLE OVERWHELMING.
WELL, WE'RE READY.
OPEN THE BIFROST TO JOTUNHEIM!

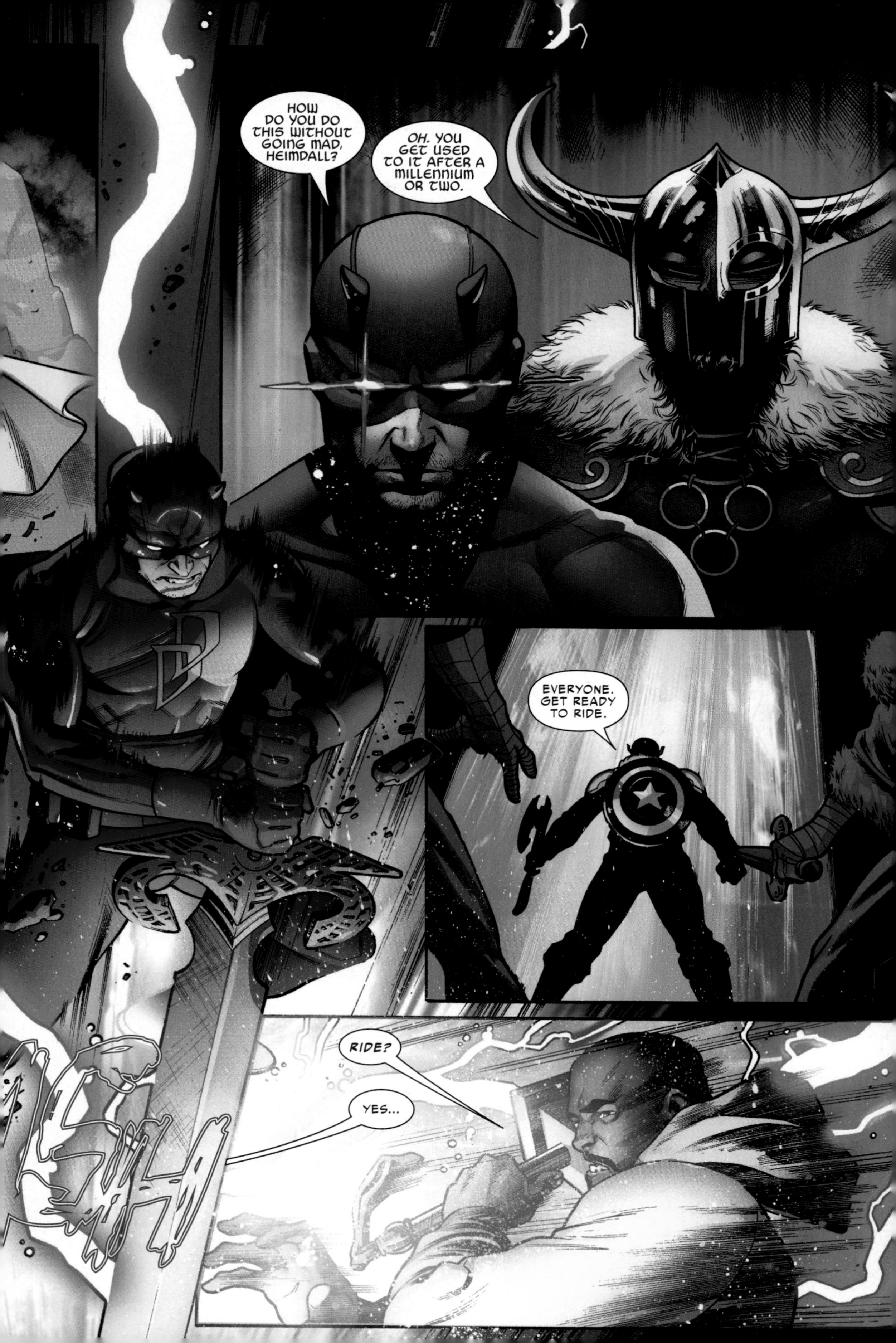
HOW DO YOU DO THIS WITHOUT GOING MAD, HEIMDALL?
OH. YOU GET USED TO IT AFTER A MILLENNIUM OR TWO.
EVERYONE. GET READY TO RIDE.
RIDE?
YES...

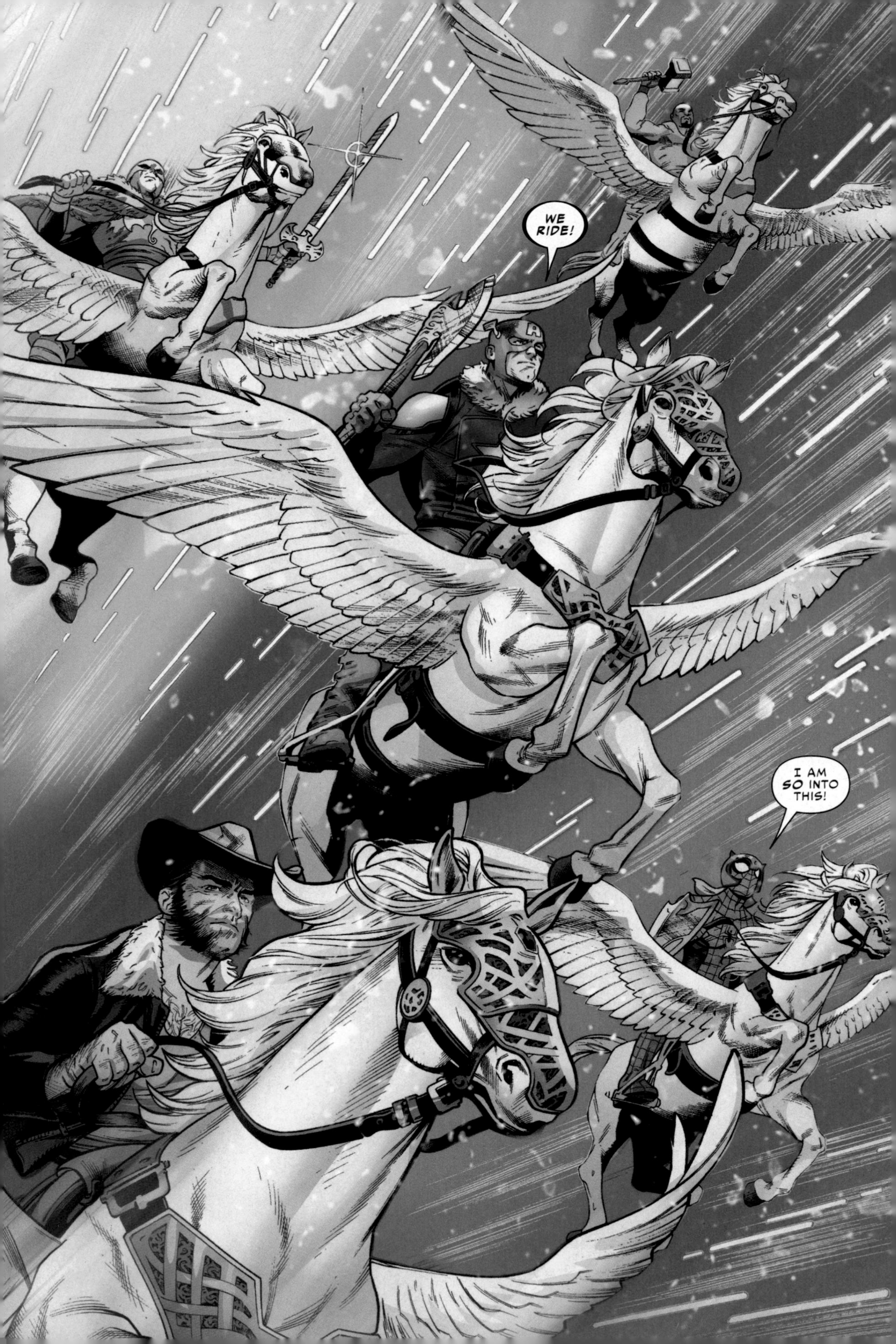
WE RIDE!
I AM SO INTO THIS!

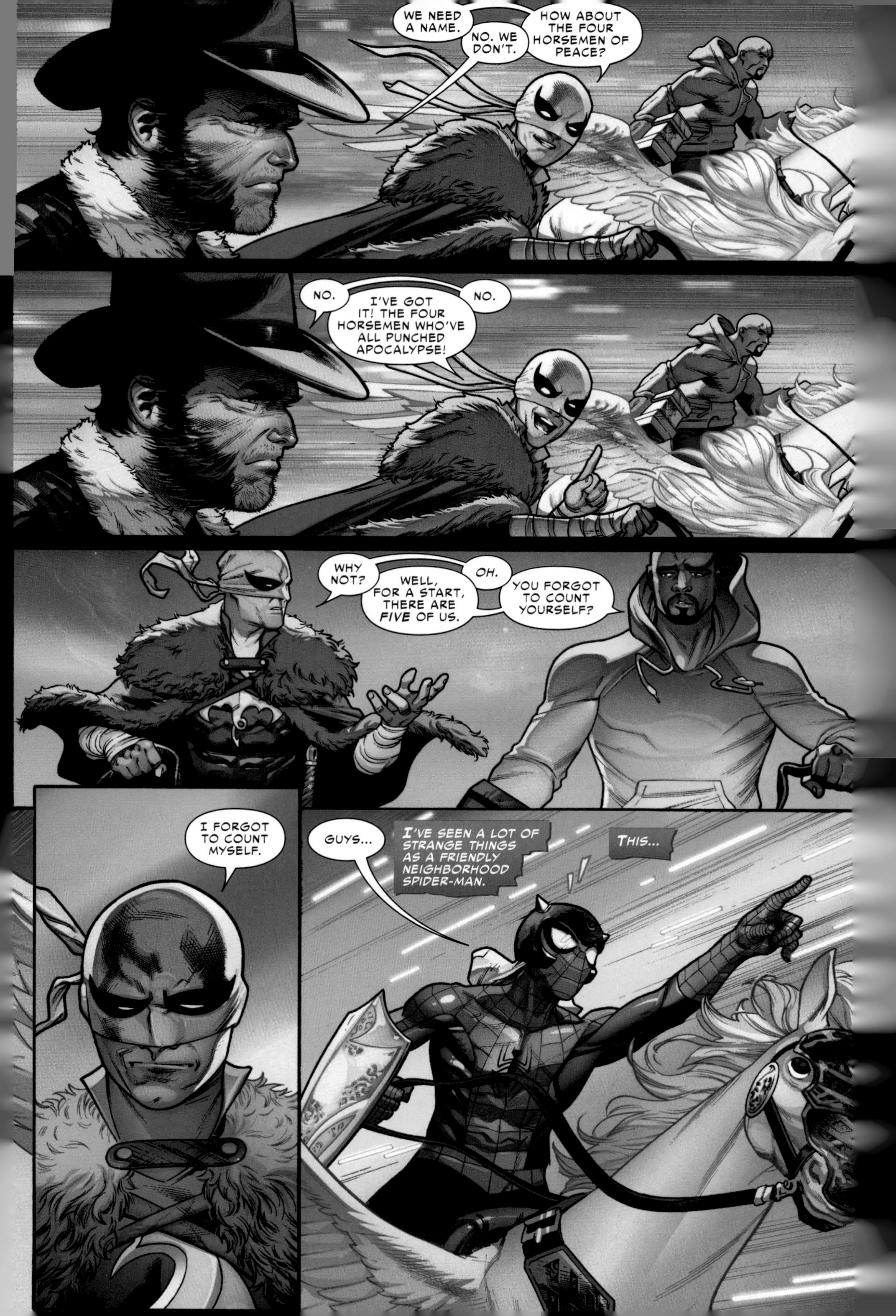
WE NEED A NAME.
HOW ABOUT THE FOUR HORSEMEN OF PEACE?
NO. WE DON'T.
NO.
I'VE GOT IT! THE FOUR HORSEMEN WHO'VE ALL PUNCHED APOCALYPSE!
NO.
WHY NOT?
WELL, FOR A START, THERE ARE FIVE OF US.
OH.
YOU FORGOT TO COUNT YOURSELF?
I FORGOT TO COUNT MYSELF.
GUYS...
I'VE SEEN A LOT OF STRANGE THINGS AS A FRIENDLY NEIGHBORHOOD SPIDER-MAN.
THIS...

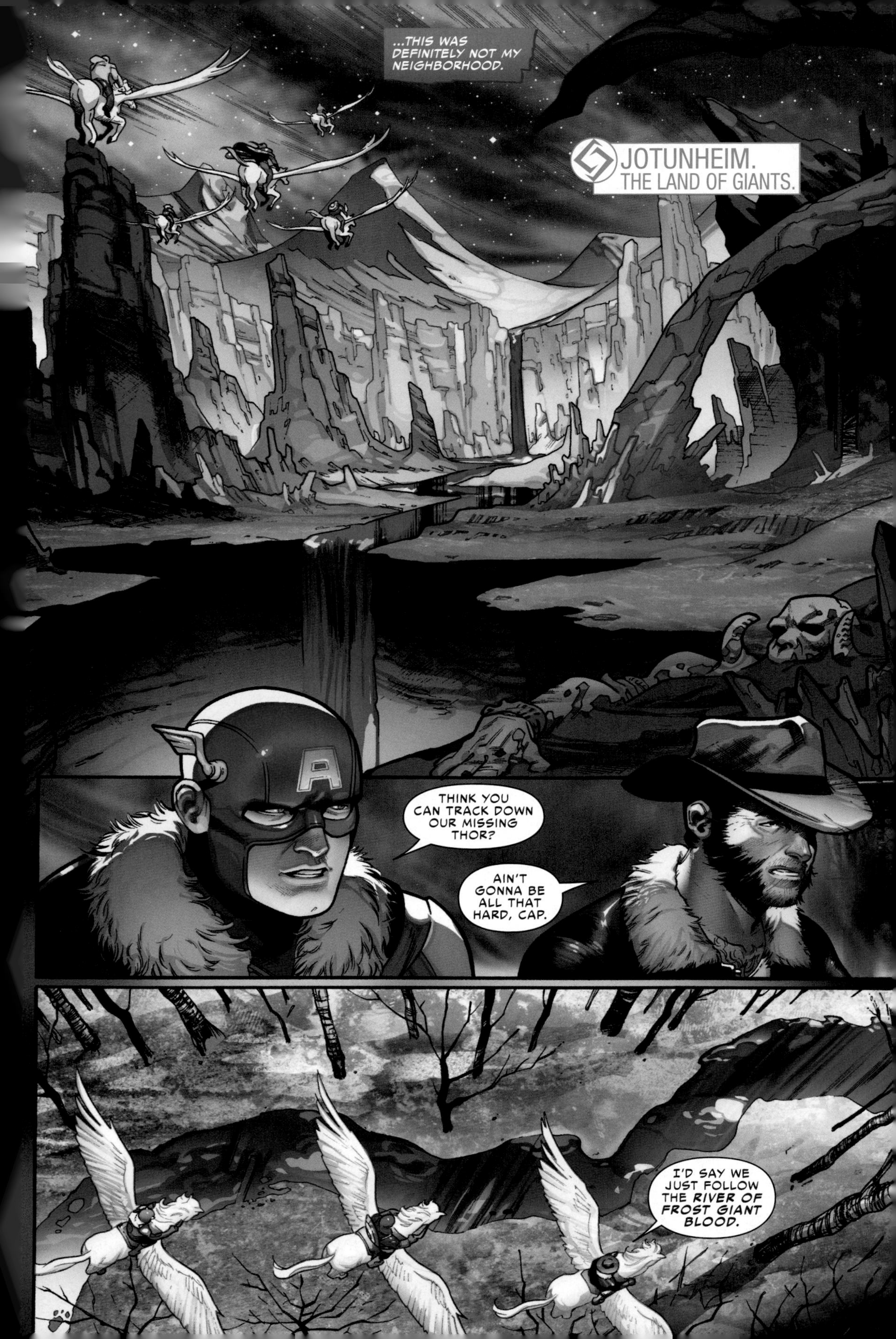
...THIS WAS DEFINITELY NOT MY NEIGHBORHOOD.
JOTUNHEIM. THE LAND OF GIANTS.
THINK YOU CAN TRACK DOWN OUR MISSING THOR?
AIN'T GONNA BE ALL THAT HARD, CAP.
I'D SAY WE JUST FOLLOW THE RIVER OF FROST GIANT BLOOD.

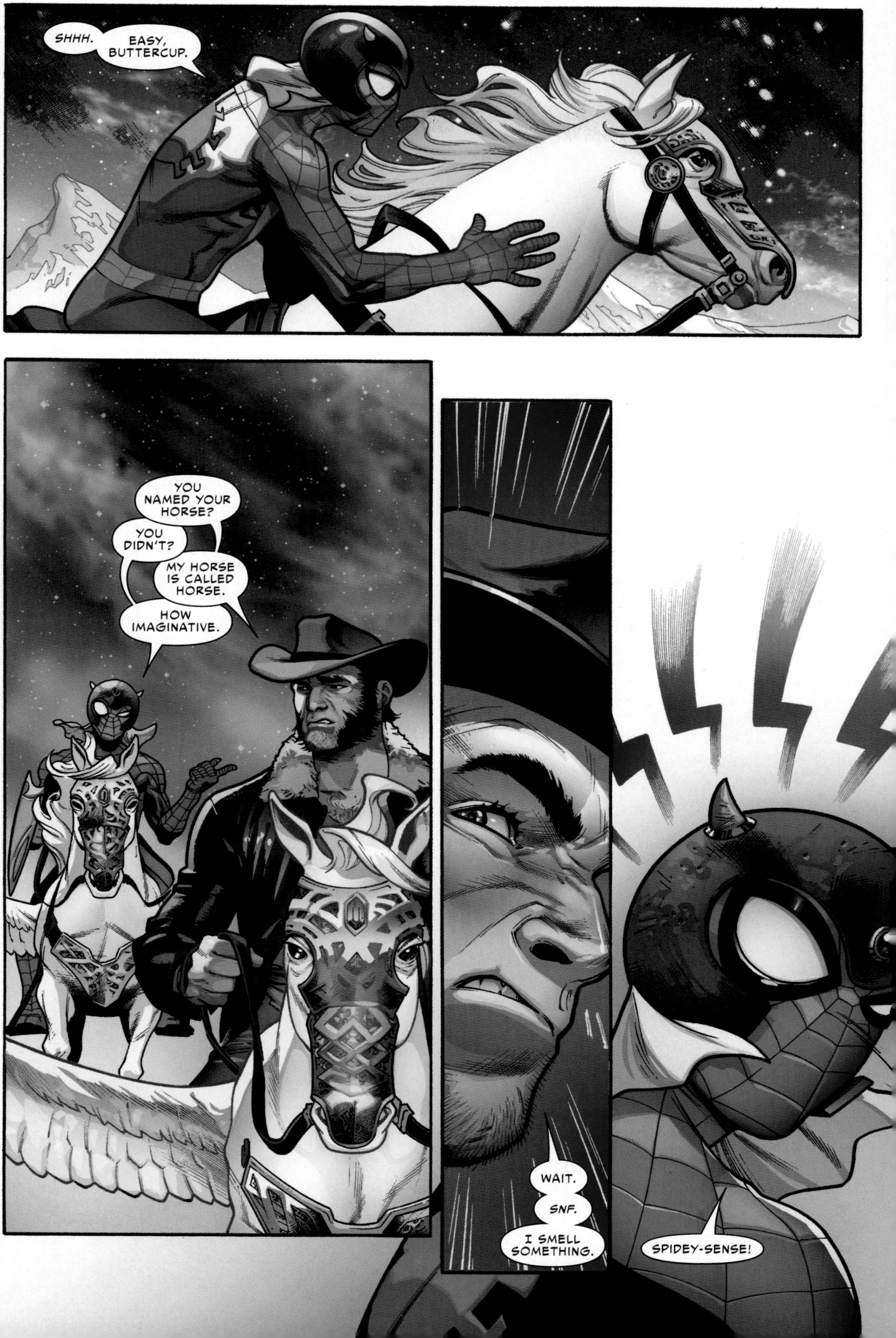
SHHH.
EASY, BUTTERCUP.
YOU NAMED YOUR HORSE?
YOU DIDN'T?
MY HORSE IS CALLED HORSE.
HOW IMAGINATIVE.
WAIT.
SNF.
I SMELL SOMETHING.
SPIDEY-SENSE!

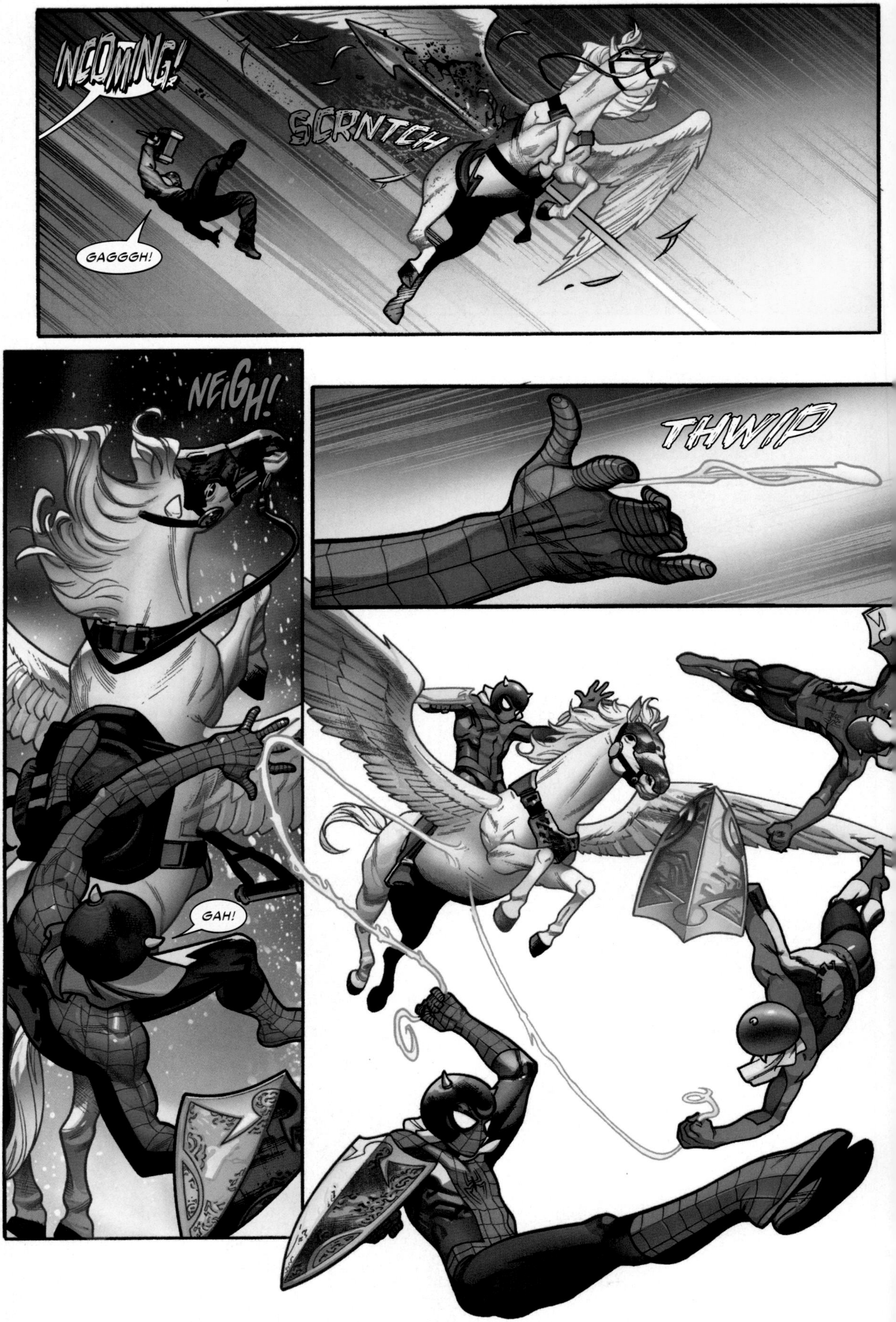
INCOMING!
SCRNTCH
GAGGGH!
NEIGH!
THWIP
GAH!

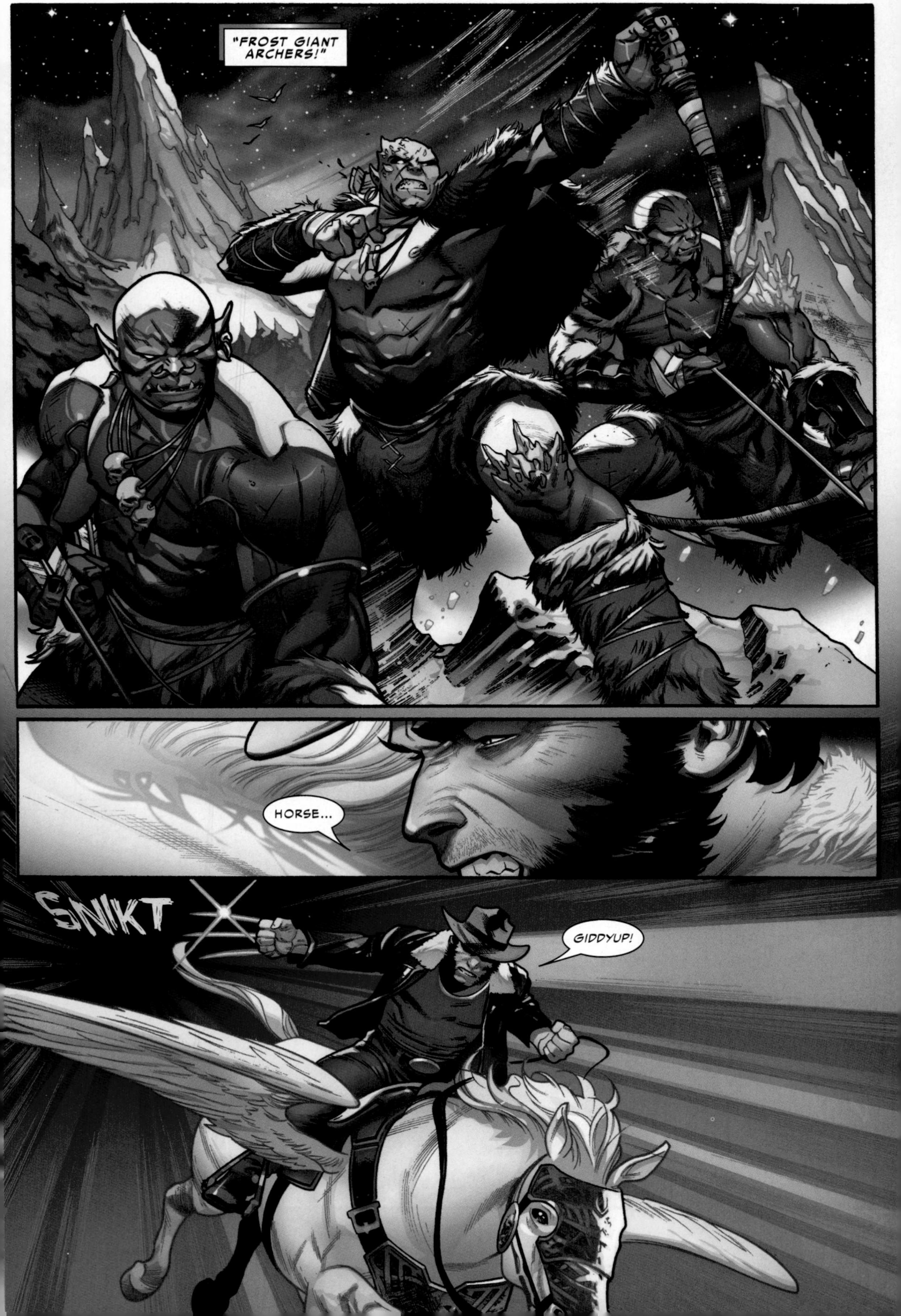
"FROST GIANT ARCHERS!"
HORSE...
SNIKT
GIDDYUP!

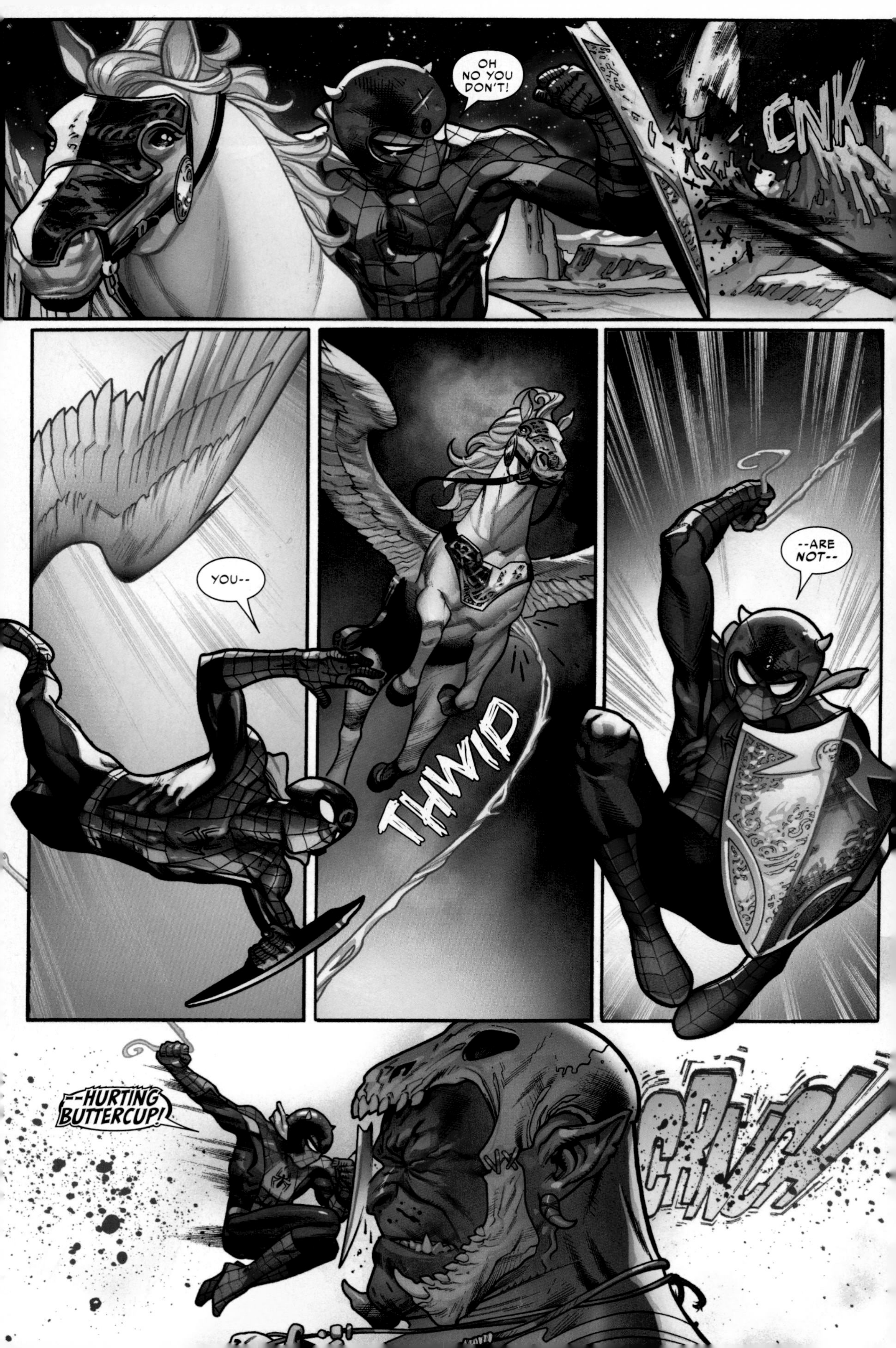
OH NO YOU DON'T!
CNK
YOU--
THWIP
--ARE NOT--
--HURTING BUTTERCUP!

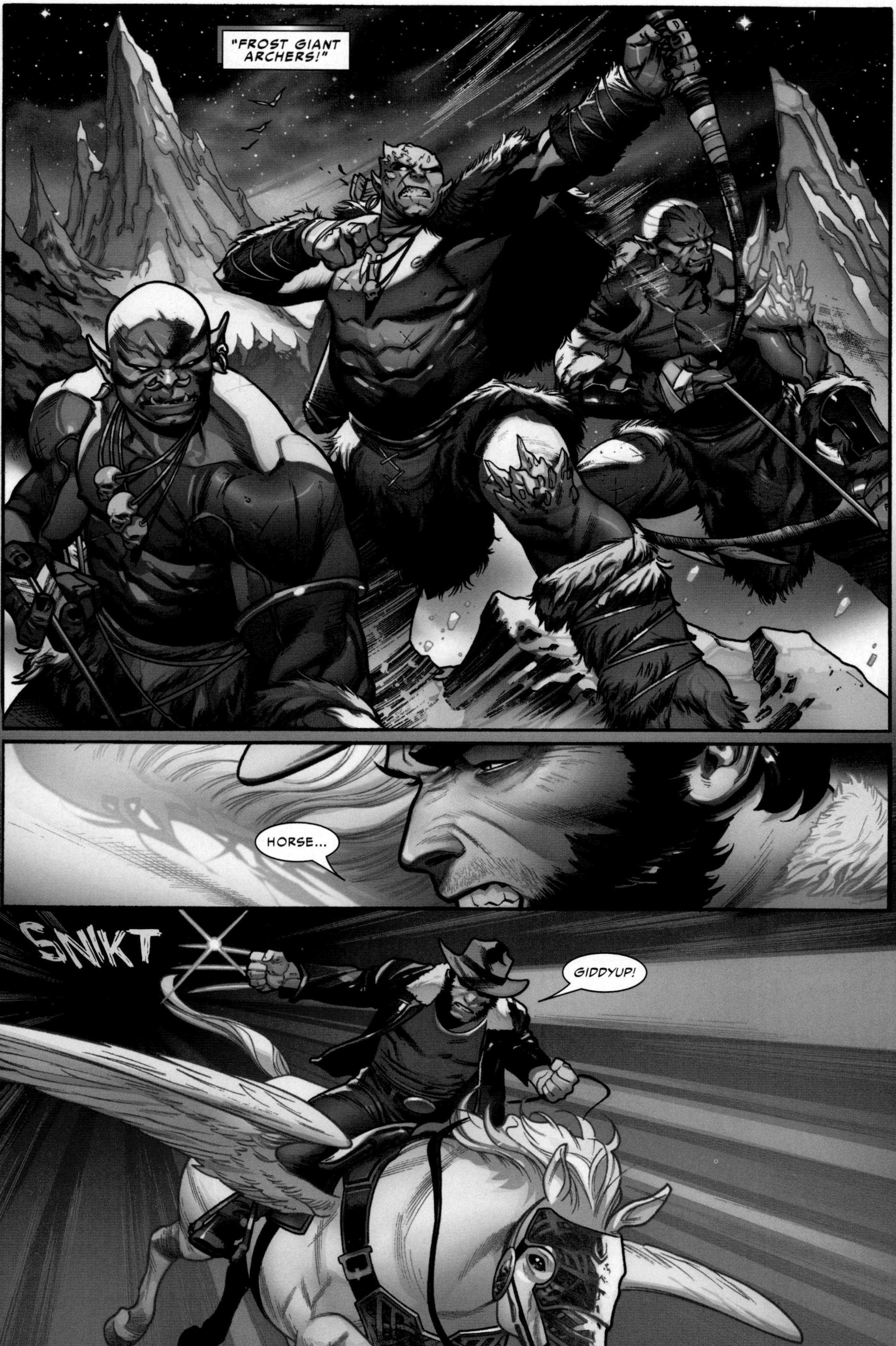
"FROST GIANT ARCHERS!"
HORSE...
SNIKT
GIDDYUP!

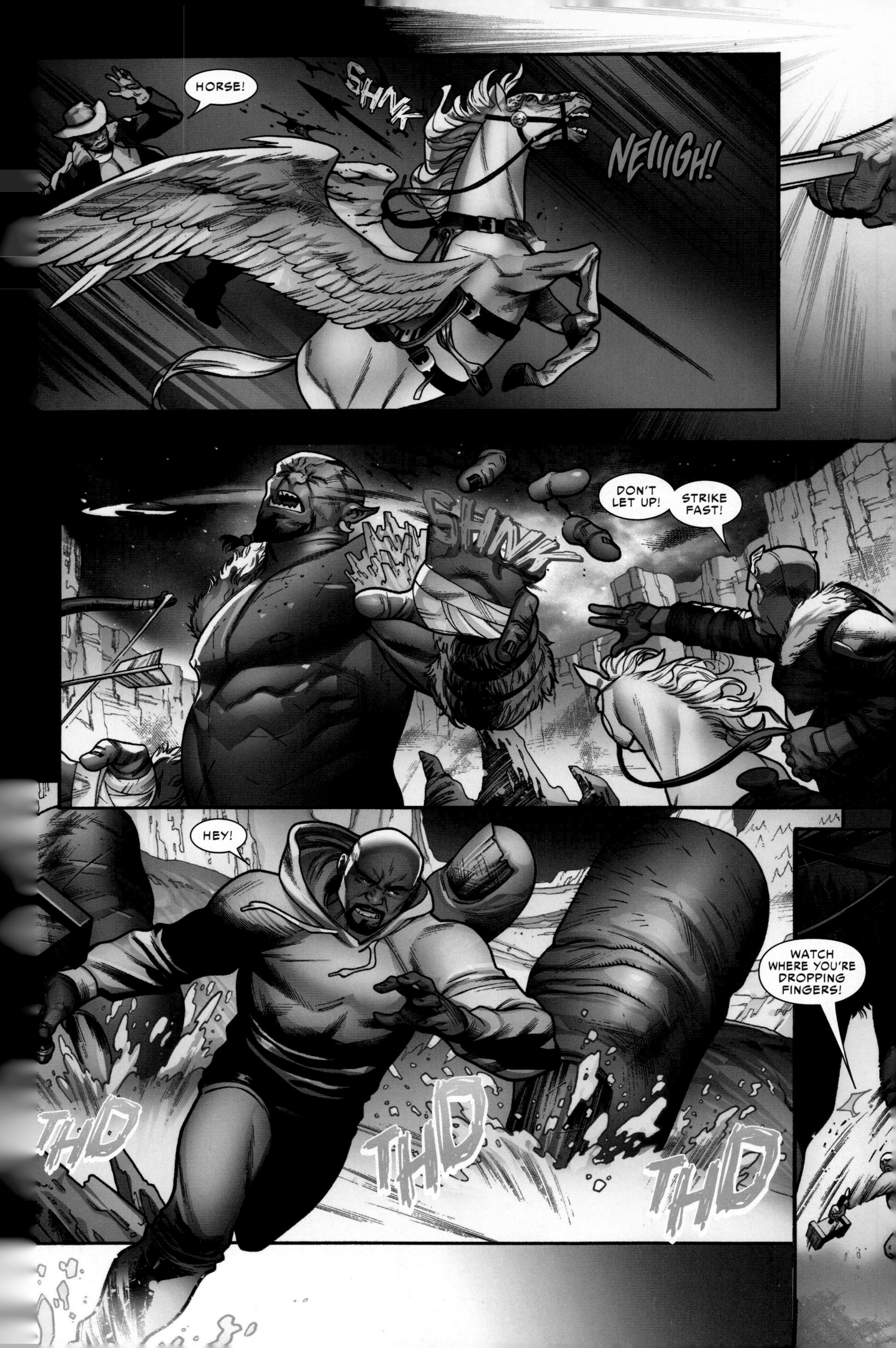
HORSE!
SHNK
NEIIIGH!
DON'T LET UP!
STRIKE FAST!
SHNK
HEY!
WATCH WHERE YOU'RE DROPPING FINGERS!
THD
THD
THD

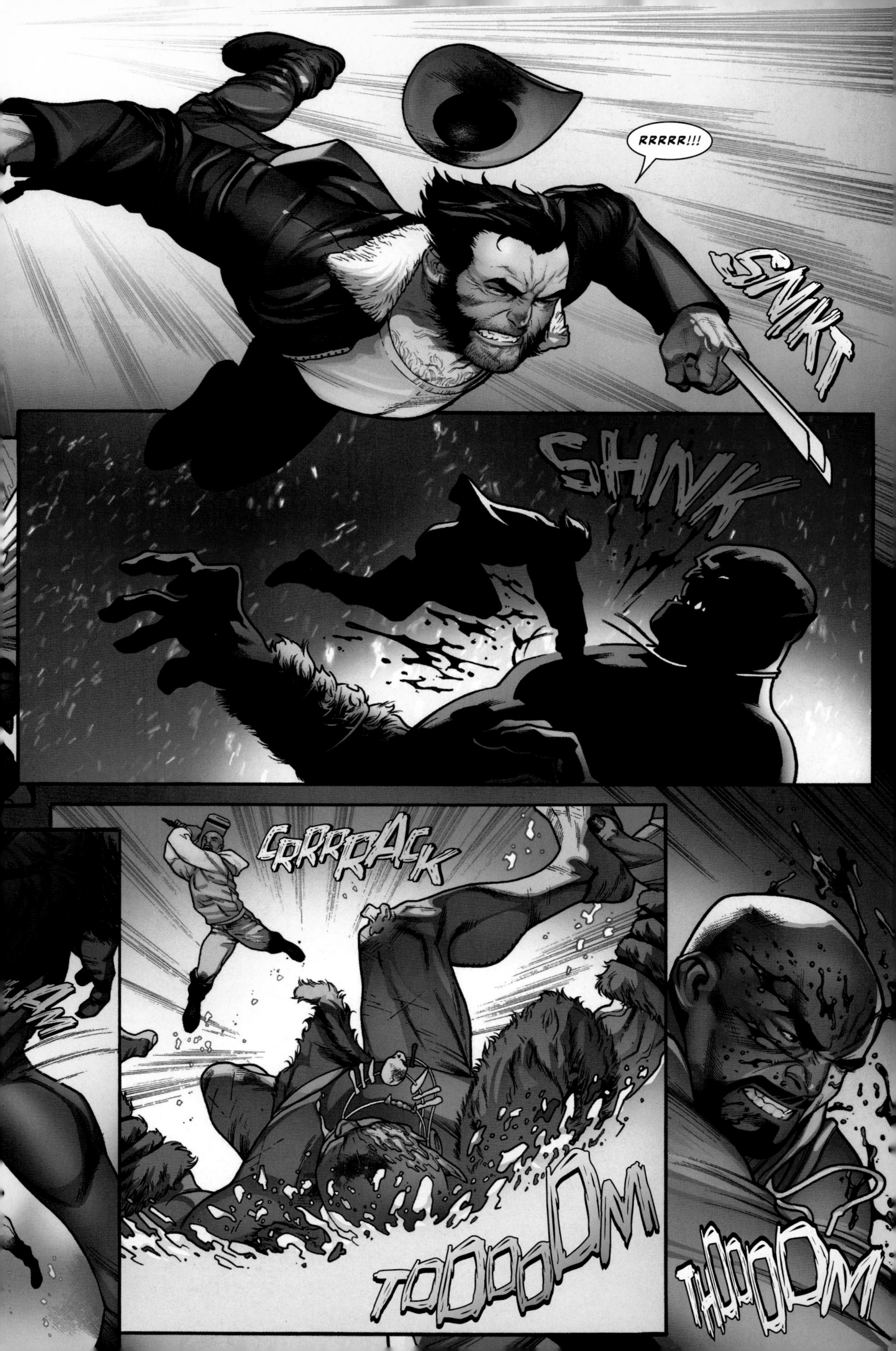
RRRRR!!!
SNIKT
SHNK
CRRRRACK
TOOOOOM
THOOOOM

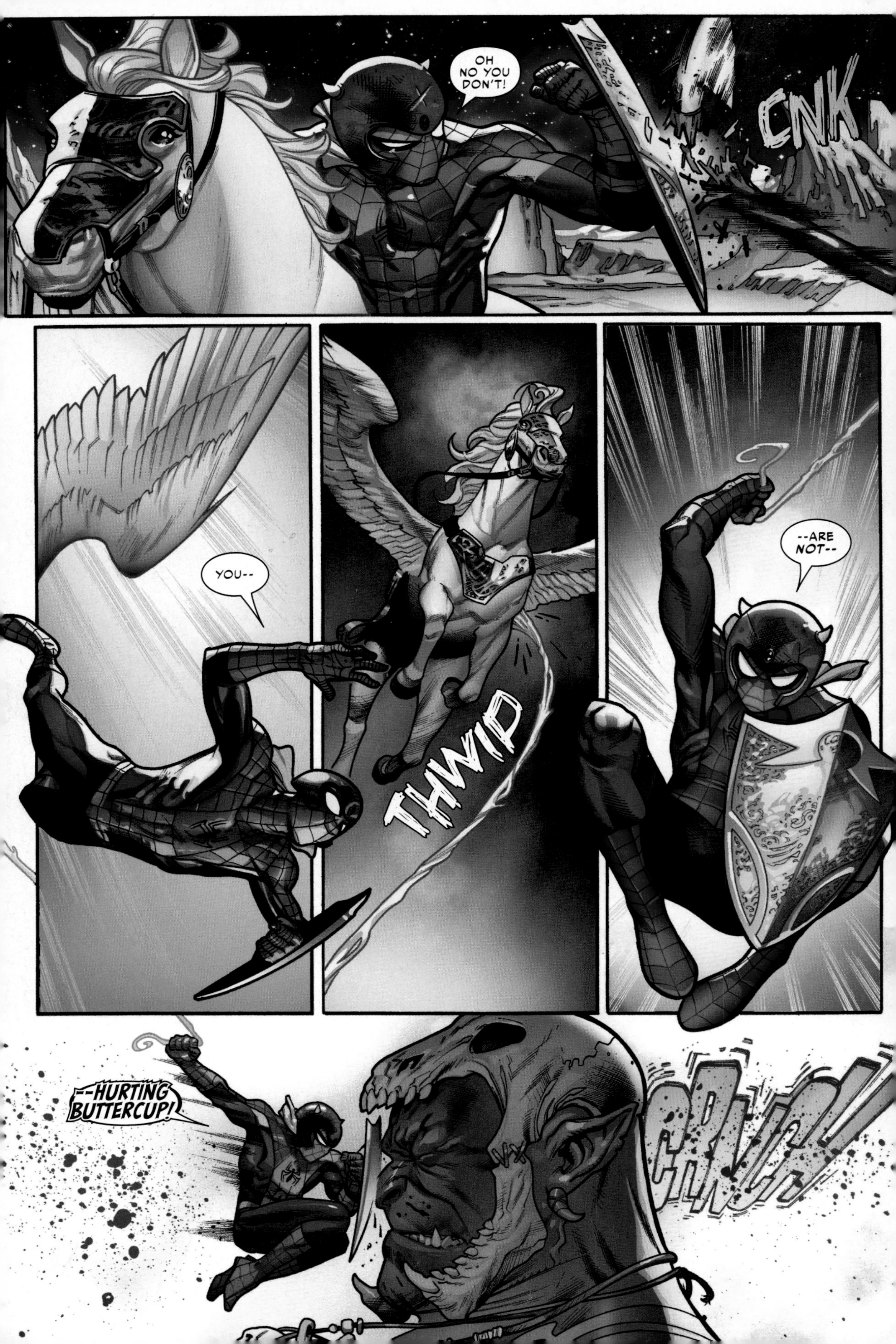

OH NO YOU DON'T!
CNK
YOU--
THWIP
--ARE NOT--
--HURTING BUTTERCUP!

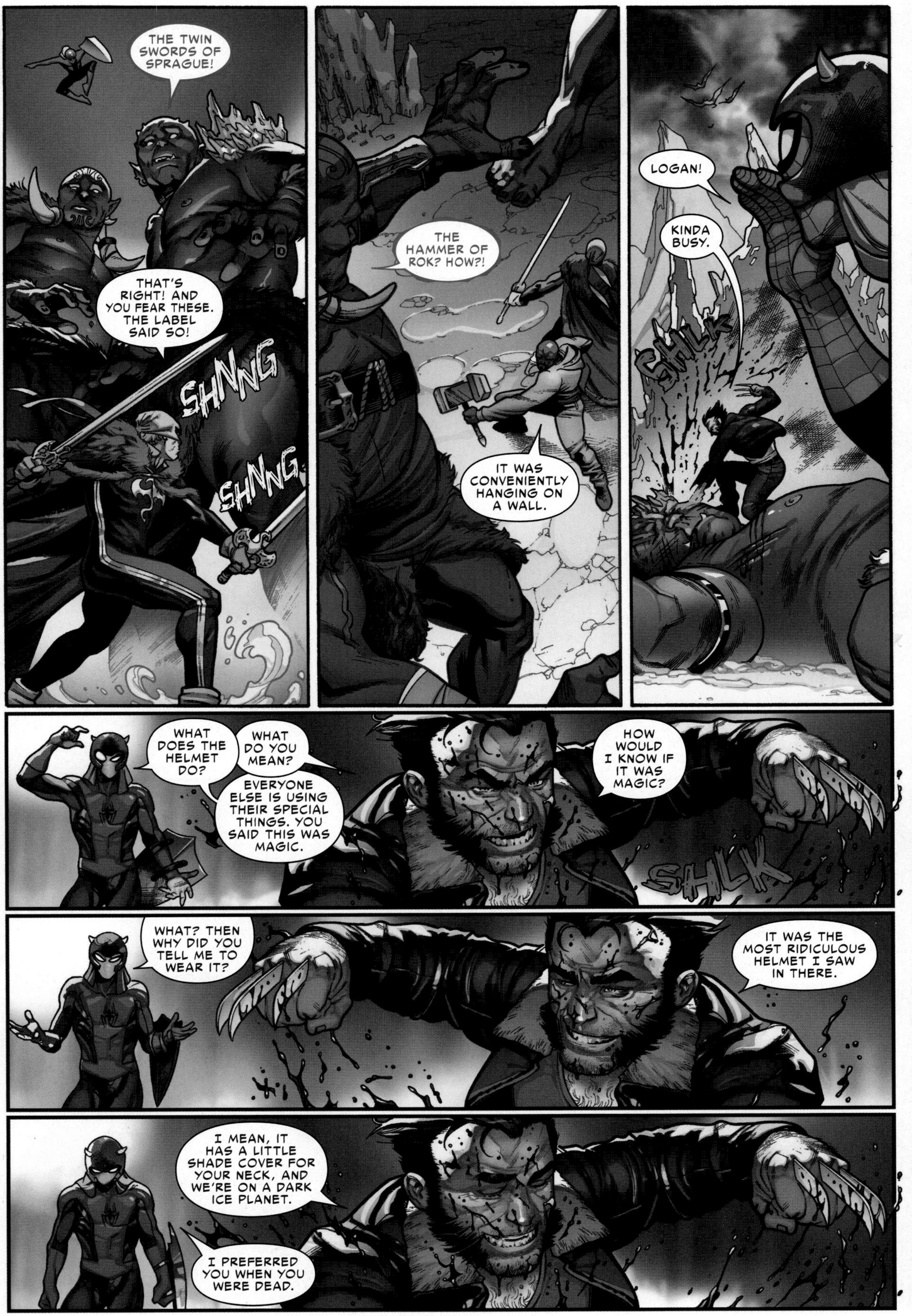
THE TWIN SWORDS OF SPRAGUE!
THAT'S RIGHT! AND YOU FEAR THESE. THE LABEL SAID SO!
SHNNG
SHNNG
THE HAMMER OF ROK? HOW?!
IT WAS CONVENIENTLY HANGING ON A WALL.
LOGAN!
KINDA BUSY.
SHLK
WHAT DOES THE HELMET DO?
WHAT DO YOU MEAN?
EVERYONE ELSE IS USING THEIR SPECIAL THINGS. YOU SAID THIS WAS MAGIC.
HOW WOULD I KNOW IF IT WAS MAGIC?
SHLK
WHAT? THEN WHY DID YOU TELL ME TO WEAR IT?
IT WAS THE MOST RIDICULOUS HELMET I SAW IN THERE.
I MEAN, IT HAS A LITTLE SHADE COVER FOR YOUR NECK, AND WE'RE ON A DARK ICE PLANET.
I PREFERRED YOU WHEN YOU WERE DEAD.

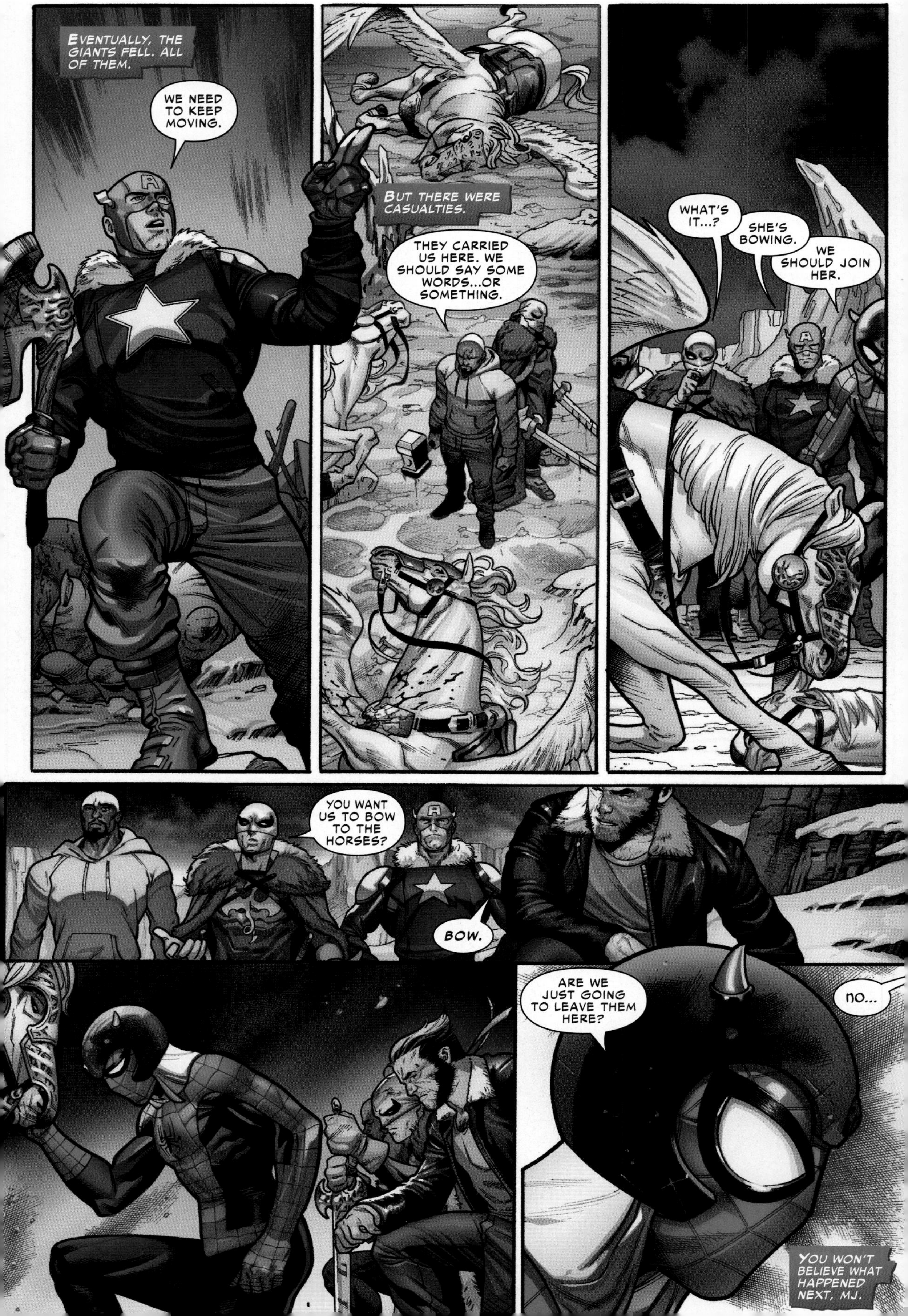

EVENTUALLY, THE GIANTS FELL. ALL OF THEM.
WE NEED TO KEEP MOVING.
BUT THERE WERE CASUALTIES.
THEY CARRIED US HERE. WE SHOULD SAY SOME WORDS...OR SOMETHING.
WHAT'S IT...?
SHE'S BOWING.
WE SHOULD JOIN HER.
YOU WANT US TO BOW TO THE HORSES?
BOW.
ARE WE JUST GOING TO LEAVE THEM HERE?
no...
YOU WON'T BELIEVE WHAT HAPPENED NEXT, MJ.

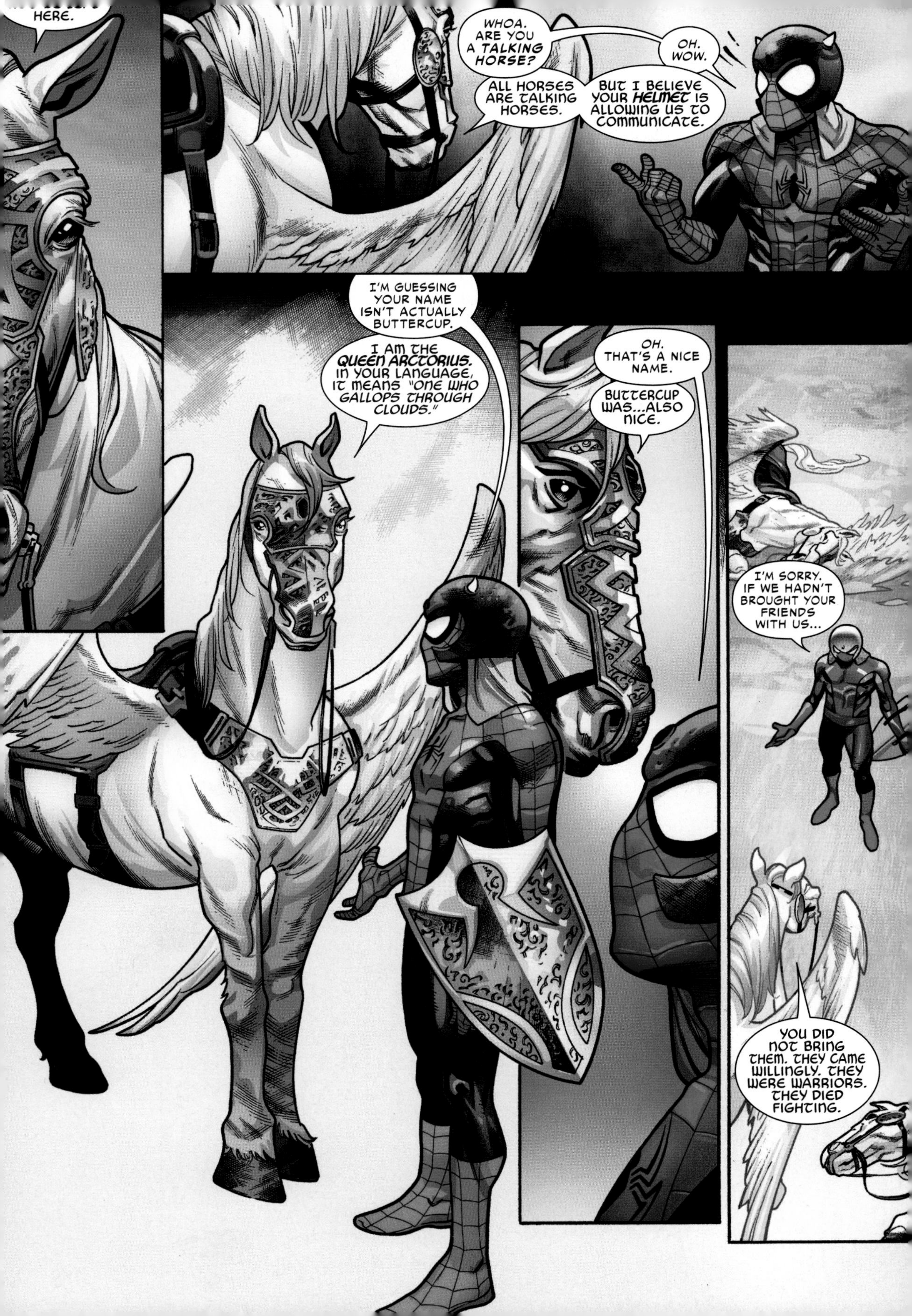

HERE.
WHOA. ARE YOU A TALKING HORSE?
ALL HORSES ARE TALKING HORSES.
OH. WOW.
BUT I BELIEVE YOUR HELMET IS ALLOWING US TO COMMUNICATE.
I'M GUESSING YOUR NAME ISN'T ACTUALLY BUTTERCUP.
I AM THE QUEEN ARCTORIUS. IN YOUR LANGUAGE, IT MEANS "ONE WHO GALLOPS THROUGH CLOUDS."
OH. THAT'S A NICE NAME.
BUTTERCUP WAS...ALSO NICE.
I'M SORRY. IF WE HADN'T BROUGHT YOUR FRIENDS WITH US...
YOU DID NOT BRING THEM. THEY CAME WILLINGLY. THEY WERE WARRIORS. THEY DIED FIGHTING.

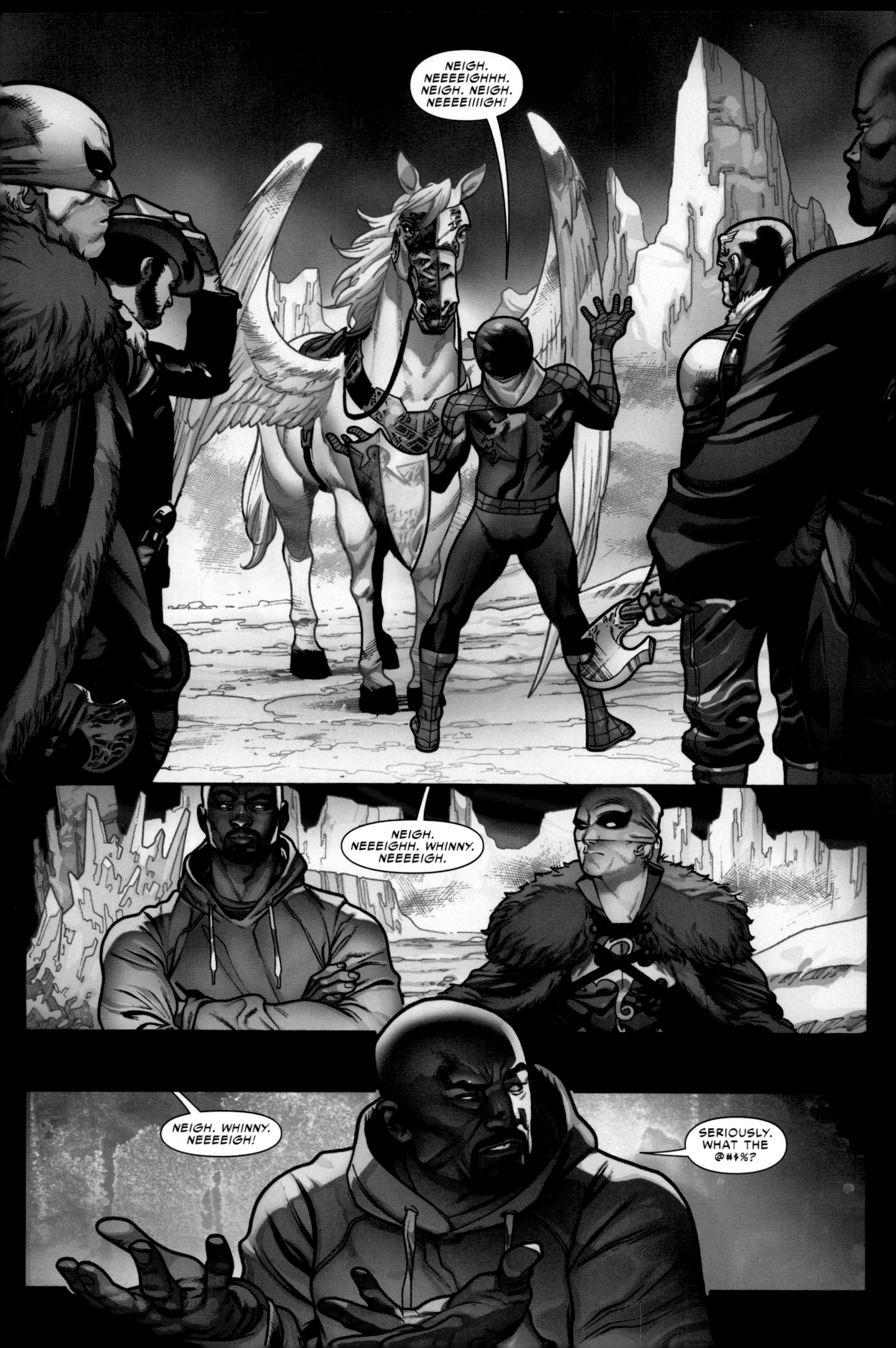
NEIGH. NEEEEIGHHH. NEIGH. NEIGH. NEEEEIIIIGH!
NEIGH. NEEEEIGHH. WHINNY. NEEEEIGH.
NEIGH. WHINNY. NEEEEIGH!
SERIOUSLY. WHAT THE @#$%?

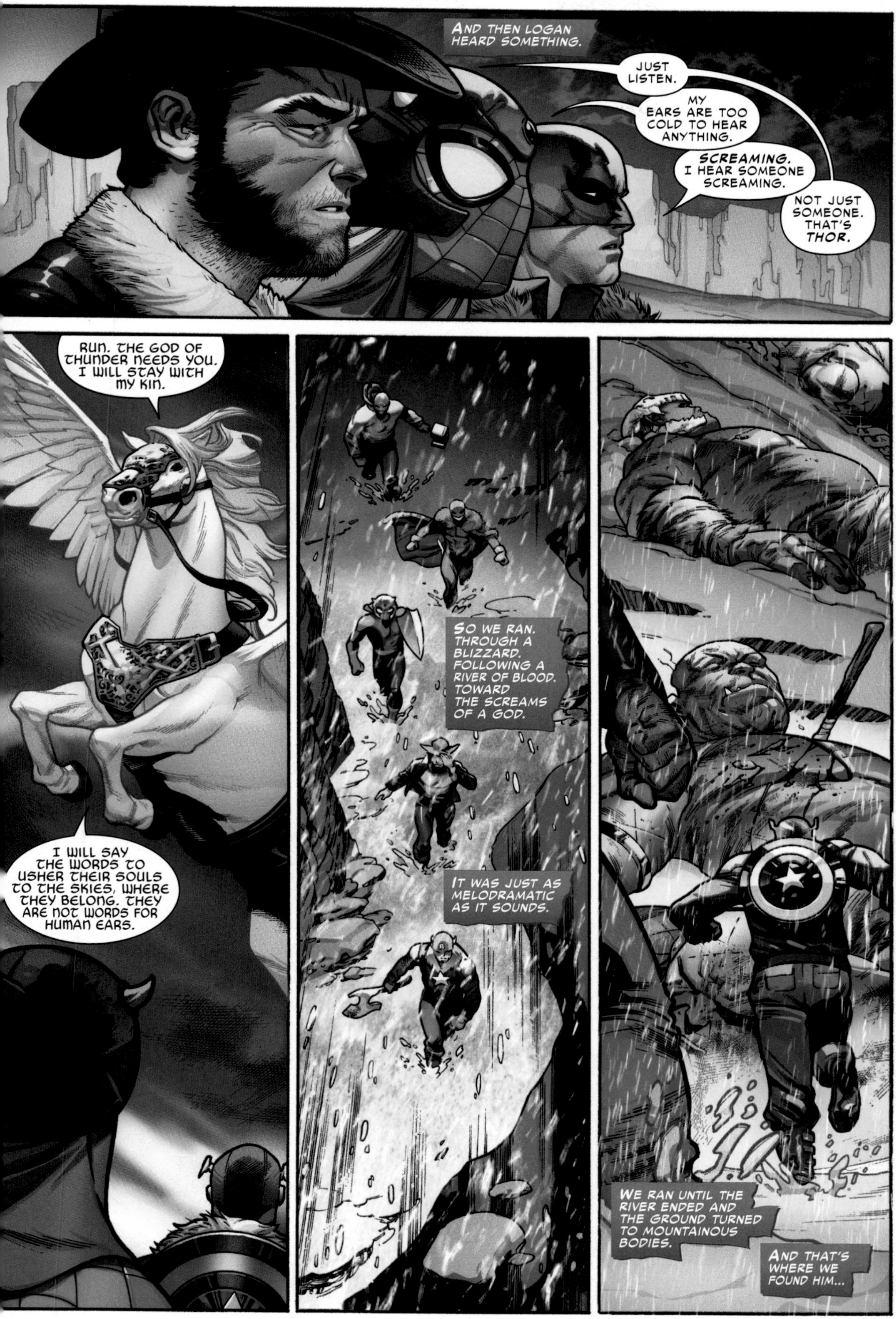
AND THEN LOGAN HEARD SOMETHING.
JUST LISTEN.
MY EARS ARE TOO COLD TO HEAR ANYTHING.
SCREAMING. I HEAR SOMEONE SCREAMING.
NOT JUST SOMEONE. THAT'S *THOR.*
RUN. THE GOD OF THUNDER NEEDS YOU. I WILL STAY WITH MY KIN.
I WILL SAY THE WORDS TO USHER THEIR SOULS TO THE SKIES, WHERE THEY BELONG. THEY ARE NOT WORDS FOR HUMAN EARS.
SO WE RAN. THROUGH A BLIZZARD. FOLLOWING A RIVER OF BLOOD. TOWARD THE SCREAMS OF A GOD.
IT WAS JUST AS MELODRAMATIC AS IT SOUNDS.
WE RAN UNTIL THE RIVER ENDED AND THE GROUND TURNED TO MOUNTAINOUS BODIES.
AND THAT'S WHERE WE FOUND HIM...

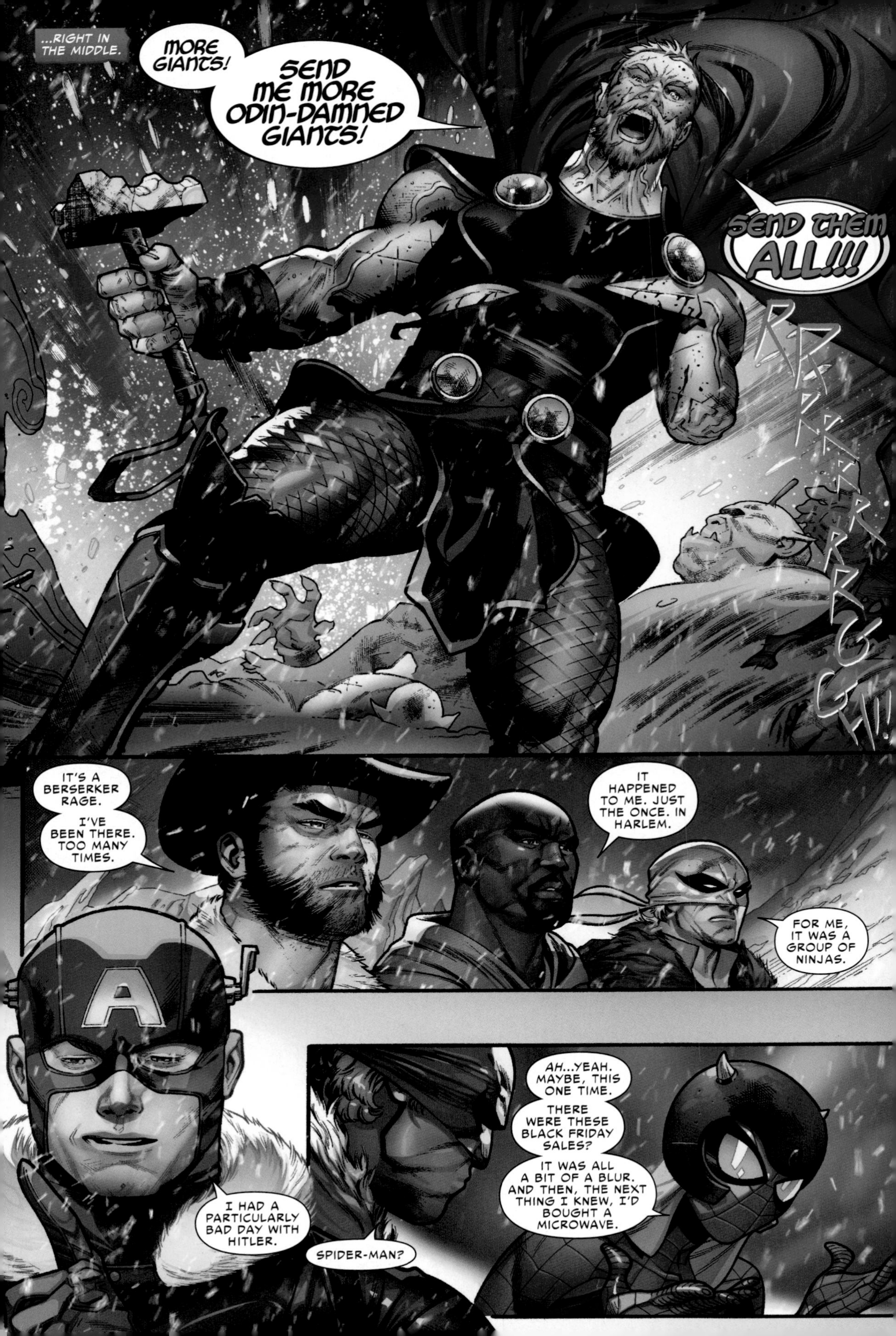
...RIGHT IN THE MIDDLE.
MORE GIANTS!
SEND ME MORE ODIN-DAMNED GIANTS!
SEND THEM ALL!!!
RRRRRRRRRRRGGGH!!
IT'S A BERSERKER RAGE.
I'VE BEEN THERE. TOO MANY TIMES.
IT HAPPENED TO ME. JUST THE ONCE. IN HARLEM.
FOR ME, IT WAS A GROUP OF NINJAS.
I HAD A PARTICULARLY BAD DAY WITH HITLER.
SPIDER-MAN?
AH...YEAH. MAYBE, THIS ONE TIME.
THERE WERE THESE BLACK FRIDAY SALES?
IT WAS ALL A BIT OF A BLUR. AND THEN, THE NEXT THING I KNEW, I'D BOUGHT A MICROWAVE.

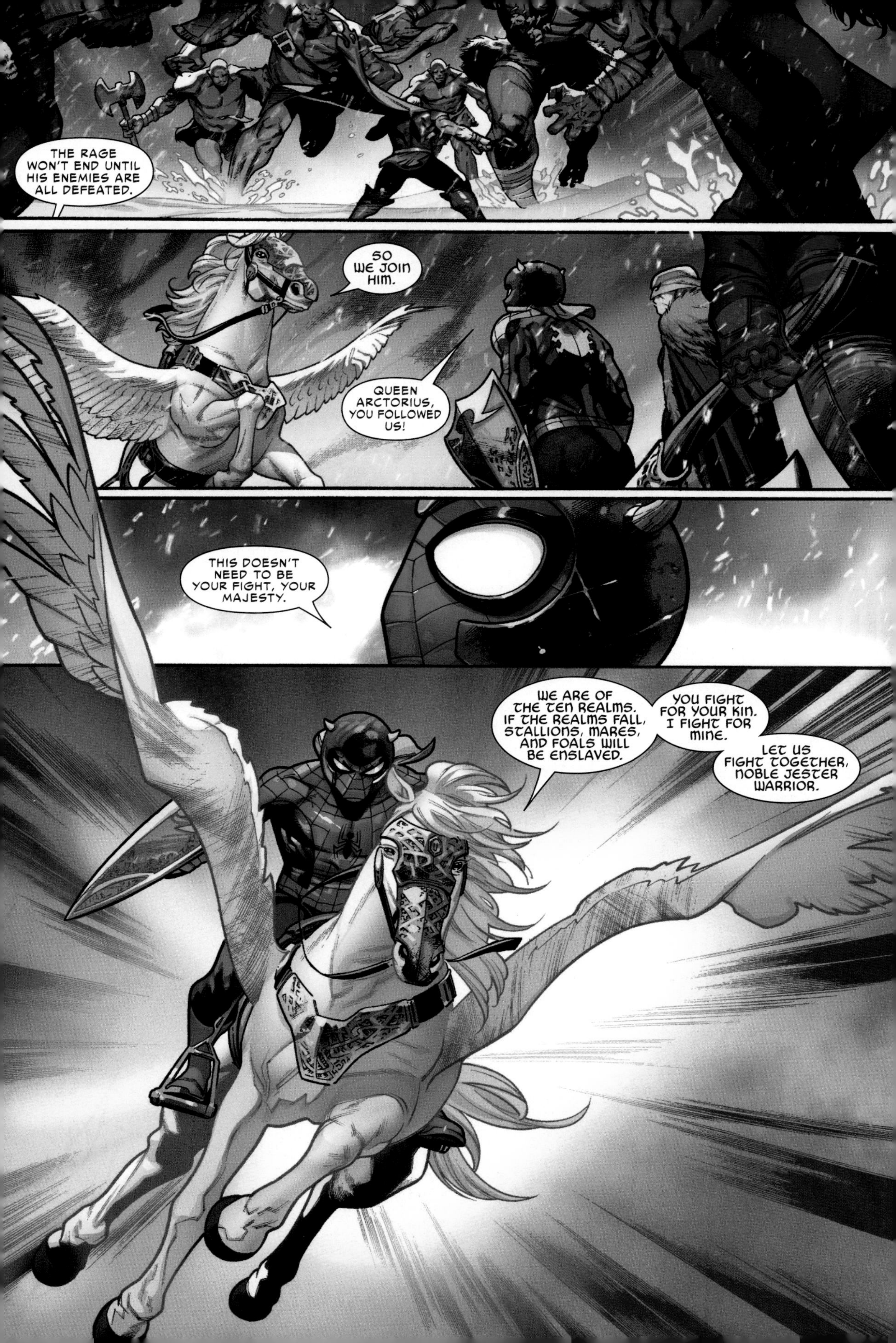
THE RAGE WON'T END UNTIL HIS ENEMIES ARE ALL DEFEATED.
SO WE JOIN HIM.
QUEEN ARCTORIUS, YOU FOLLOWED US!
THIS DOESN'T NEED TO BE YOUR FIGHT, YOUR MAJESTY.
WE ARE OF THE TEN REALMS. IF THE REALMS FALL, STALLIONS, MARES, AND FOALS WILL BE ENSLAVED.
YOU FIGHT FOR YOUR KIN. I FIGHT FOR MINE.
LET US FIGHT TOGETHER, NOBLE JESTER WARRIOR.

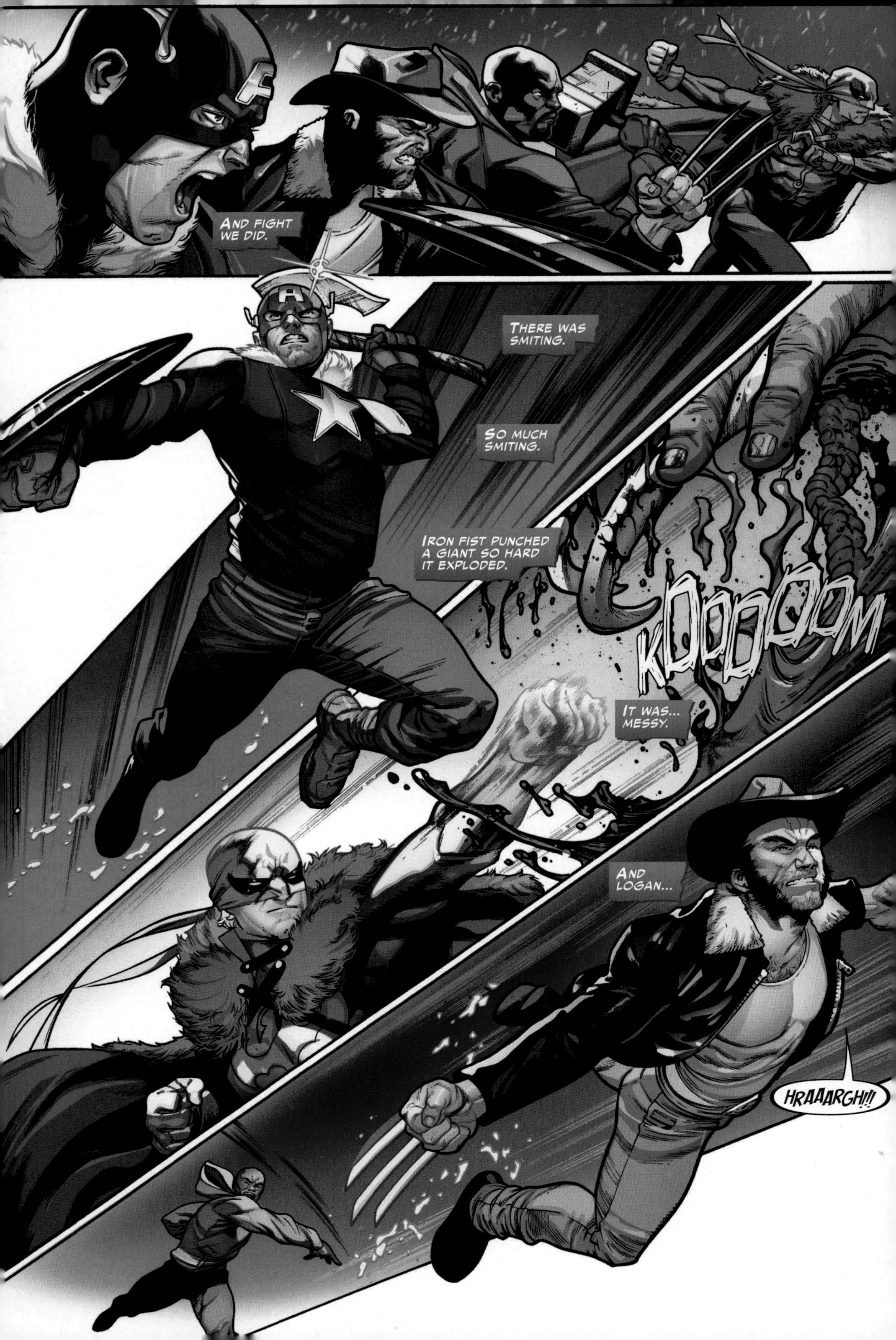

AND FIGHT WE DID.
THERE WAS SMITING.
SO MUCH SMITING.
IRON FIST PUNCHED A GIANT SO HARD IT EXPLODED.
KDOOOOOM
IT WAS... MESSY.
AND LOGAN...
HRAAARGH!!!

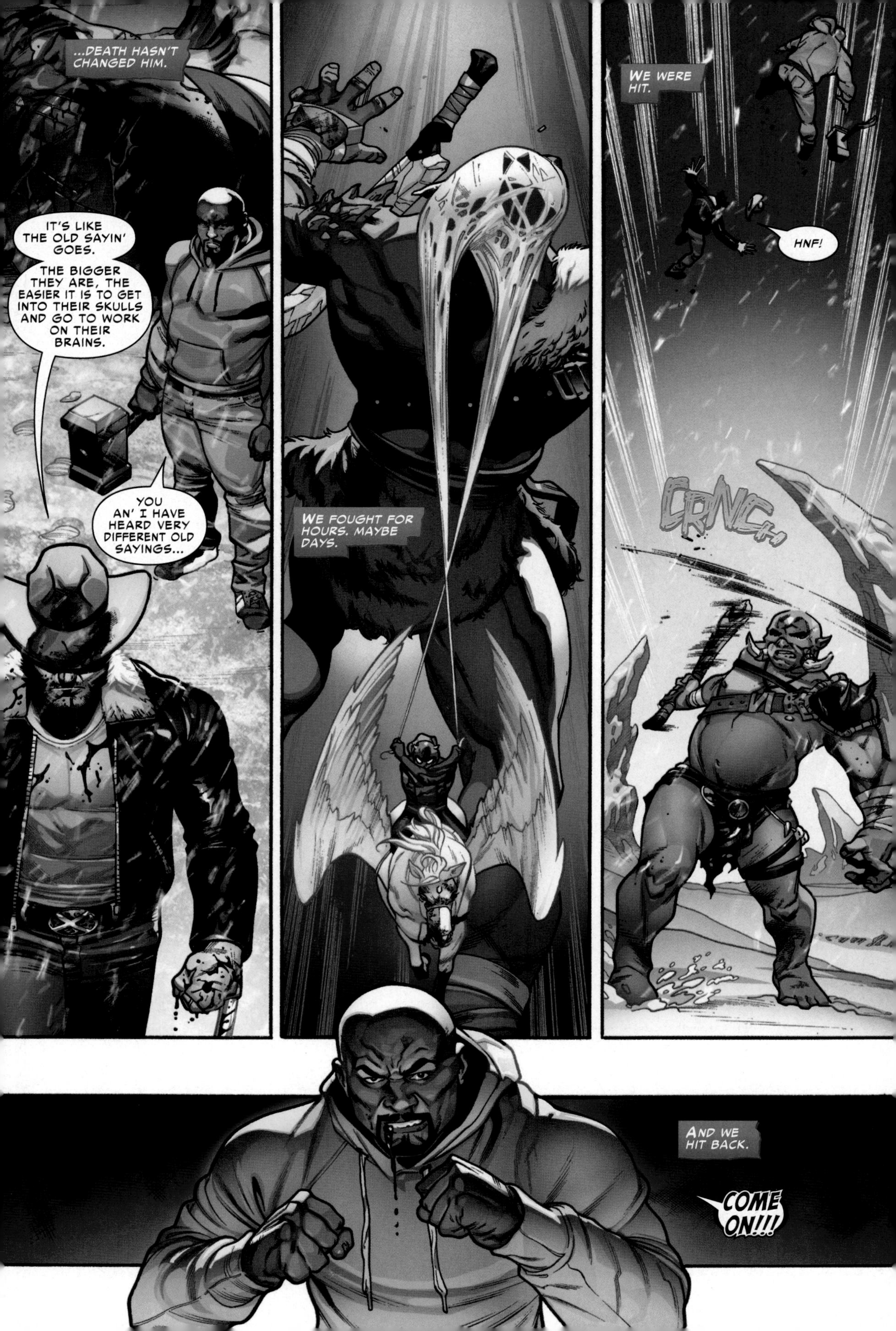
...DEATH HASN'T CHANGED HIM.
IT'S LIKE THE OLD SAYIN' GOES.
THE BIGGER THEY ARE, THE EASIER IT IS TO GET INTO THEIR SKULLS AND GO TO WORK ON THEIR BRAINS.
YOU AN' I HAVE HEARD VERY DIFFERENT OLD SAYINGS...
WE FOUGHT FOR HOURS. MAYBE DAYS.
WE WERE HIT.
HNF!
CRNCH
AND WE HIT BACK.
COME ON!!!

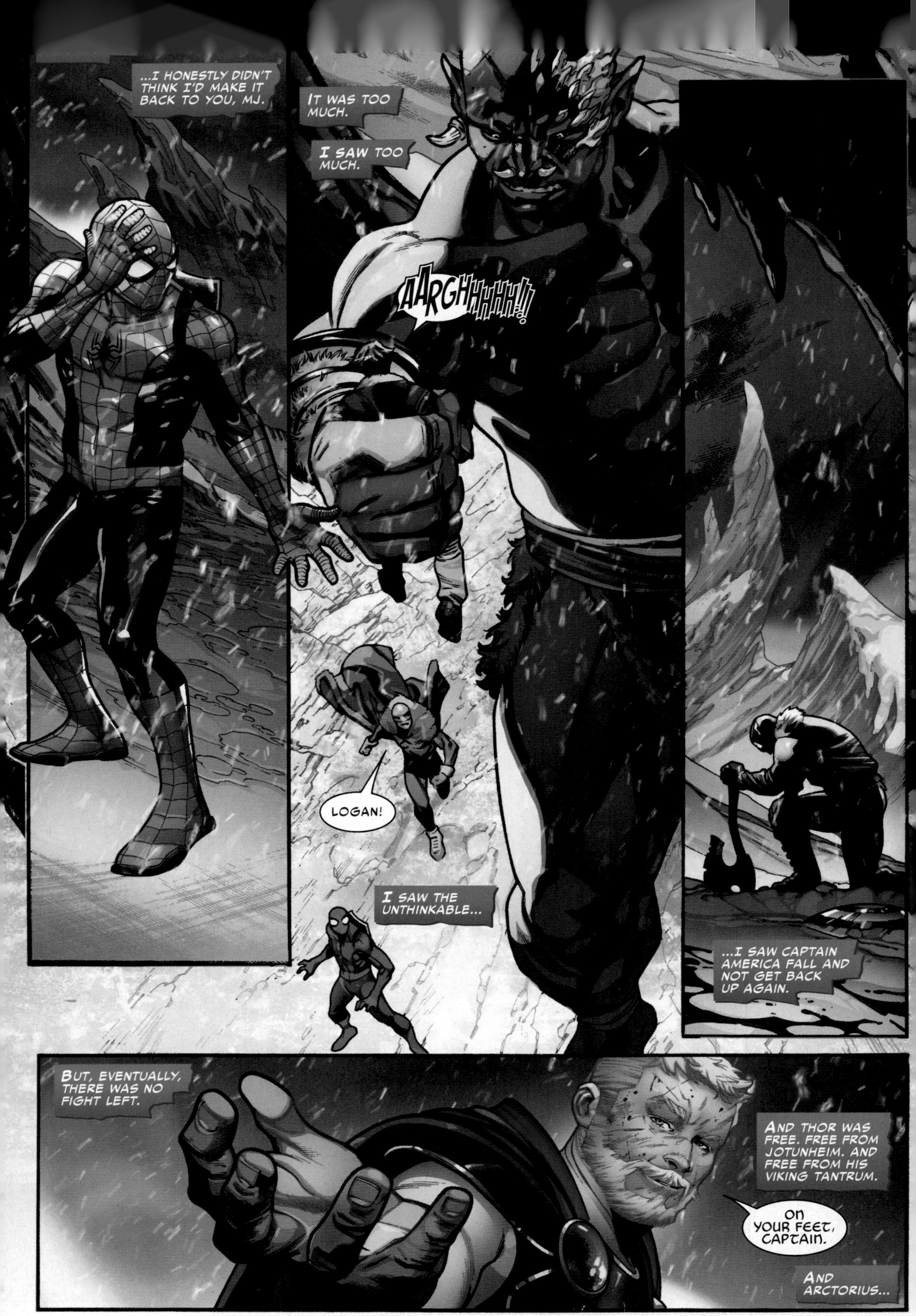

...I HONESTLY DIDN'T THINK I'D MAKE IT BACK TO YOU, MJ.
IT WAS TOO MUCH.
I SAW TOO MUCH.
AARGHHHHH!!
LOGAN!
I SAW THE UNTHINKABLE...
...I SAW CAPTAIN AMERICA FALL AND NOT GET BACK UP AGAIN.
BUT, EVENTUALLY, THERE WAS NO FIGHT LEFT.
AND THOR WAS FREE. FREE FROM JOTUNHEIM. AND FREE FROM HIS VIKING TANTRUM.
ON YOUR FEET, CAPTAIN.
AND ARCTORIUS...

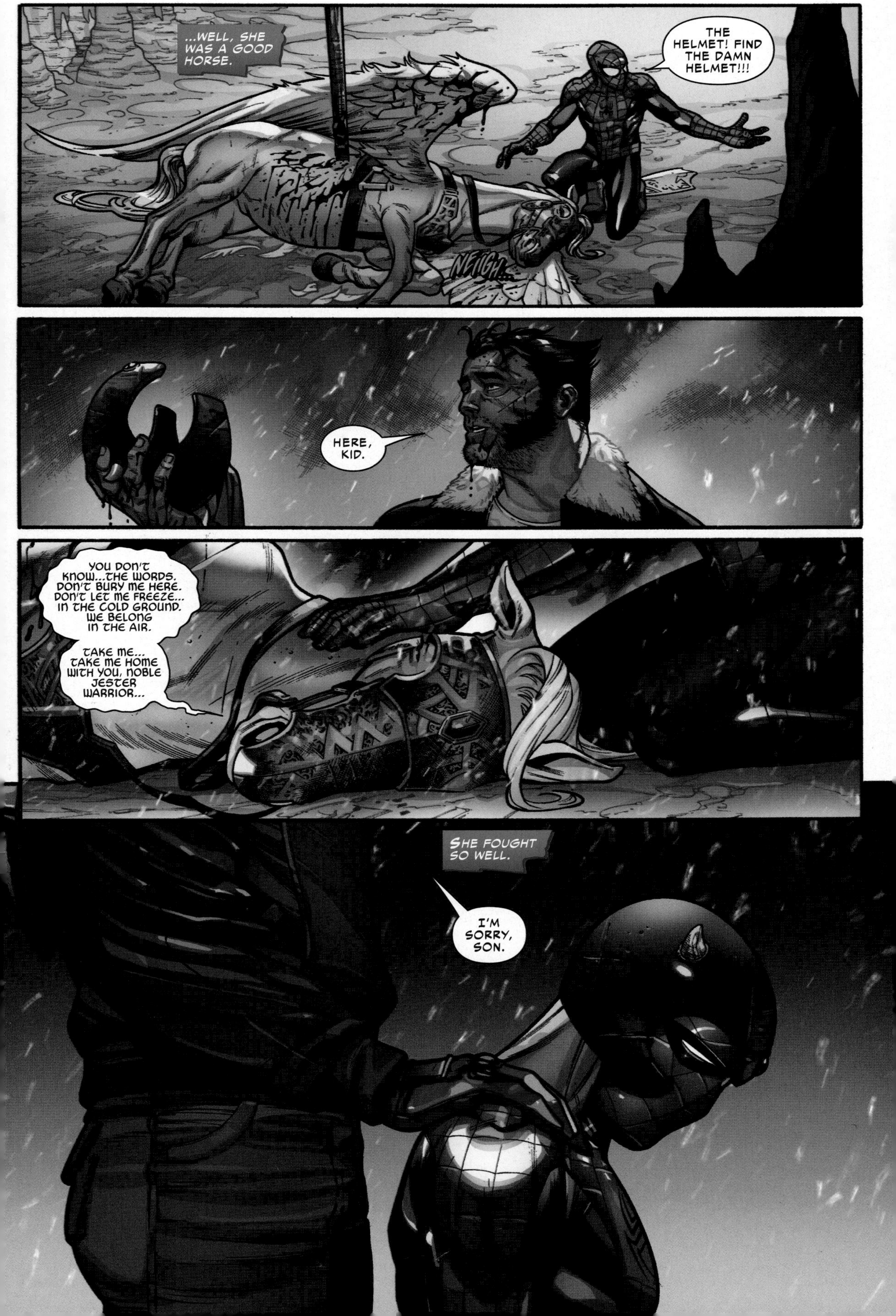
...WELL, SHE WAS A GOOD HORSE.
THE HELMET! FIND THE DAMN HELMET!!!
NEIGH...
HERE, KID.
YOU DON'T KNOW...THE WORDS. DON'T BURY ME HERE. DON'T LET ME FREEZE... IN THE COLD GROUND. WE BELONG IN THE AIR.
TAKE ME... TAKE ME HOME WITH YOU, NOBLE JESTER WARRIOR...
SHE FOUGHT SO WELL.
I'M SORRY, SON.

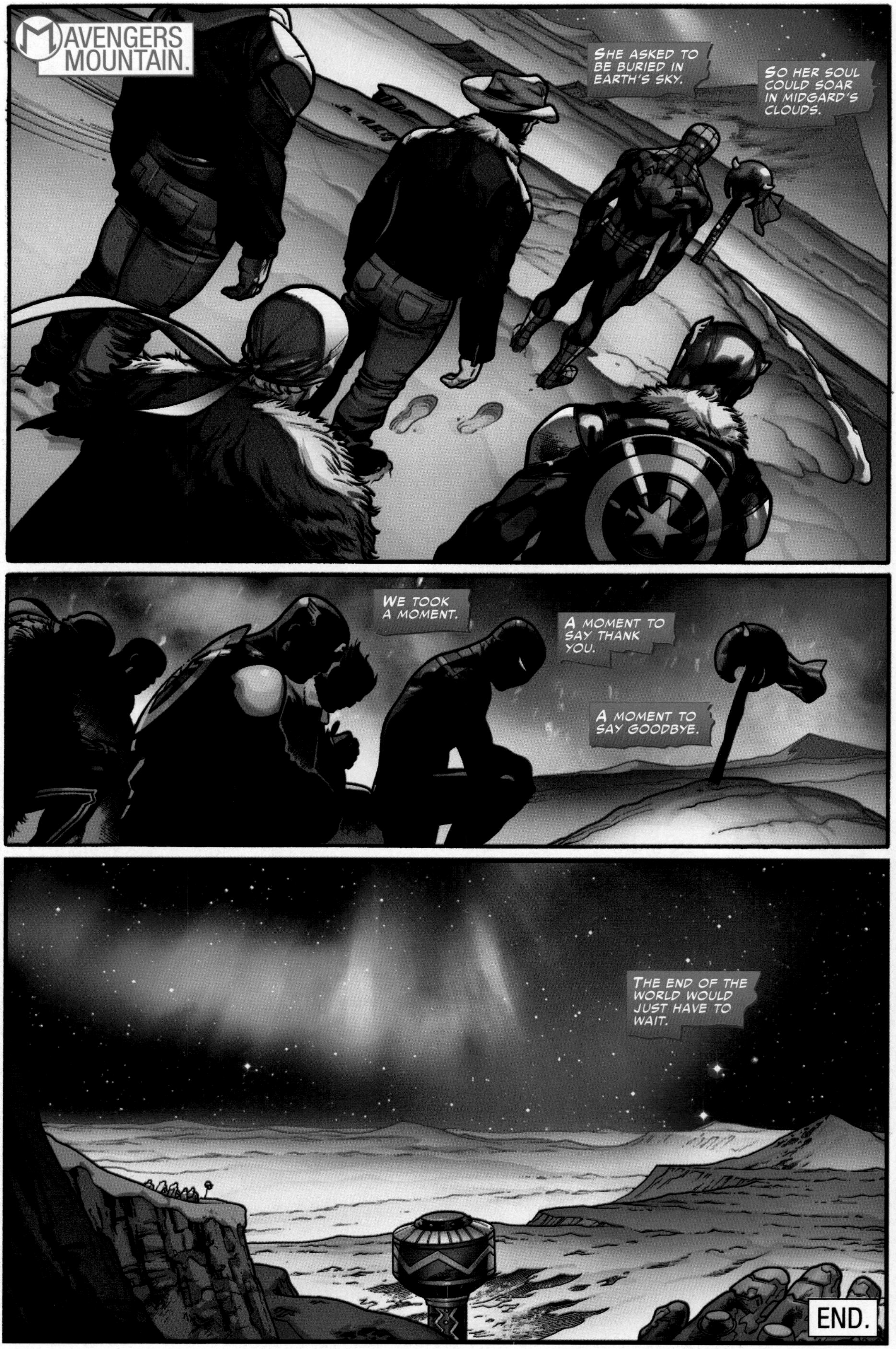
AVENGERS MOUNTAIN.
SHE ASKED TO BE BURIED IN EARTH'S SKY.
SO HER SOUL COULD SOAR IN MIDGARD'S CLOUDS.
WE TOOK A MOMENT.
A MOMENT TO SAY THANK YOU.
A MOMENT TO SAY GOODBYE.
THE END OF THE WORLD WOULD JUST HAVE TO WAIT.
END.

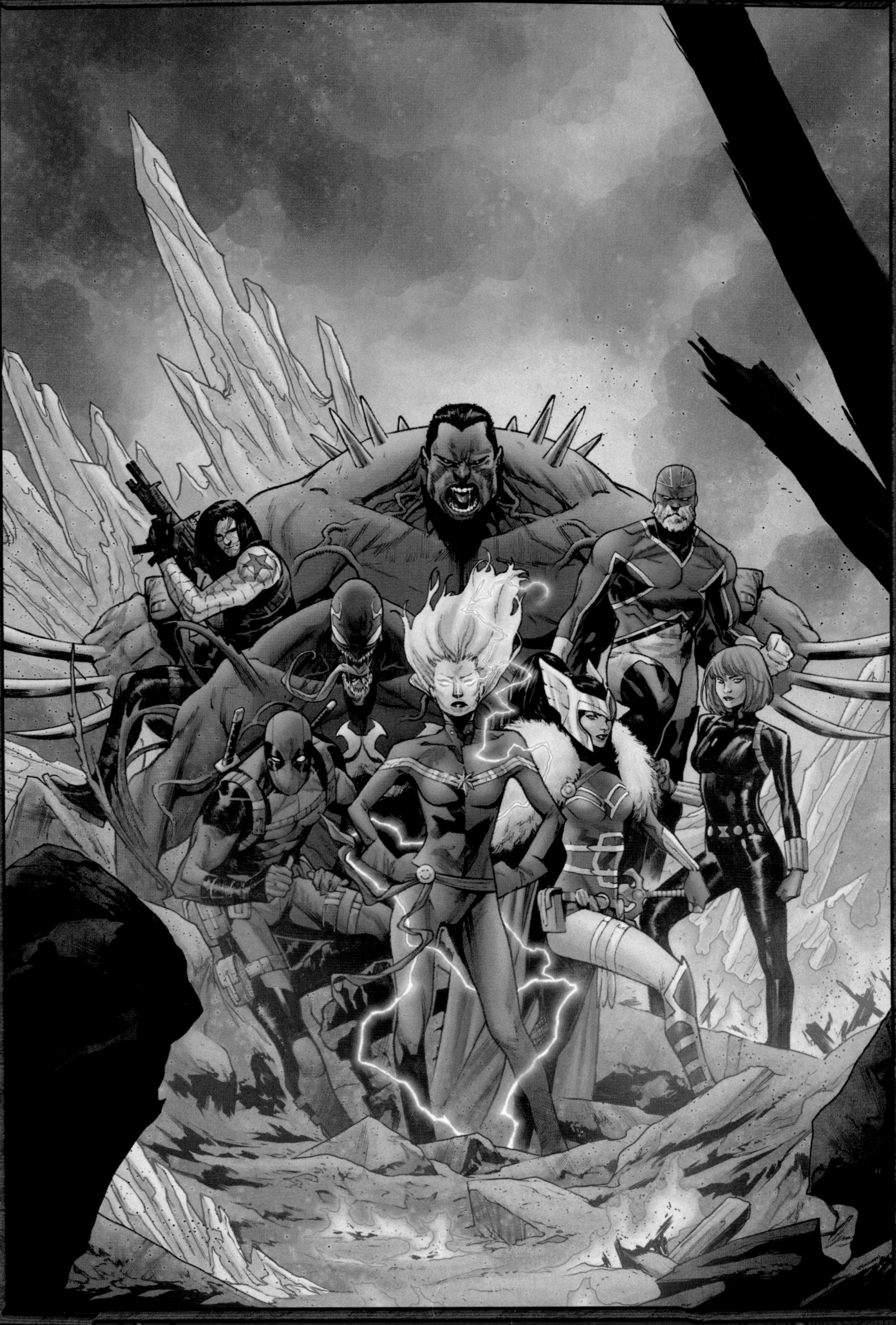

The War Avengers

The war has already spread across the globe—and thanks to his
Black Bifrost, Malekith's army is only growing.

While Lady Freyja leads a mission to Svartalfheim to shut down the
Black Bifrost and Captain America takes a team to rescue Thor from Jotunheim,
Captain Marvel will lead the heroes she has left into the front lines on Earth.
For this is war. And war requires a whole different kind of avenging....

THE WAR OF THE REALMS

STRIKEFORCE
THE WAR AVENGERS

written by
DENNIS "HOPELESS" HALLUM
drawn by
KIM JACINTO & ARIO ANINDITO
colored by
JAVA TARTAGLIA & FELIPE SOBREIRO
lettered by
VC's JOE SABINO
cover artists
KIM JACINTO & MATT HOLLINGSWORTH
variant cover artists
NICK BRADSHAW & LAURA MARTIN

SARAH BRUNSTAD
associate editor

WIL MOSS
editor

Note: Read WAR OF THE REALMS #1-3 before this issue.

TOM BREVOORT   C.B. CEBULSKI   JOE QUESADA   DAN BUCKLEY   ALAN FINE
executive editor   editor in chief   chief creative officer   president   executive producer

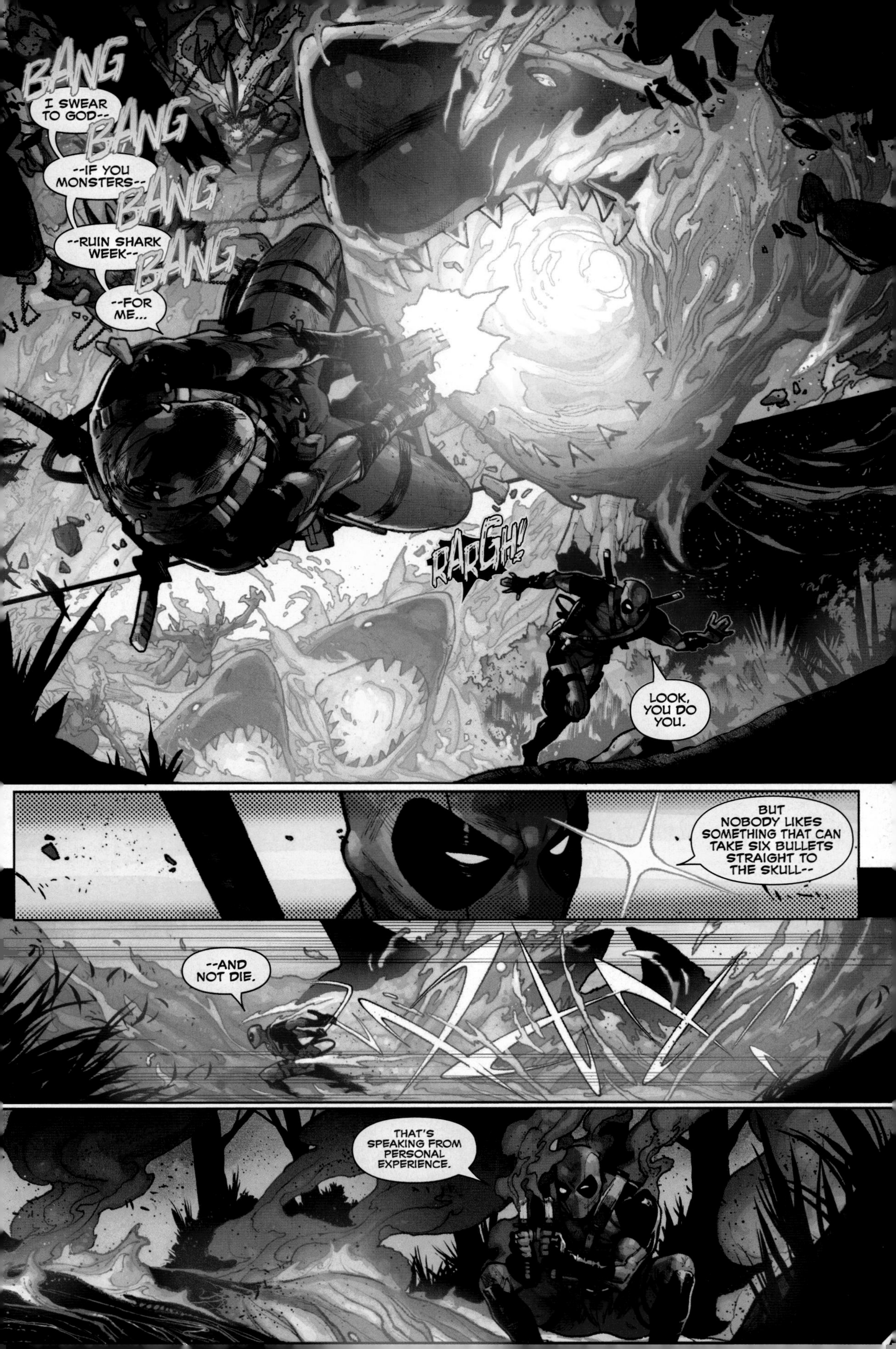
BANG
I SWEAR TO GOD--
BANG
--IF YOU MONSTERS--
BANG
--RUIN SHARK WEEK--
BANG
--FOR ME...
RARGH!
LOOK, YOU DO YOU.
BUT NOBODY LIKES SOMETHING THAT CAN TAKE SIX BULLETS STRAIGHT TO THE SKULL--
--AND NOT DIE.
THAT'S SPEAKING FROM PERSONAL EXPERIENCE.

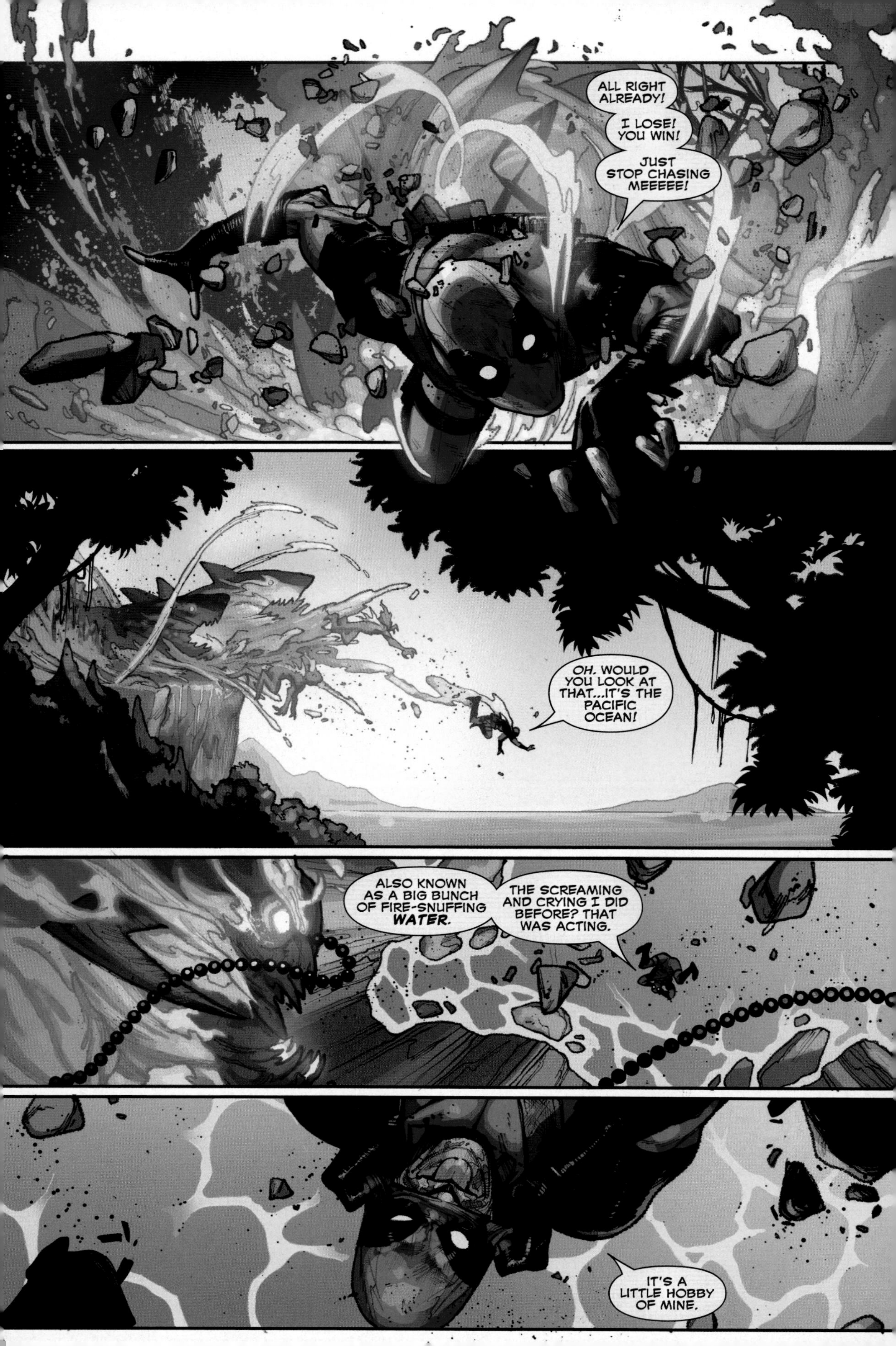
ALL RIGHT ALREADY!
I LOSE! YOU WIN!
JUST STOP CHASING MEEEEE!
OH. WOULD YOU LOOK AT THAT...IT'S THE PACIFIC OCEAN!
ALSO KNOWN AS A BIG BUNCH OF FIRE-SNUFFING WATER.
THE SCREAMING AND CRYING I DID BEFORE? THAT WAS ACTING.
IT'S A LITTLE HOBBY OF MINE.

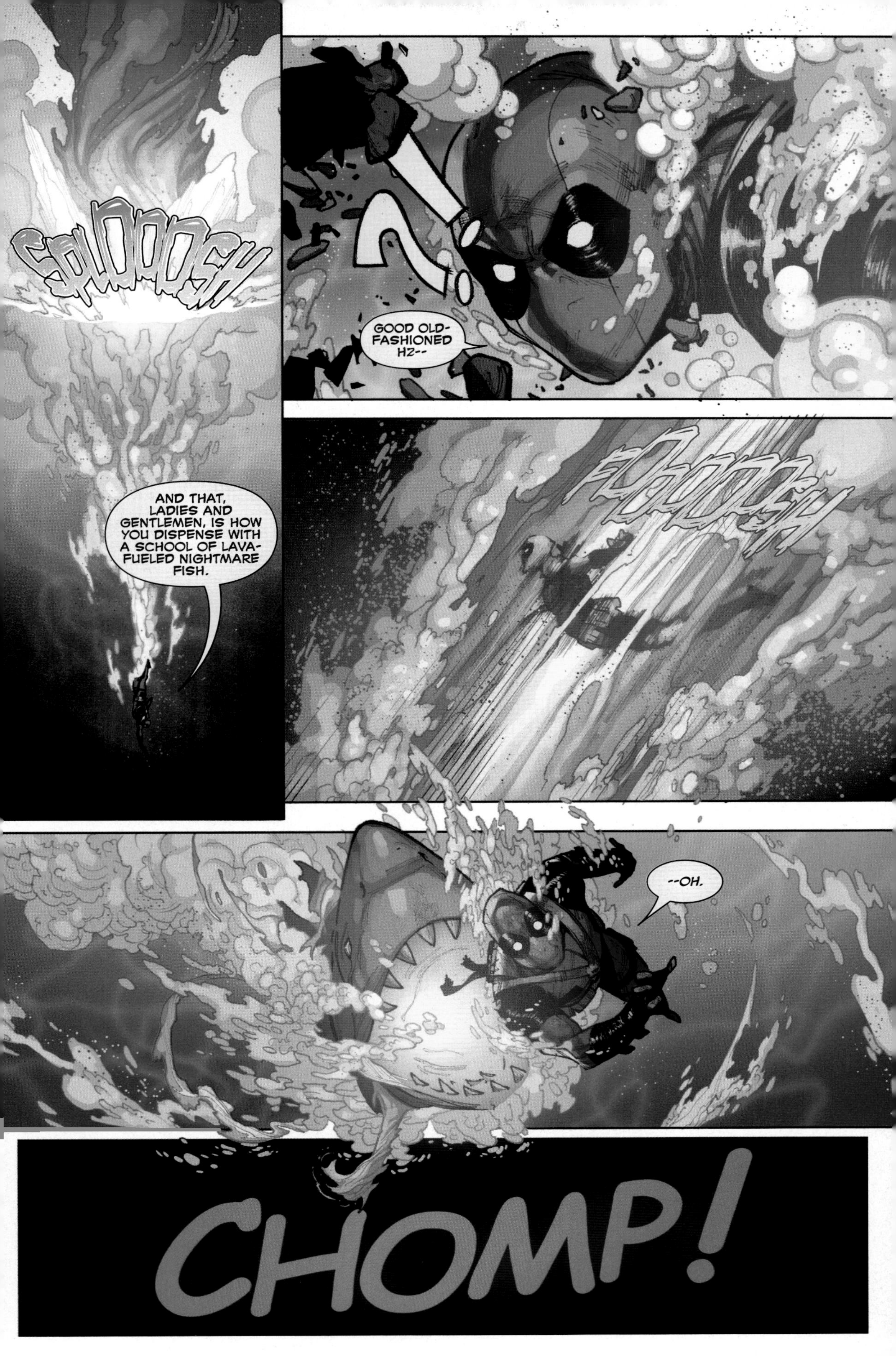
SPLOOOOSH
GOOD OLD-FASHIONED HZ--
AND THAT, LADIES AND GENTLEMEN, IS HOW YOU DISPENSE WITH A SCHOOL OF LAVA-FUELED NIGHTMARE FISH.
FOOOOOSH
--OH.
CHOMP!

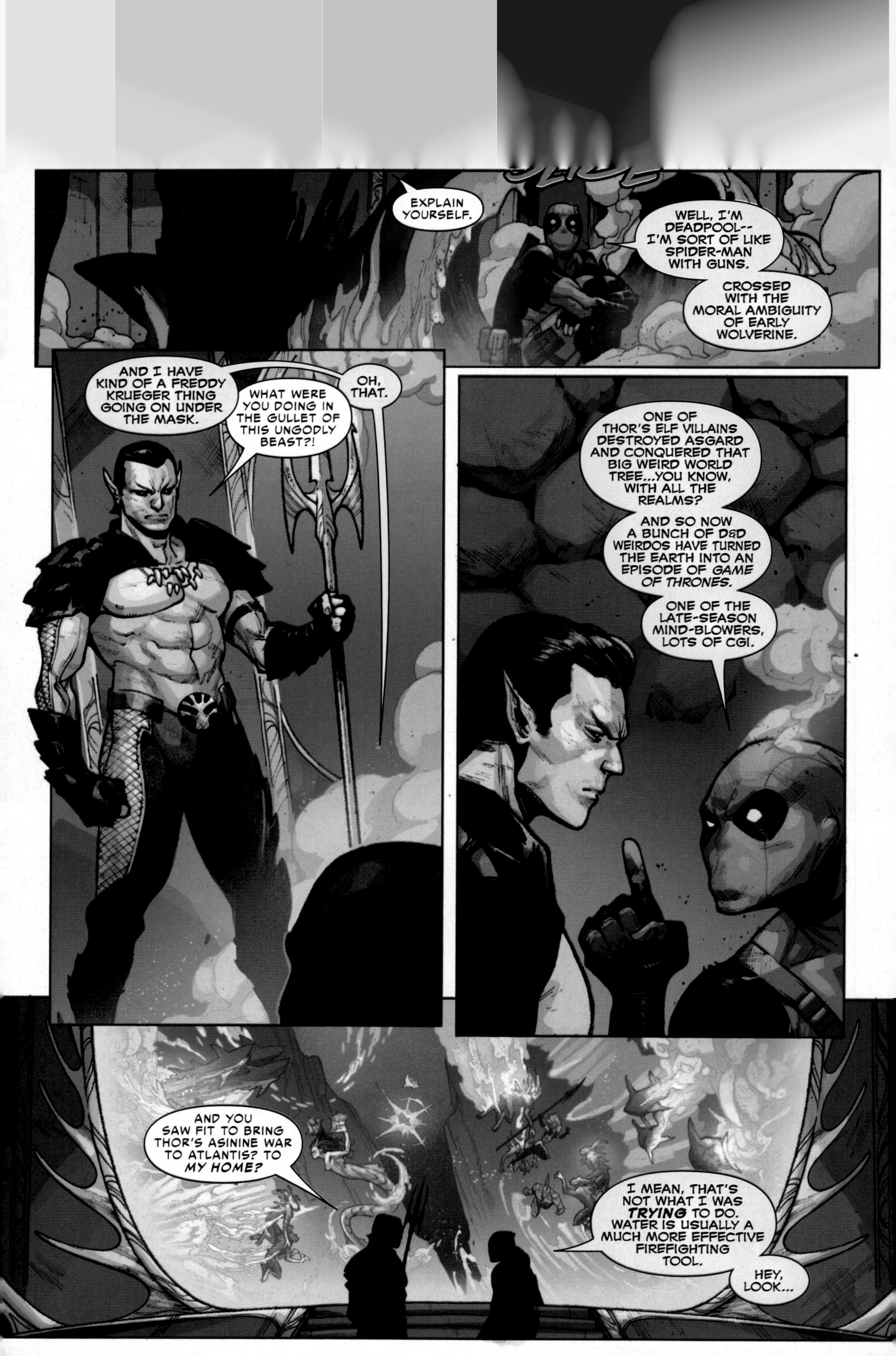
EXPLAIN YOURSELF.
WELL, I'M DEADPOOL-- I'M SORT OF LIKE SPIDER-MAN WITH GUNS.
CROSSED WITH THE MORAL AMBIGUITY OF EARLY WOLVERINE.
AND I HAVE KIND OF A FREDDY KRUEGER THING GOING ON UNDER THE MASK.
OH, THAT.
WHAT WERE YOU DOING IN THE GULLET OF THIS UNGODLY BEAST?!
ONE OF THOR'S ELF VILLAINS DESTROYED ASGARD AND CONQUERED THAT BIG WEIRD WORLD TREE...YOU KNOW, WITH ALL THE REALMS?
AND SO NOW A BUNCH OF D&D WEIRDOS HAVE TURNED THE EARTH INTO AN EPISODE OF *GAME OF THRONES.*
ONE OF THE LATE-SEASON MIND-BLOWERS, LOTS OF CGI.
AND YOU SAW FIT TO BRING THOR'S ASININE WAR TO ATLANTIS? TO *MY HOME?*
I MEAN, THAT'S NOT WHAT I WAS ***TRYING*** TO DO. WATER IS USUALLY A MUCH MORE EFFECTIVE FIREFIGHTING TOOL.
HEY, LOOK...

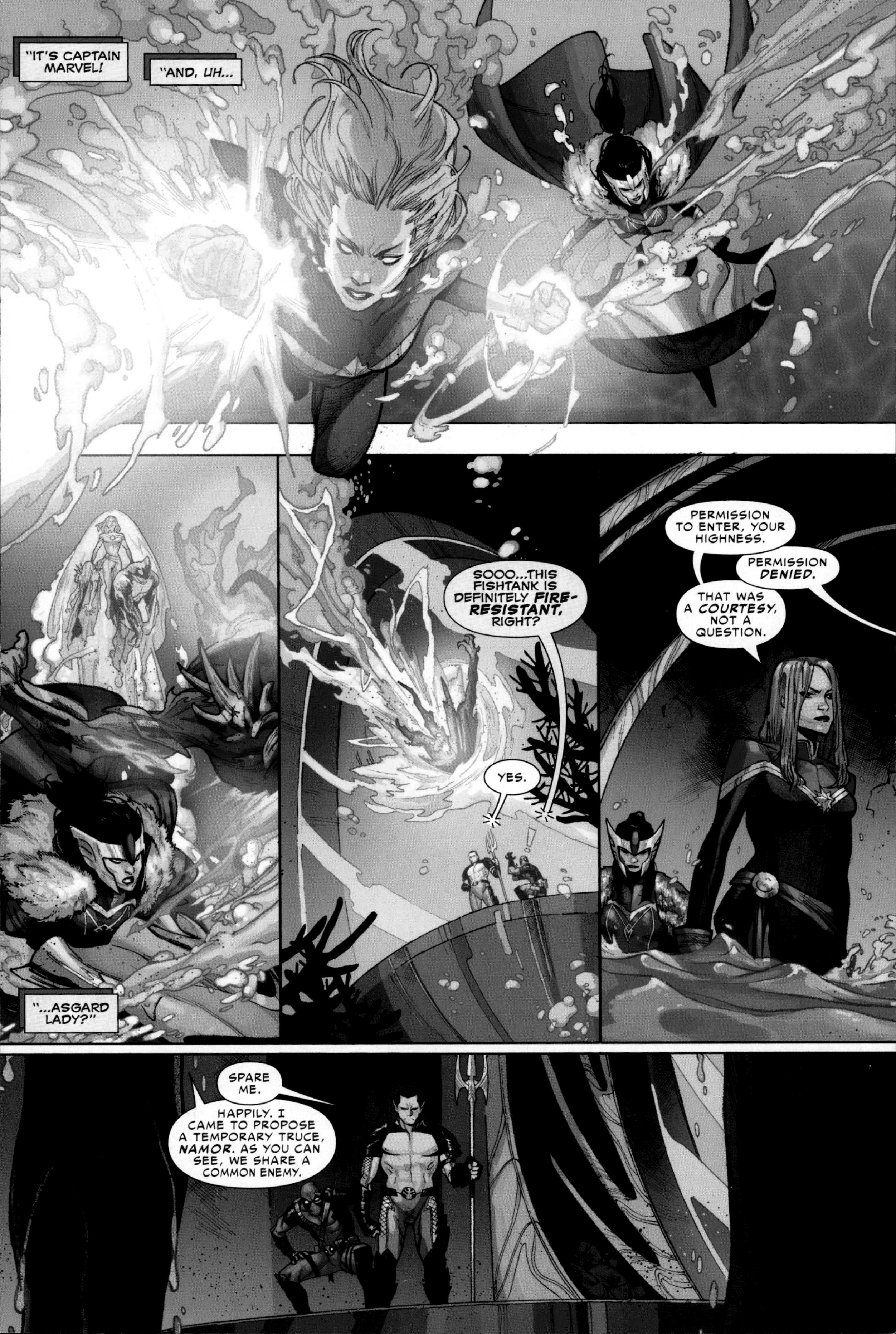

"IT'S CAPTAIN MARVEL!
"AND, UH...
"...ASGARD LADY?"
SOOO...THIS FISHTANK IS DEFINITELY FIRE-RESISTANT, RIGHT?
YES.
PERMISSION TO ENTER, YOUR HIGHNESS.
PERMISSION DENIED.
THAT WAS A COURTESY, NOT A QUESTION.
SPARE ME.
HAPPILY. I CAME TO PROPOSE A TEMPORARY TRUCE, NAMOR. AS YOU CAN SEE, WE SHARE A COMMON ENEMY.

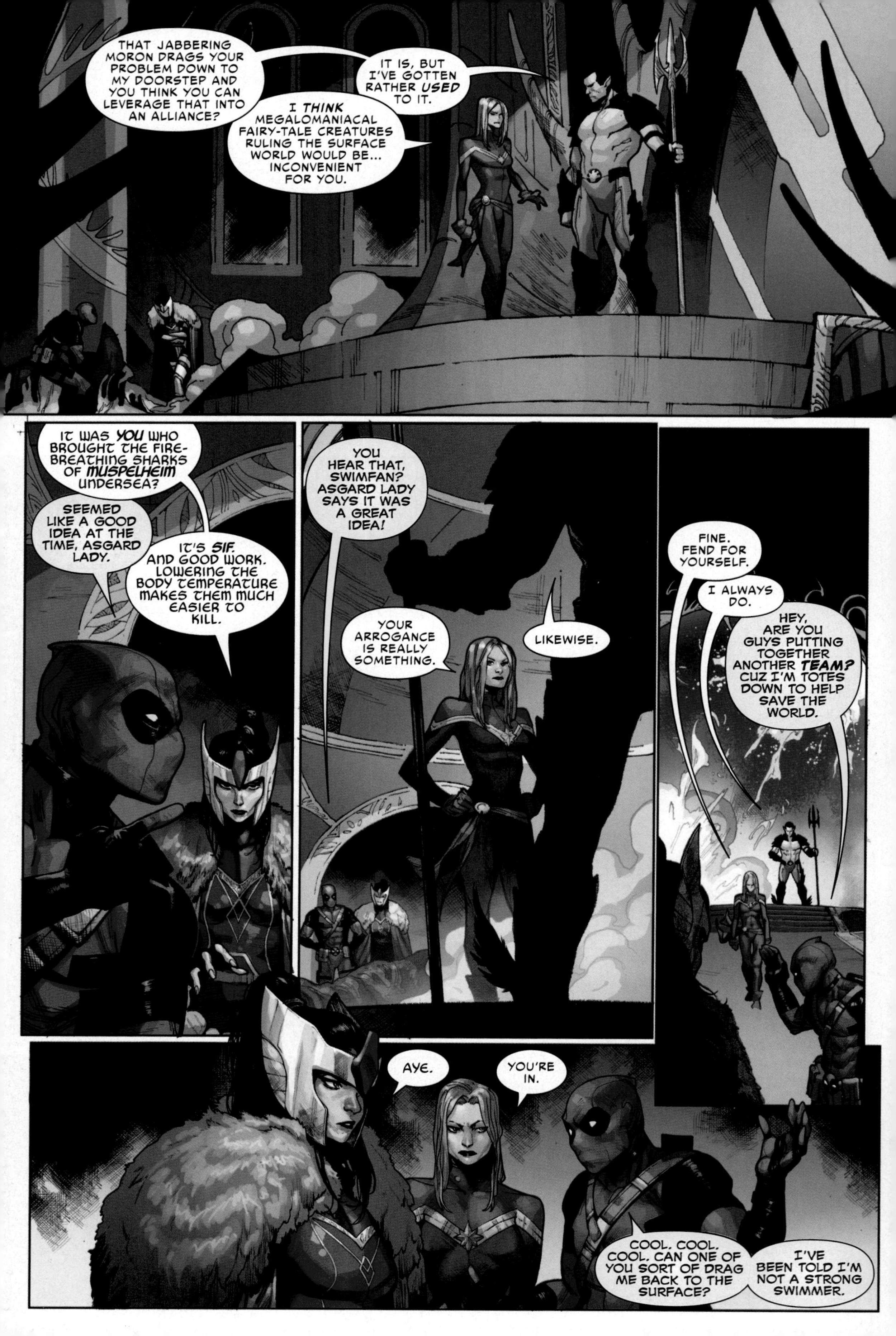

THAT JABBERING MORON DRAGS YOUR PROBLEM DOWN TO MY DOORSTEP AND YOU THINK YOU CAN LEVERAGE THAT INTO AN ALLIANCE?
IT IS, BUT I'VE GOTTEN RATHER *USED* TO IT.
I *THINK* MEGALOMANIACAL FAIRY-TALE CREATURES RULING THE SURFACE WORLD WOULD BE... INCONVENIENT FOR YOU.
IT WAS *YOU* WHO BROUGHT THE FIRE-BREATHING SHARKS OF *MUSPELHEIM* UNDERSEA?
SEEMED LIKE A GOOD IDEA AT THE TIME, ASGARD LADY.
IT'S *SIF.* AND GOOD WORK. LOWERING THE BODY TEMPERATURE MAKES THEM MUCH EASIER TO KILL.
YOU HEAR THAT, SWIMFAN? ASGARD LADY SAYS IT WAS A GREAT IDEA!
YOUR ARROGANCE IS REALLY SOMETHING.
LIKEWISE.
FINE. FEND FOR YOURSELF.
I ALWAYS DO.
HEY, ARE YOU GUYS PUTTING TOGETHER ANOTHER *TEAM?* CUZ I'M TOTES DOWN TO HELP SAVE THE WORLD.
AYE.
YOU'RE IN.
COOL. COOL. COOL. CAN ONE OF YOU SORT OF DRAG ME BACK TO THE SURFACE?
I'VE BEEN TOLD I'M NOT A STRONG SWIMMER.

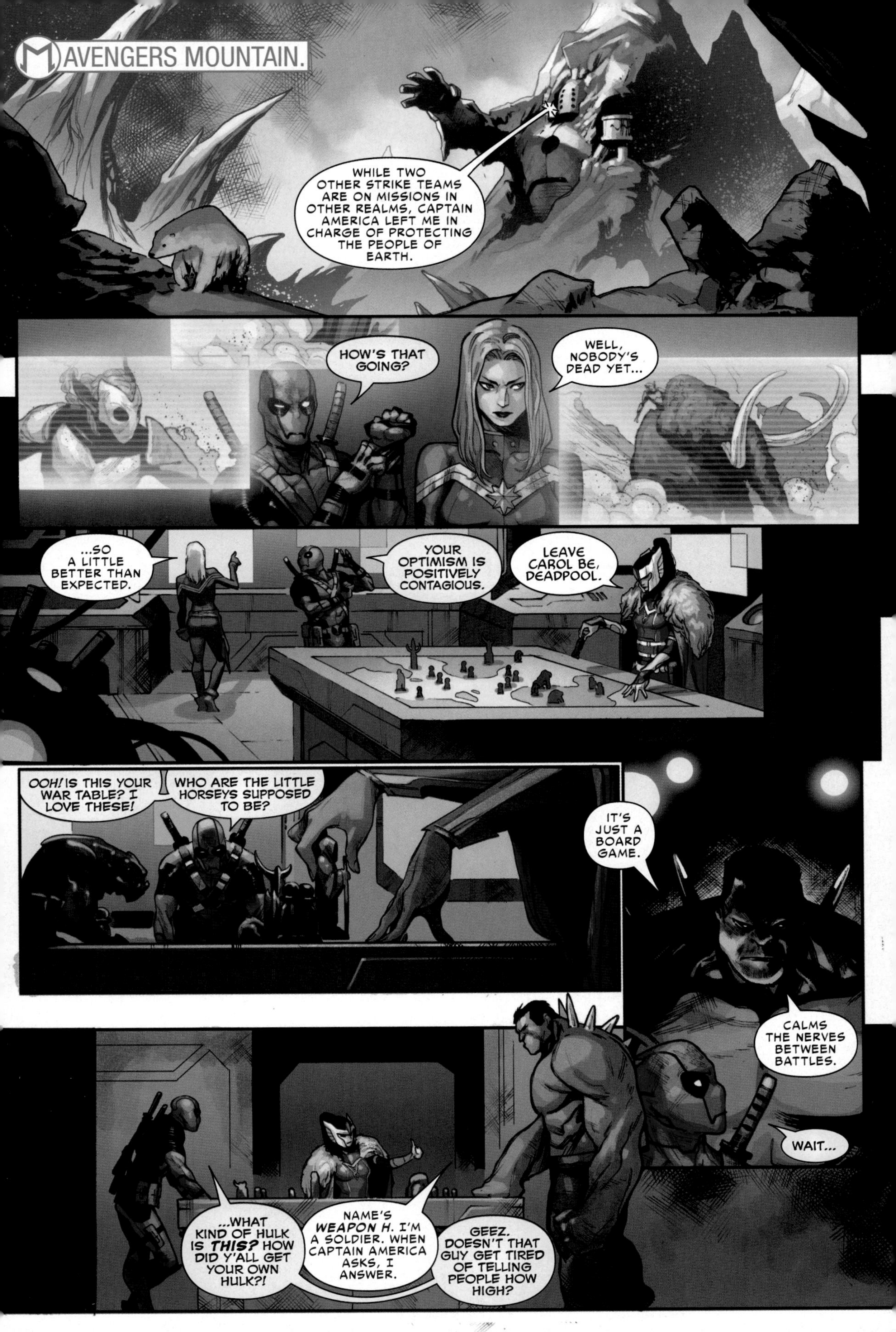

AVENGERS MOUNTAIN.
WHILE TWO OTHER STRIKE TEAMS ARE ON MISSIONS IN OTHER REALMS, CAPTAIN AMERICA LEFT ME IN CHARGE OF PROTECTING THE PEOPLE OF EARTH.
HOW'S THAT GOING?
WELL, NOBODY'S DEAD YET...
...SO A LITTLE BETTER THAN EXPECTED.
YOUR OPTIMISM IS POSITIVELY CONTAGIOUS.
LEAVE CAROL BE, DEADPOOL.
OOH! IS THIS YOUR WAR TABLE? I LOVE THESE!
WHO ARE THE LITTLE HORSEYS SUPPOSED TO BE?
IT'S JUST A BOARD GAME.
CALMS THE NERVES BETWEEN BATTLES.
WAIT...
...WHAT KIND OF HULK IS THIS? HOW DID Y'ALL GET YOUR OWN HULK?!
NAME'S WEAPON H. I'M A SOLDIER. WHEN CAPTAIN AMERICA ASKS, I ANSWER.
GEEZ. DOESN'T THAT GUY GET TIRED OF TELLING PEOPLE HOW HIGH?

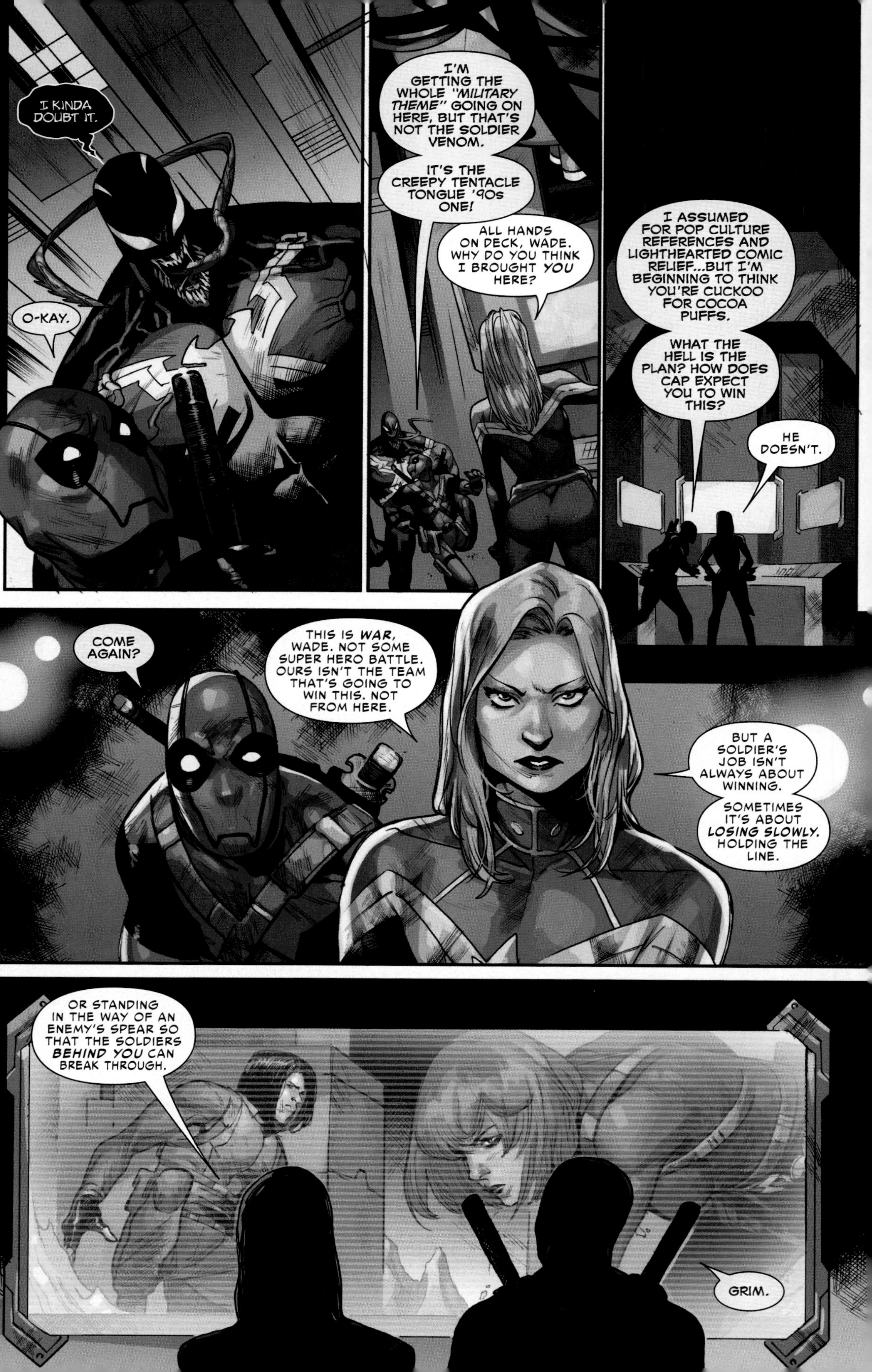

I KINDA DOUBT IT.
O-KAY.
I'M GETTING THE WHOLE "MILITARY THEME" GOING ON HERE, BUT THAT'S NOT THE SOLDIER VENOM.
IT'S THE CREEPY TENTACLE TONGUE '90s ONE!
ALL HANDS ON DECK, WADE. WHY DO YOU THINK I BROUGHT YOU HERE?
I ASSUMED FOR POP CULTURE REFERENCES AND LIGHTHEARTED COMIC RELIEF...BUT I'M BEGINNING TO THINK YOU'RE CUCKOO FOR COCOA PUFFS.
WHAT THE HELL IS THE PLAN? HOW DOES CAP EXPECT YOU TO WIN THIS?
HE DOESN'T.
COME AGAIN?
THIS IS WAR, WADE. NOT SOME SUPER HERO BATTLE. OURS ISN'T THE TEAM THAT'S GOING TO WIN THIS. NOT FROM HERE.
BUT A SOLDIER'S JOB ISN'T ALWAYS ABOUT WINNING.
SOMETIMES IT'S ABOUT LOSING SLOWLY. HOLDING THE LINE.
OR STANDING IN THE WAY OF AN ENEMY'S SPEAR SO THAT THE SOLDIERS BEHIND YOU CAN BREAK THROUGH.
GRIM.

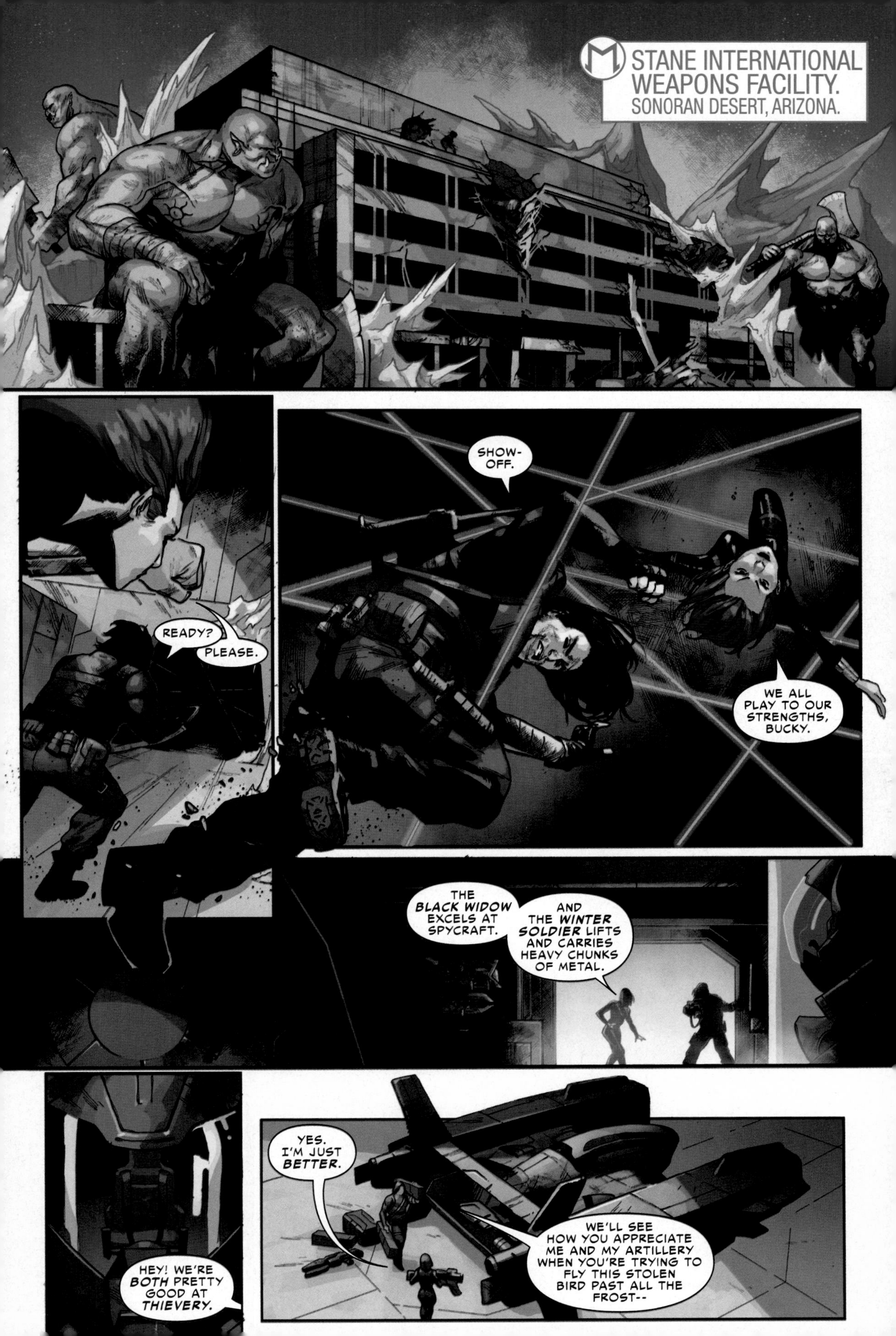
STANE INTERNATIONAL WEAPONS FACILITY. SONORAN DESERT, ARIZONA.
READY?
PLEASE.
SHOW-OFF.
WE ALL PLAY TO OUR STRENGTHS, BUCKY.
THE BLACK WIDOW EXCELS AT SPYCRAFT.
AND THE WINTER SOLDIER LIFTS AND CARRIES HEAVY CHUNKS OF METAL.
HEY! WE'RE BOTH PRETTY GOOD AT THIEVERY.
YES. I'M JUST BETTER.
WE'LL SEE HOW YOU APPRECIATE ME AND MY ARTILLERY WHEN YOU'RE TRYING TO FLY THIS STOLEN BIRD PAST ALL THE FROST--

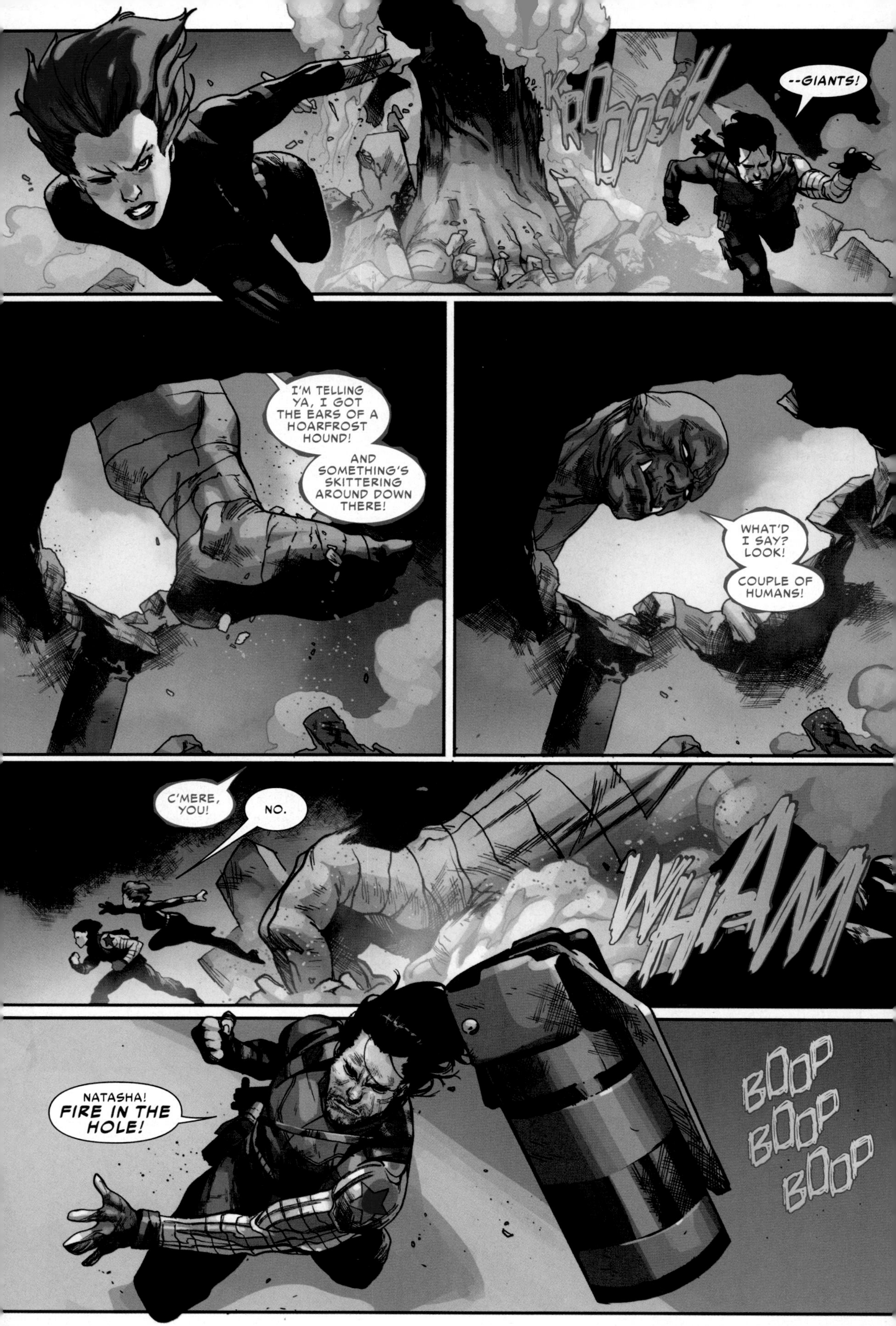
KROOOOSH
--GIANTS!
I'M TELLING YA, I GOT THE EARS OF A HOARFROST HOUND!
AND SOMETHING'S SKITTERING AROUND DOWN THERE!
WHAT'D I SAY? LOOK!
COUPLE OF HUMANS!
C'MERE, YOU!
NO.
WHAM
NATASHA! FIRE IN THE HOLE!
BOOP BOOP BOOP

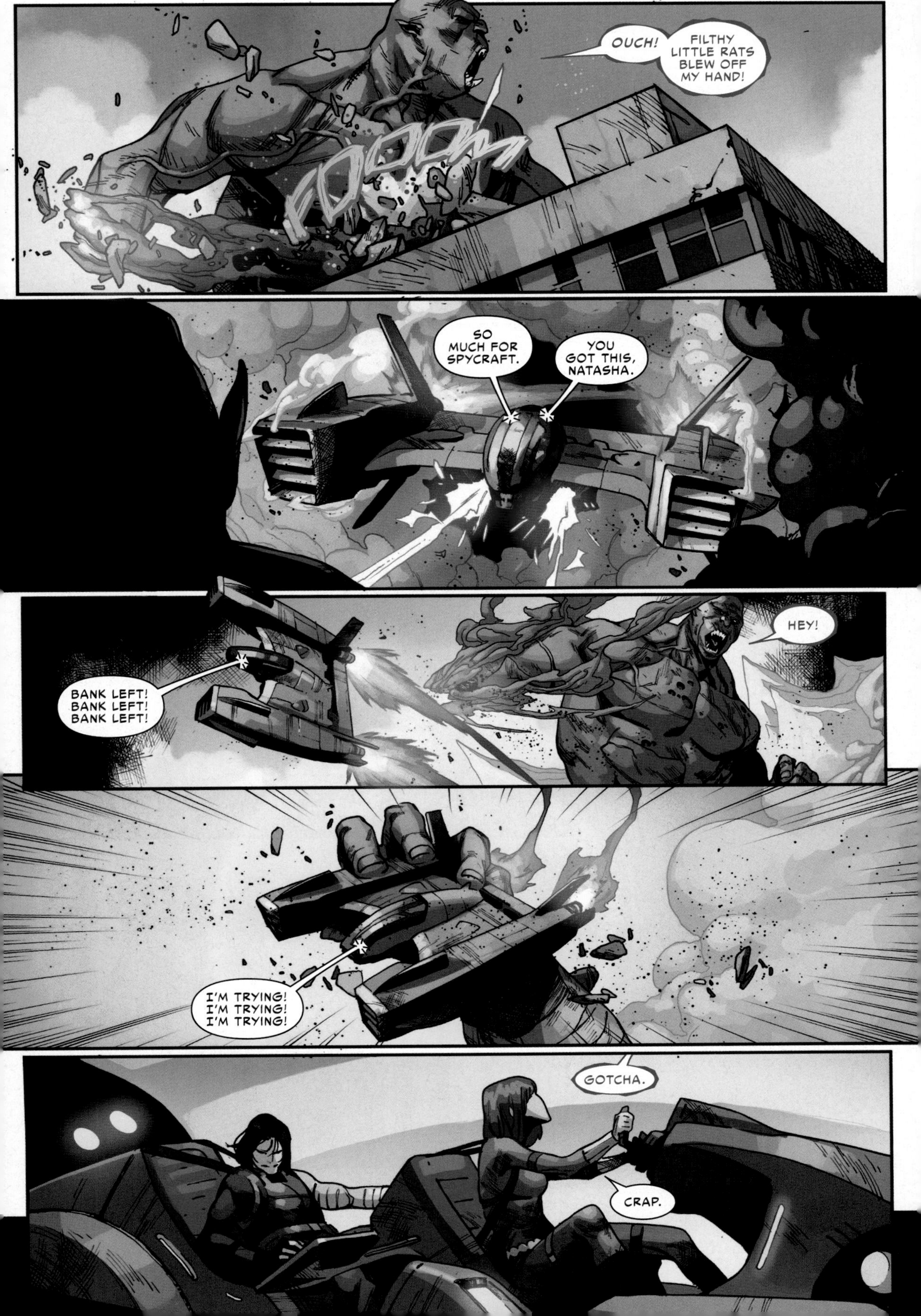
OUCH!
FILTHY LITTLE RATS BLEW OFF MY HAND!
FOOOM
SO MUCH FOR SPYCRAFT.
YOU GOT THIS, NATASHA.
HEY!
BANK LEFT! BANK LEFT! BANK LEFT!
I'M TRYING! I'M TRYING! I'M TRYING!
GOTCHA.
CRAP.

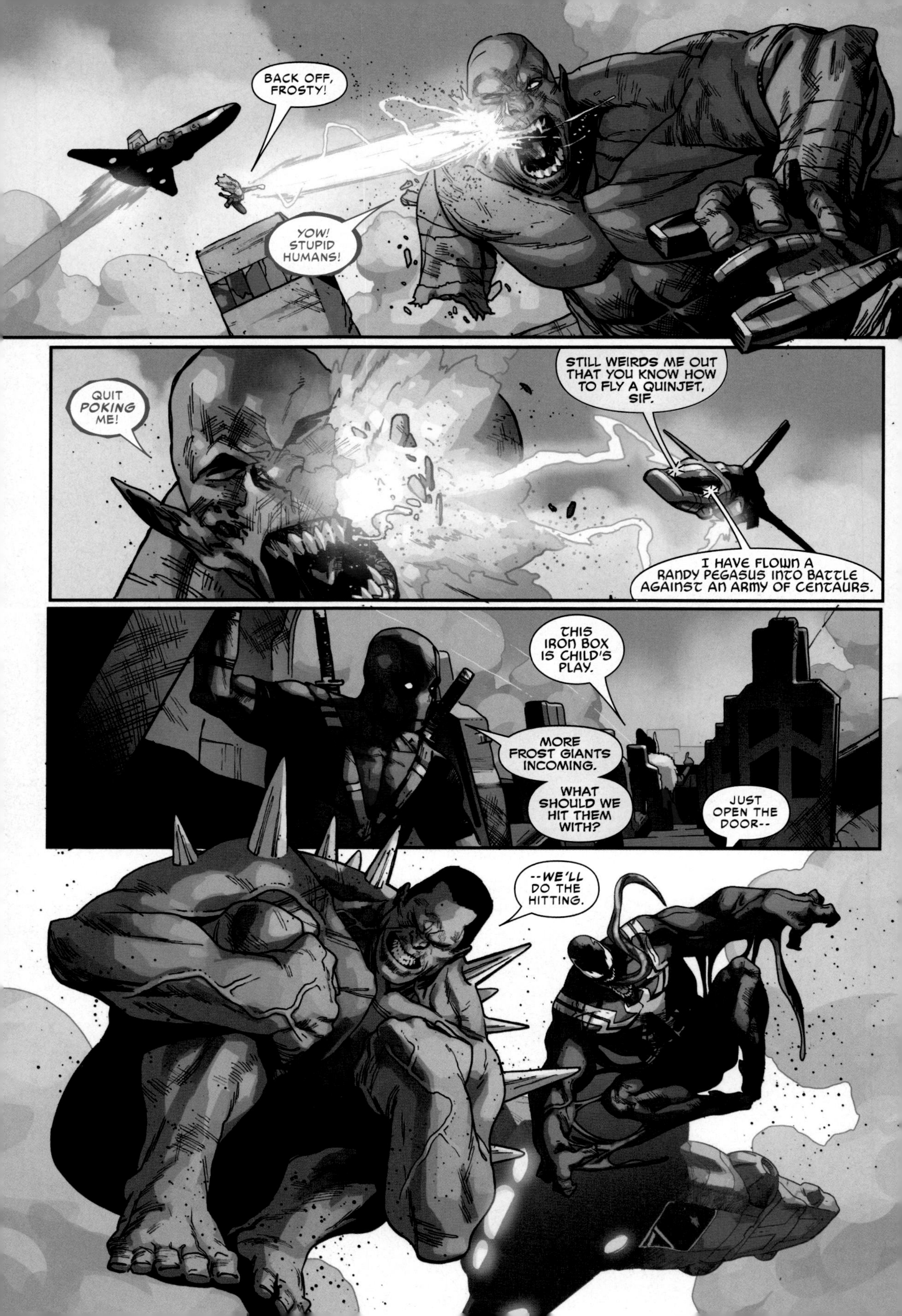
BACK OFF, FROSTY!
YOW! STUPID HUMANS!
QUIT POKING ME!
STILL WEIRDS ME OUT THAT YOU KNOW HOW TO FLY A QUINJET, SIF.
I HAVE FLOWN A RANDY PEGASUS INTO BATTLE AGAINST AN ARMY OF CENTAURS.
THIS IRON BOX IS CHILD'S PLAY.
MORE FROST GIANTS INCOMING.
WHAT SHOULD WE HIT THEM WITH?
JUST OPEN THE DOOR--
--WE'LL DO THE HITTING.

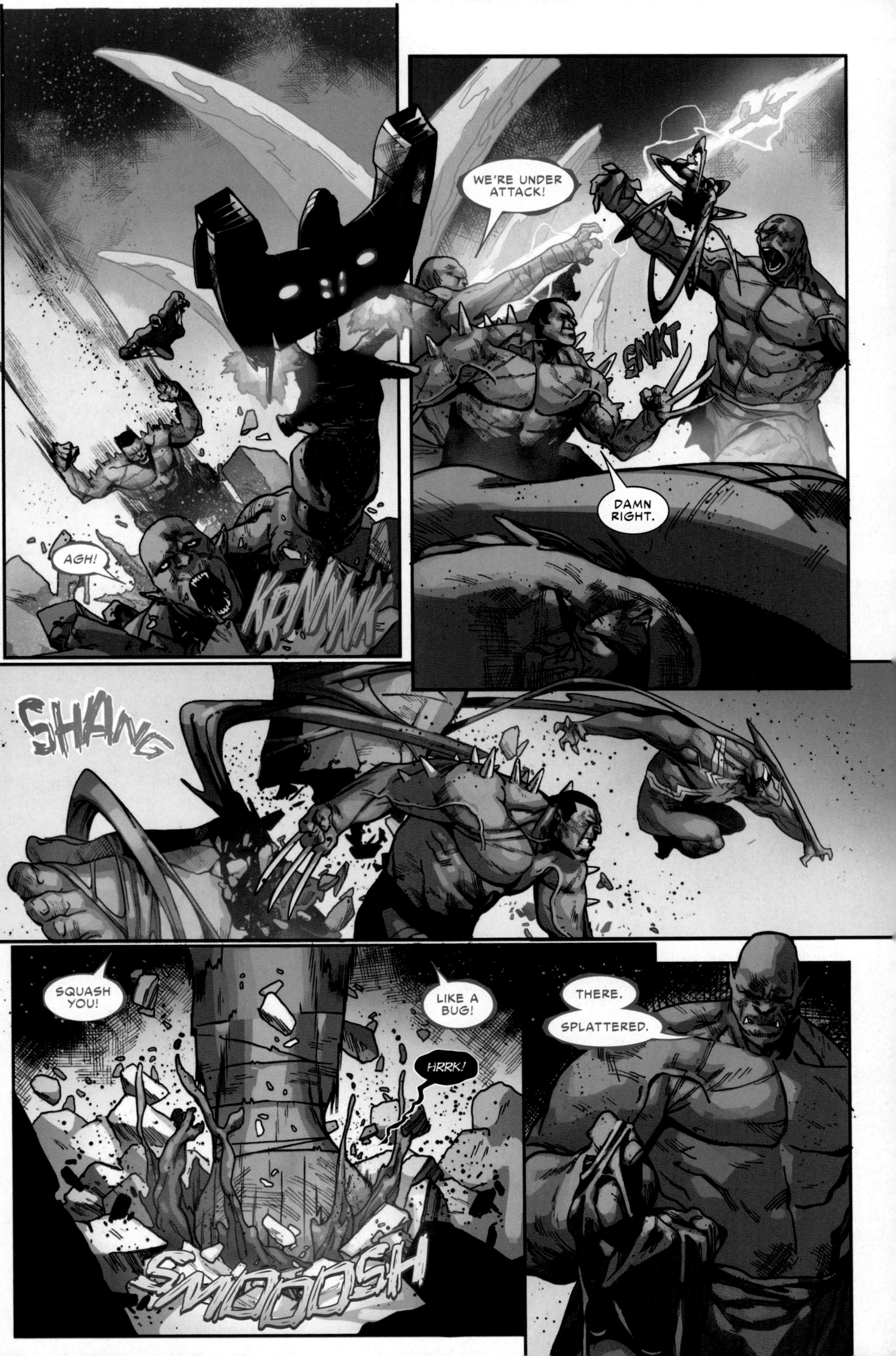
AGH!
KRNNNK
WE'RE UNDER ATTACK!
SNIKT
DAMN RIGHT.
SHANG
SQUASH YOU!
LIKE A BUG!
HRRK!
SMOOOSH
THERE.
SPLATTERED.

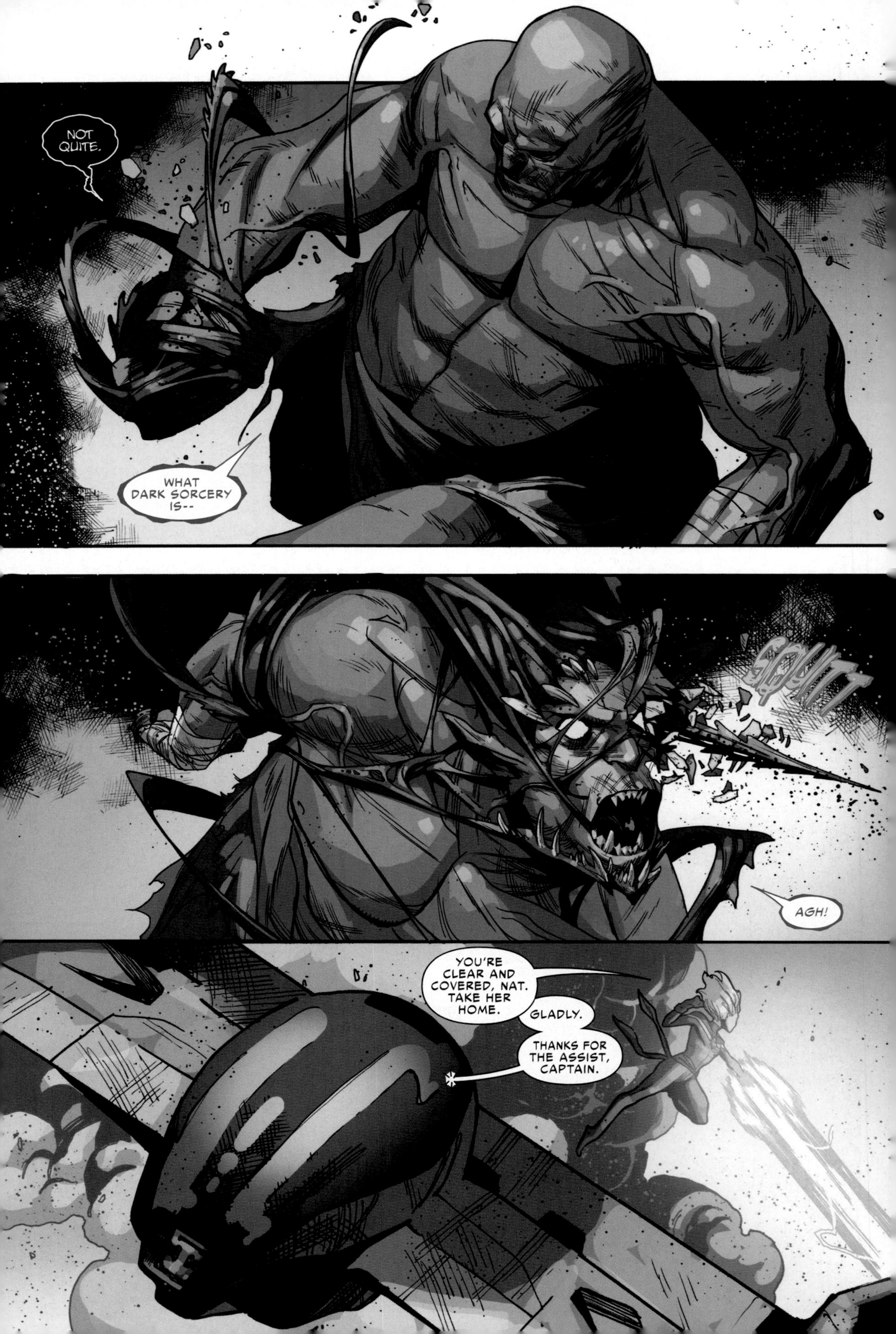
NOT QUITE.
WHAT DARK SORCERY IS--
AGH!
YOU'RE CLEAR AND COVERED, NAT. TAKE HER HOME.
GLADLY.
THANKS FOR THE ASSIST, CAPTAIN.

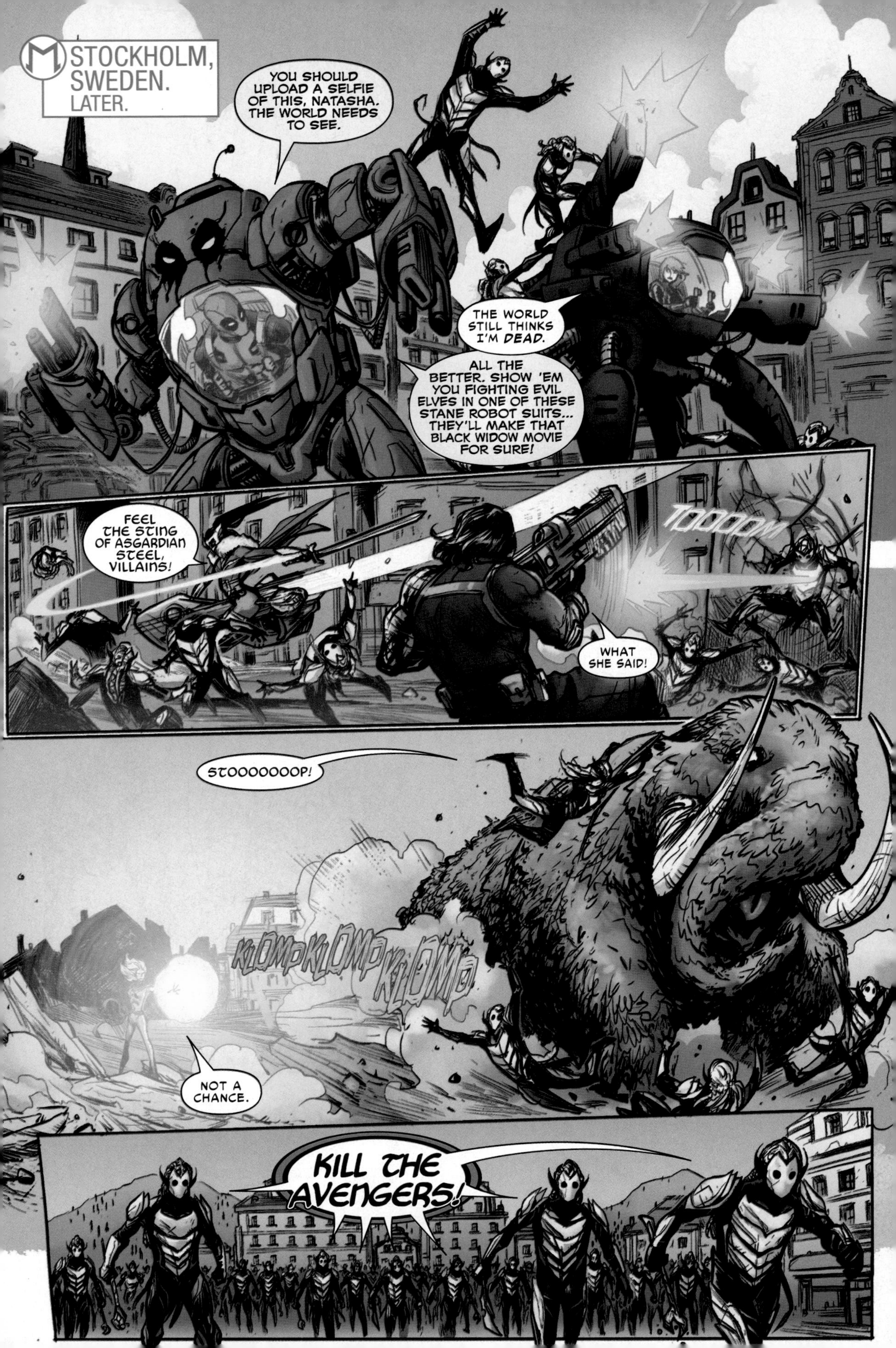
STOCKHOLM, SWEDEN. LATER.
YOU SHOULD UPLOAD A SELFIE OF THIS, NATASHA. THE WORLD NEEDS TO SEE.
THE WORLD STILL THINKS I'M DEAD.
ALL THE BETTER. SHOW 'EM YOU FIGHTING EVIL ELVES IN ONE OF THESE STANE ROBOT SUITS... THEY'LL MAKE THAT BLACK WIDOW MOVIE FOR SURE!
FEEL THE STING OF ASGARDIAN STEEL, VILLAINS!
TOOOOM
WHAT SHE SAID!
STOOOOOOOP!
KLOMP KLOMP KLOMP
NOT A CHANCE.
KILL THE AVENGERS!

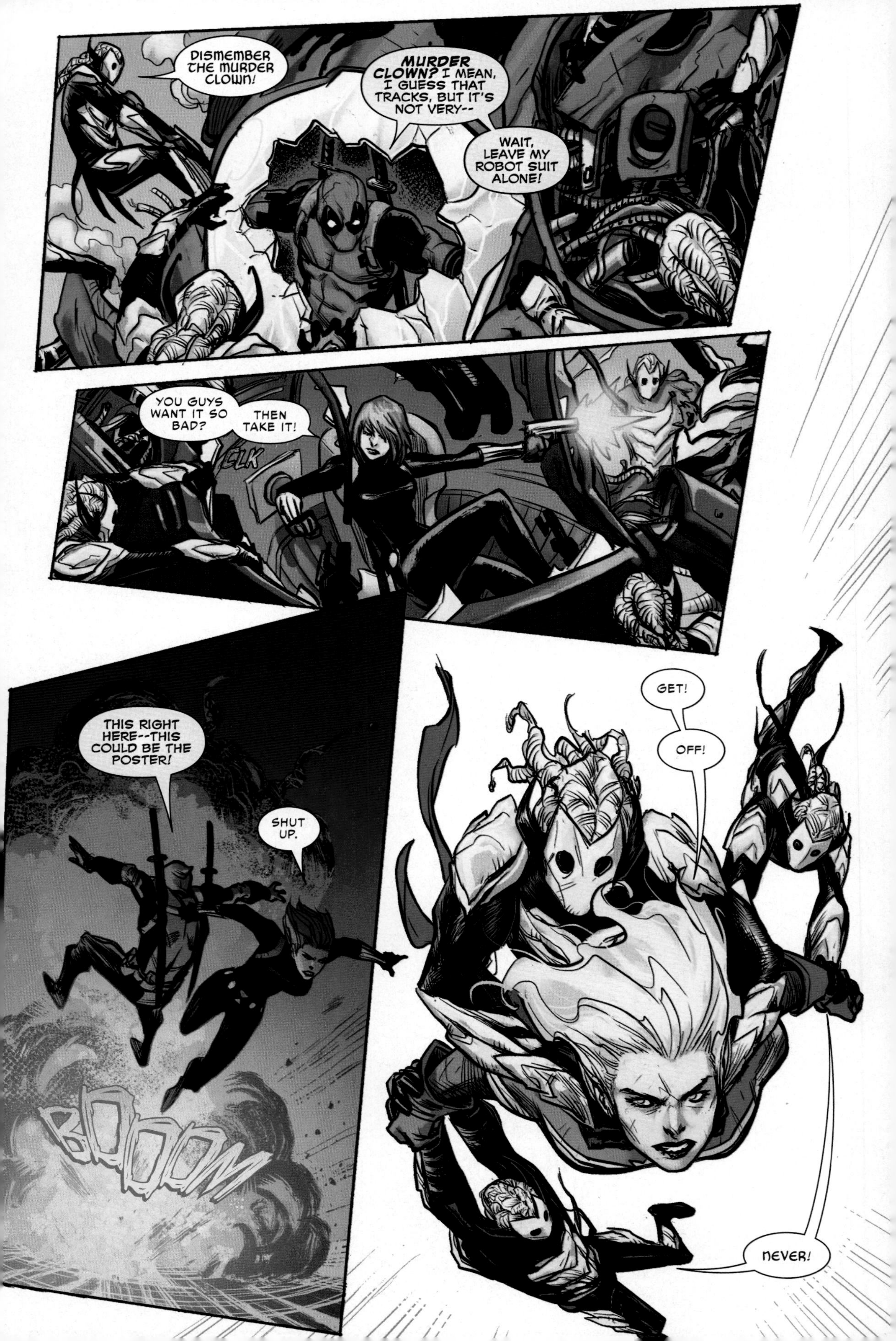
DISMEMBER THE MURDER CLOWN!
MURDER CLOWN? I MEAN, I GUESS THAT TRACKS, BUT IT'S NOT VERY--
WAIT, LEAVE MY ROBOT SUIT ALONE!
YOU GUYS WANT IT SO BAD?
THEN TAKE IT!
CLK
THIS RIGHT HERE--THIS COULD BE THE POSTER!
SHUT UP.
BOOOM
GET!
OFF!
NEVER!

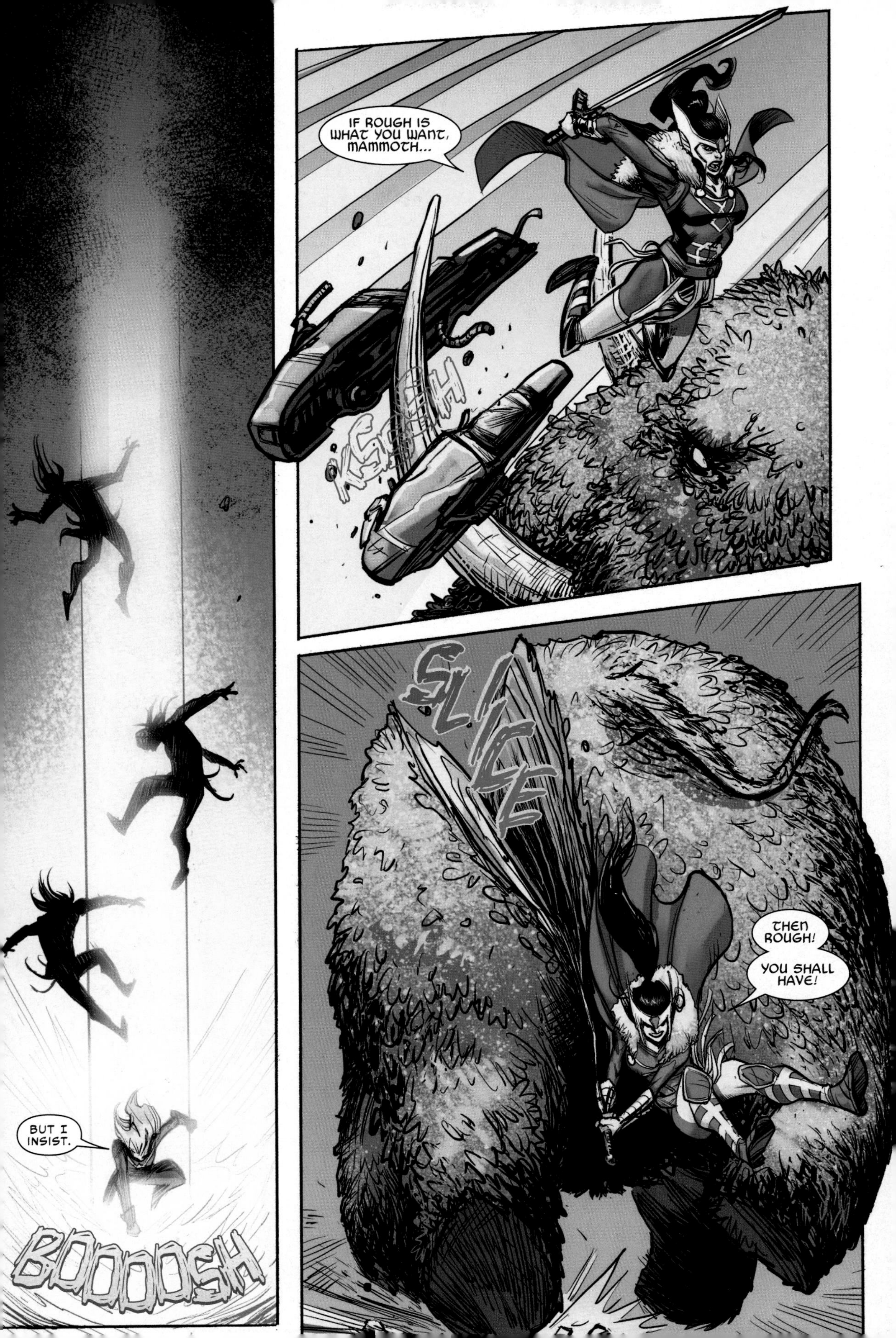
BUT I INSIST.
BOOOOSH
IF ROUGH IS WHAT YOU WANT, MAMMOTH...
SLICE
THEN ROUGH!
YOU SHALL HAVE!

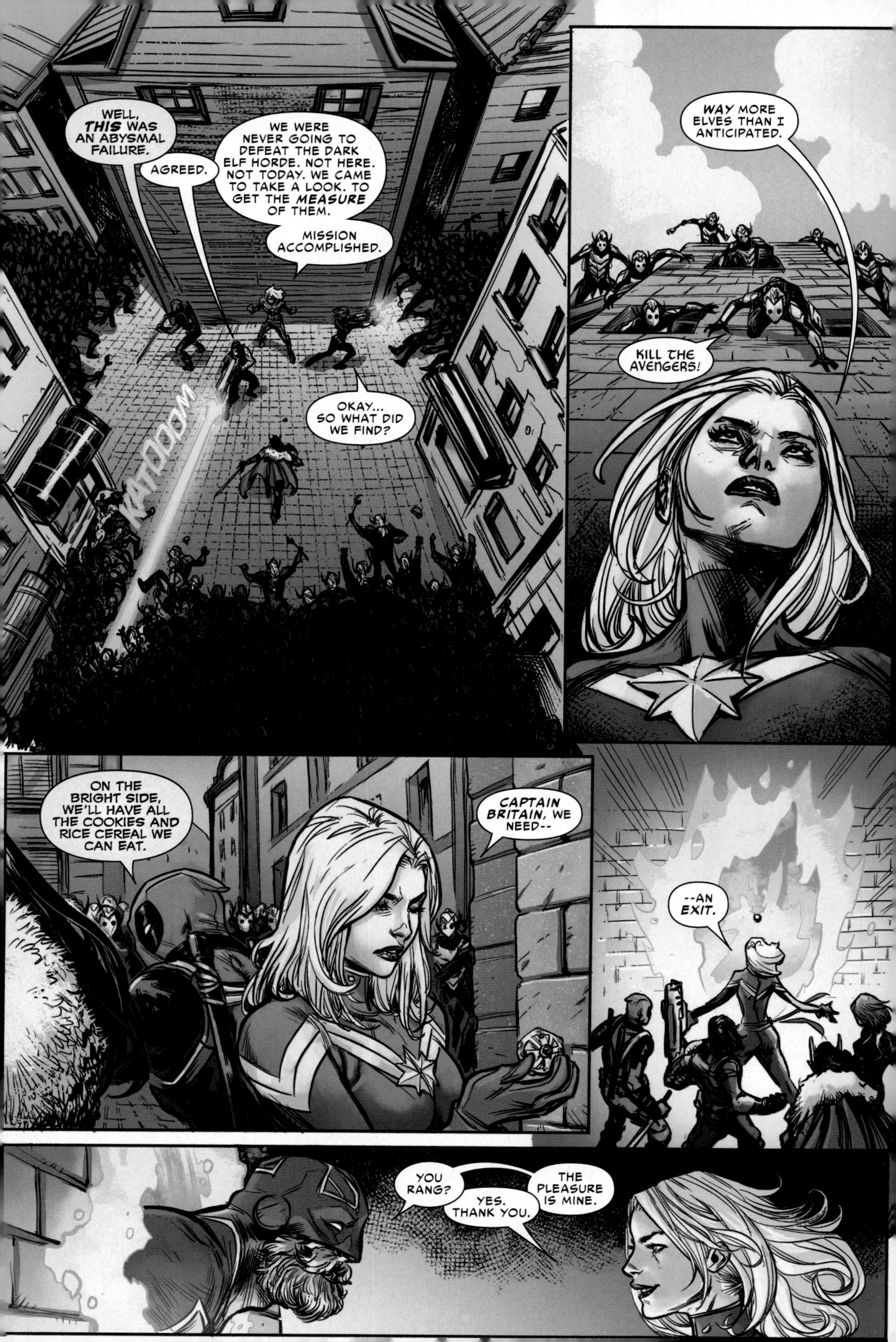
WELL, THIS WAS AN ABYSMAL FAILURE.
AGREED.
WE WERE NEVER GOING TO DEFEAT THE DARK ELF HORDE. NOT HERE. NOT TODAY. WE CAME TO TAKE A LOOK. TO GET THE MEASURE OF THEM.
MISSION ACCOMPLISHED.
OKAY... SO WHAT DID WE FIND?
KATOOOM
WAY MORE ELVES THAN I ANTICIPATED.
KILL THE AVENGERS!
ON THE BRIGHT SIDE, WE'LL HAVE ALL THE COOKIES AND RICE CEREAL WE CAN EAT.
CAPTAIN BRITAIN, WE NEED--
--AN EXIT.
YOU RANG?
YES. THANK YOU.
THE PLEASURE IS MINE.

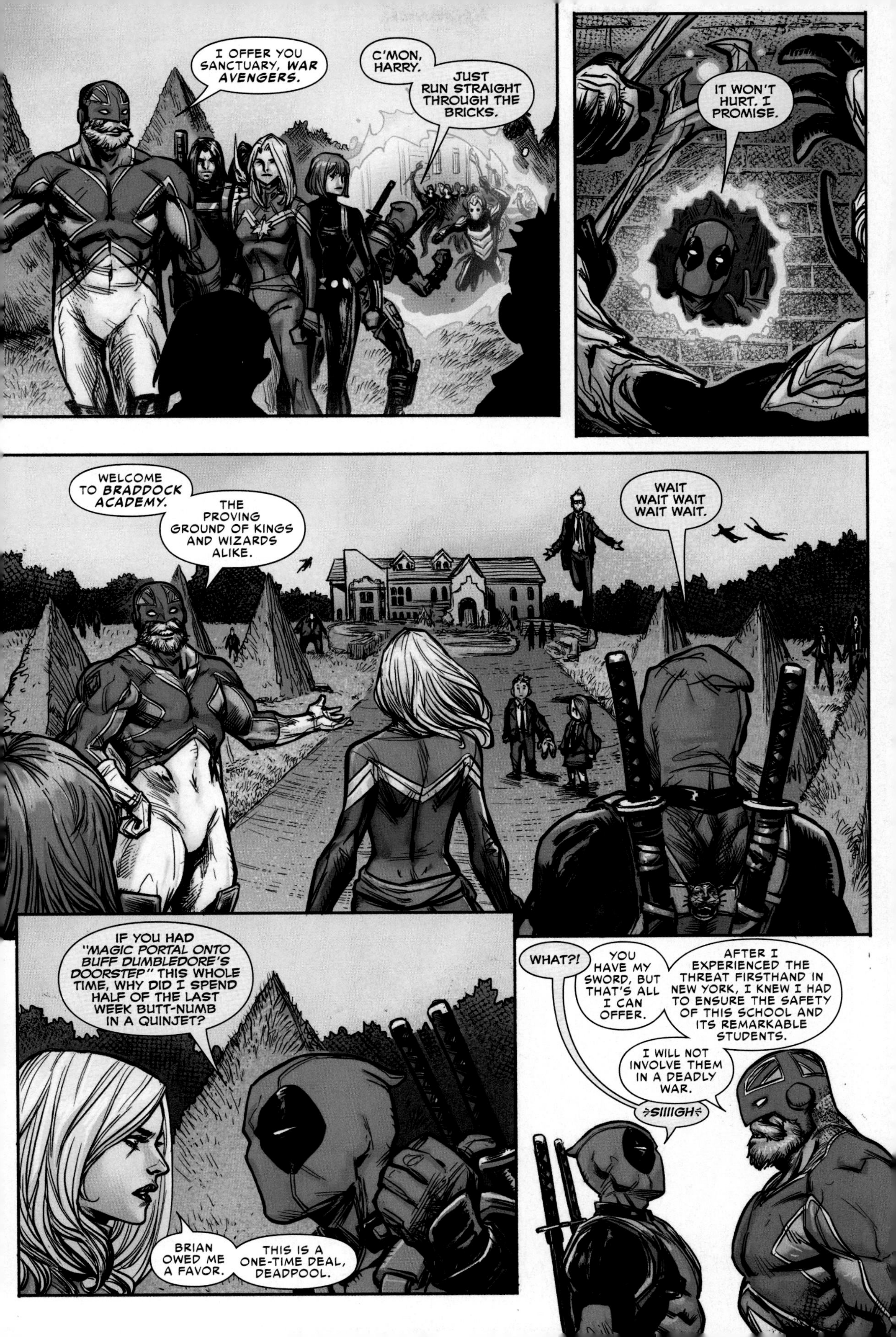
I OFFER YOU SANCTUARY, WAR AVENGERS.
C'MON, HARRY.
JUST RUN STRAIGHT THROUGH THE BRICKS.
IT WON'T HURT. I PROMISE.
WELCOME TO BRADDOCK ACADEMY.
THE PROVING GROUND OF KINGS AND WIZARDS ALIKE.
WAIT WAIT WAIT WAIT WAIT.
IF YOU HAD "MAGIC PORTAL ONTO BUFF DUMBLEDORE'S DOORSTEP" THIS WHOLE TIME, WHY DID I SPEND HALF OF THE LAST WEEK BUTT-NUMB IN A QUINJET?
BRIAN OWED ME A FAVOR.
THIS IS A ONE-TIME DEAL, DEADPOOL.
AFTER I EXPERIENCED THE THREAT FIRSTHAND IN NEW YORK, I KNEW I HAD TO ENSURE THE SAFETY OF THIS SCHOOL AND ITS REMARKABLE STUDENTS.
I WILL NOT INVOLVE THEM IN A DEADLY WAR.
YOU HAVE MY SWORD, BUT THAT'S ALL I CAN OFFER.
WHAT?!
SIIIIGH

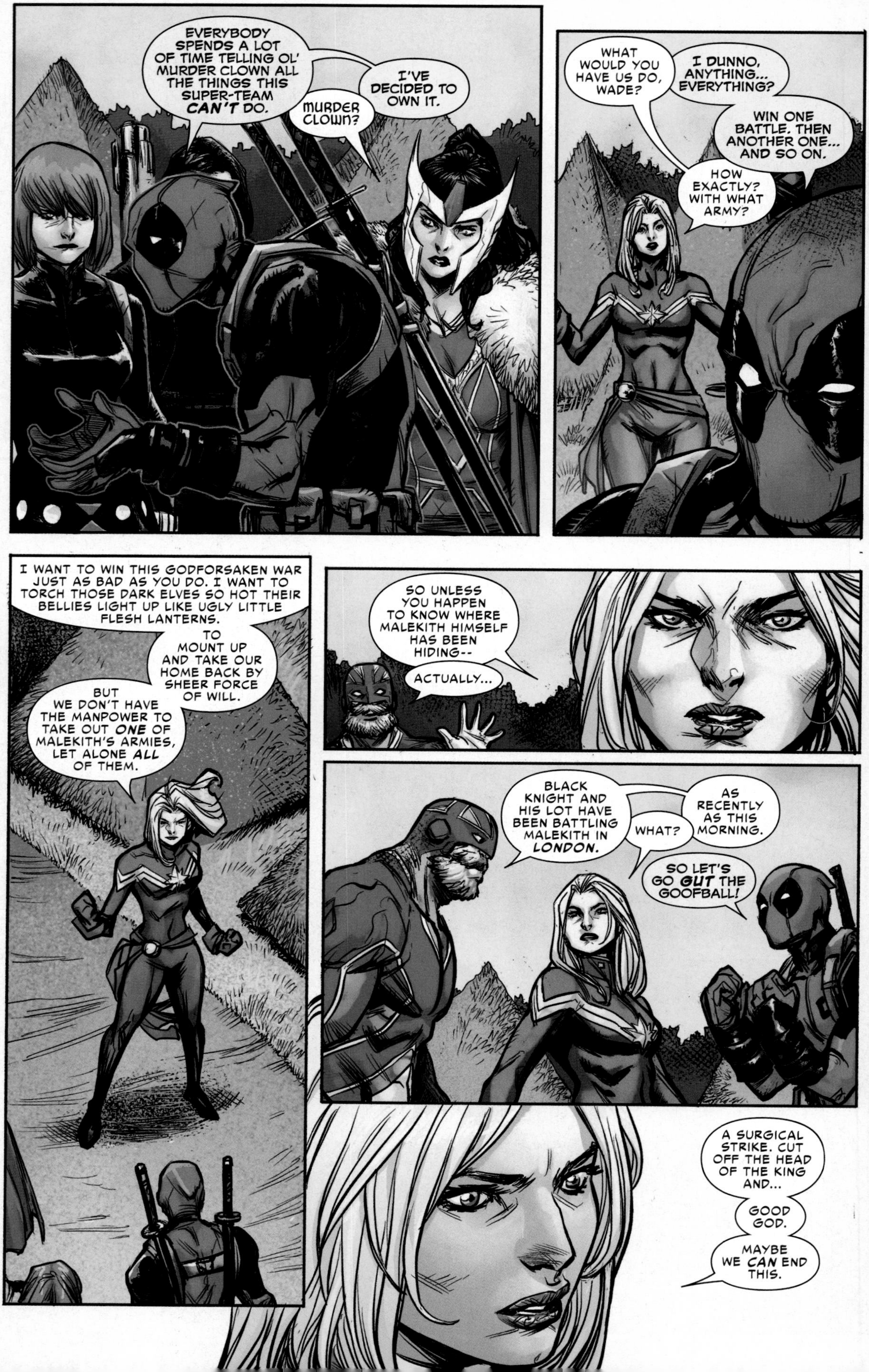
EVERYBODY SPENDS A LOT OF TIME TELLING OL' MURDER CLOWN ALL THE THINGS THIS SUPER-TEAM CAN'T DO.
I'VE DECIDED TO OWN IT.
MURDER CLOWN?
WHAT WOULD YOU HAVE US DO, WADE?
I DUNNO, ANYTHING... EVERYTHING?
WIN ONE BATTLE. THEN ANOTHER ONE... AND SO ON.
HOW EXACTLY? WITH WHAT ARMY?
I WANT TO WIN THIS GODFORSAKEN WAR JUST AS BAD AS YOU DO. I WANT TO TORCH THOSE DARK ELVES SO HOT THEIR BELLIES LIGHT UP LIKE UGLY LITTLE FLESH LANTERNS.
TO MOUNT UP AND TAKE OUR HOME BACK BY SHEER FORCE OF WILL.
BUT WE DON'T HAVE THE MANPOWER TO TAKE OUT ONE OF MALEKITH'S ARMIES, LET ALONE ALL OF THEM.
SO UNLESS YOU HAPPEN TO KNOW WHERE MALEKITH HIMSELF HAS BEEN HIDING--
ACTUALLY...
BLACK KNIGHT AND HIS LOT HAVE BEEN BATTLING MALEKITH IN LONDON.
WHAT?
AS RECENTLY AS THIS MORNING.
SO LET'S GO GUT THE GOOFBALL!
A SURGICAL STRIKE. CUT OFF THE HEAD OF THE KING AND...
GOOD GOD.
MAYBE WE CAN END THIS.

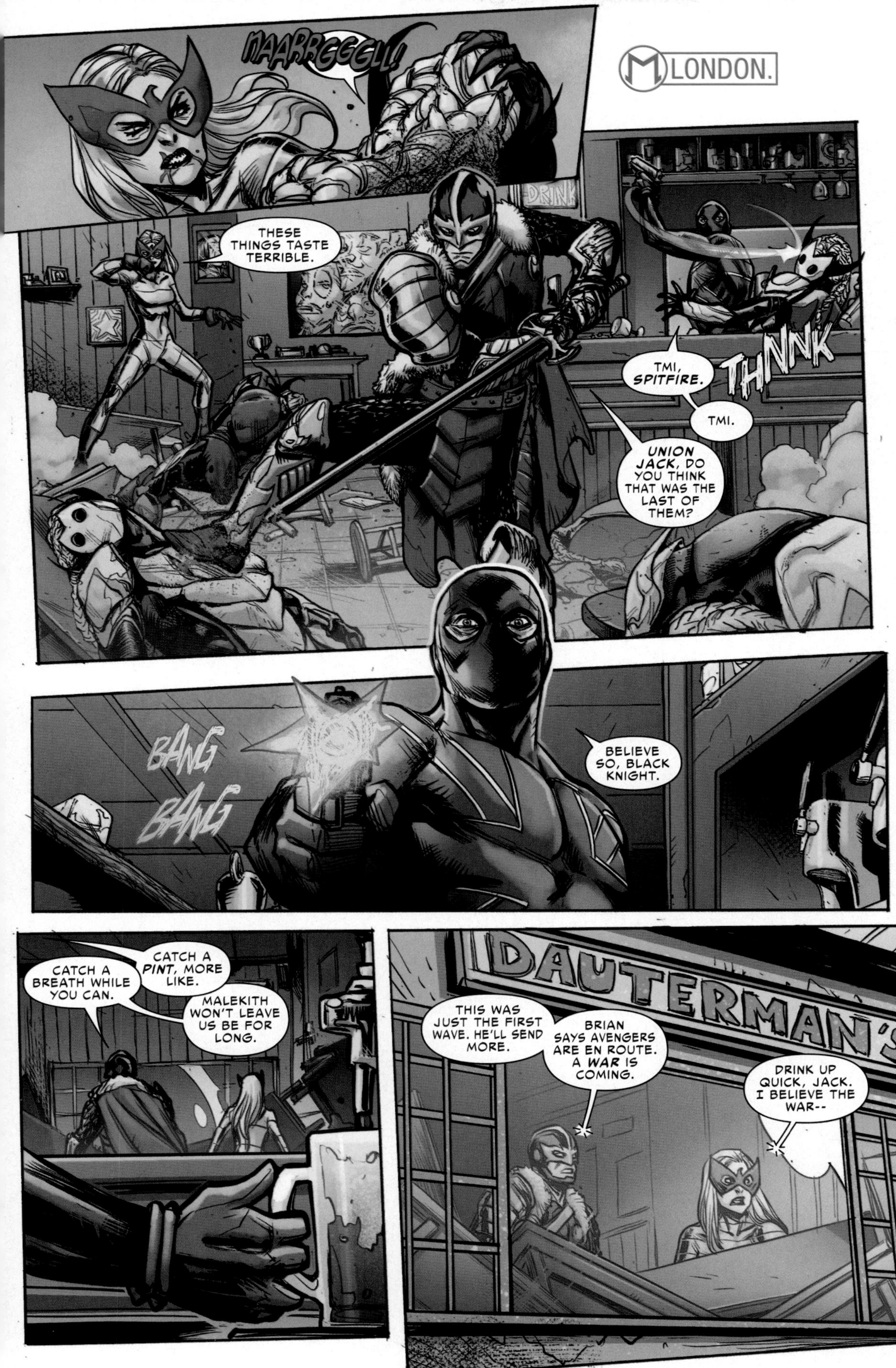
LONDON.
NAARRGGGLL!
THESE THINGS TASTE TERRIBLE.
THNNK
TMI, SPITFIRE.
TMI.
UNION JACK, DO YOU THINK THAT WAS THE LAST OF THEM?
BANG
BANG
BELIEVE SO, BLACK KNIGHT.
CATCH A BREATH WHILE YOU CAN.
CATCH A PINT, MORE LIKE.
MALEKITH WON'T LEAVE US BE FOR LONG.
DAUTERMAN'S
THIS WAS JUST THE FIRST WAVE. HE'LL SEND MORE.
BRIAN SAYS AVENGERS ARE EN ROUTE. A WAR IS COMING.
DRINK UP QUICK, JACK. I BELIEVE THE WAR--

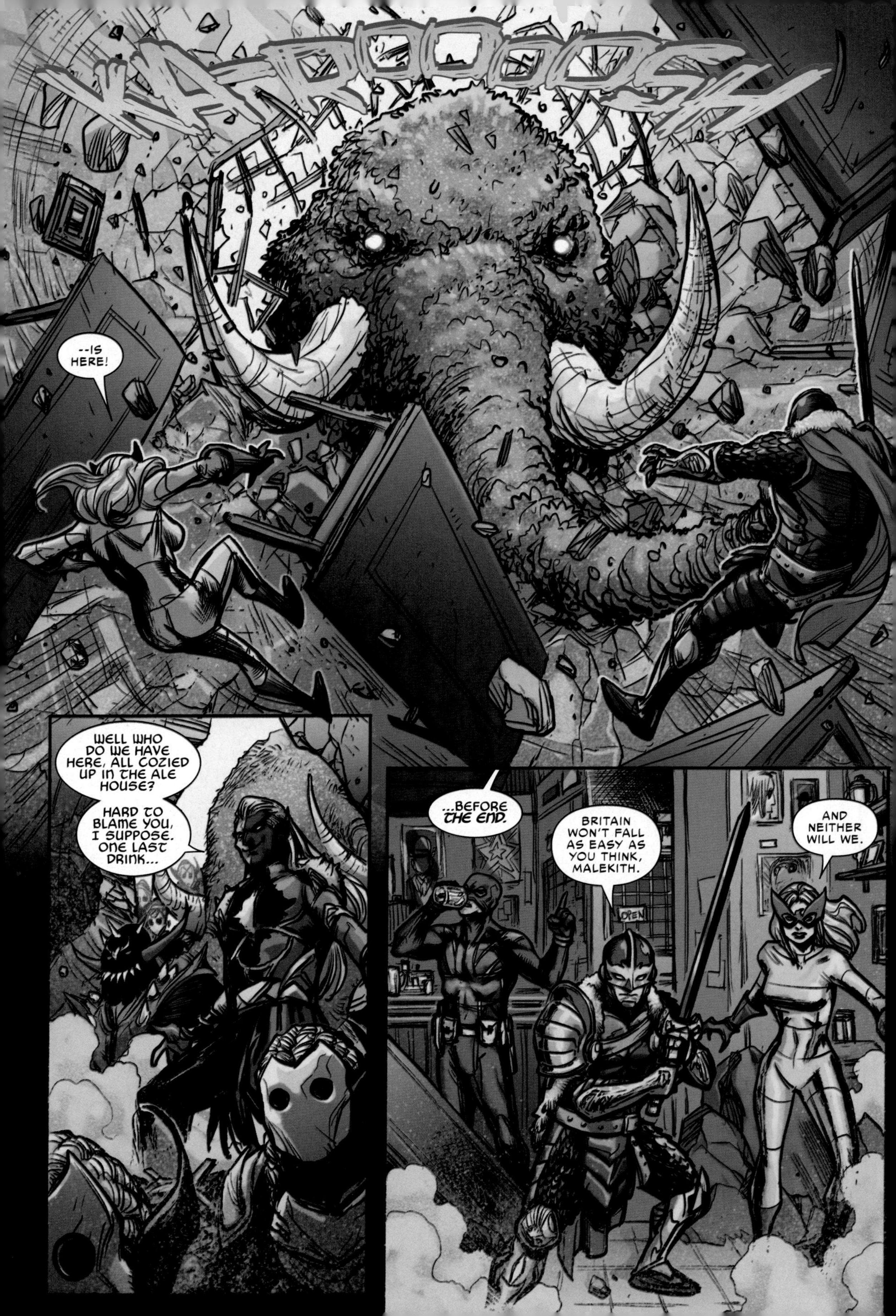
KA-DOOOOSH
--IS HERE!
WELL WHO DO WE HAVE HERE, ALL COZIED UP IN THE ALE HOUSE?
HARD TO BLAME YOU, I SUPPOSE. ONE LAST DRINK...
...BEFORE THE END.
BRITAIN WON'T FALL AS EASY AS YOU THINK, MALEKITH.
AND NEITHER WILL WE.
OPEN

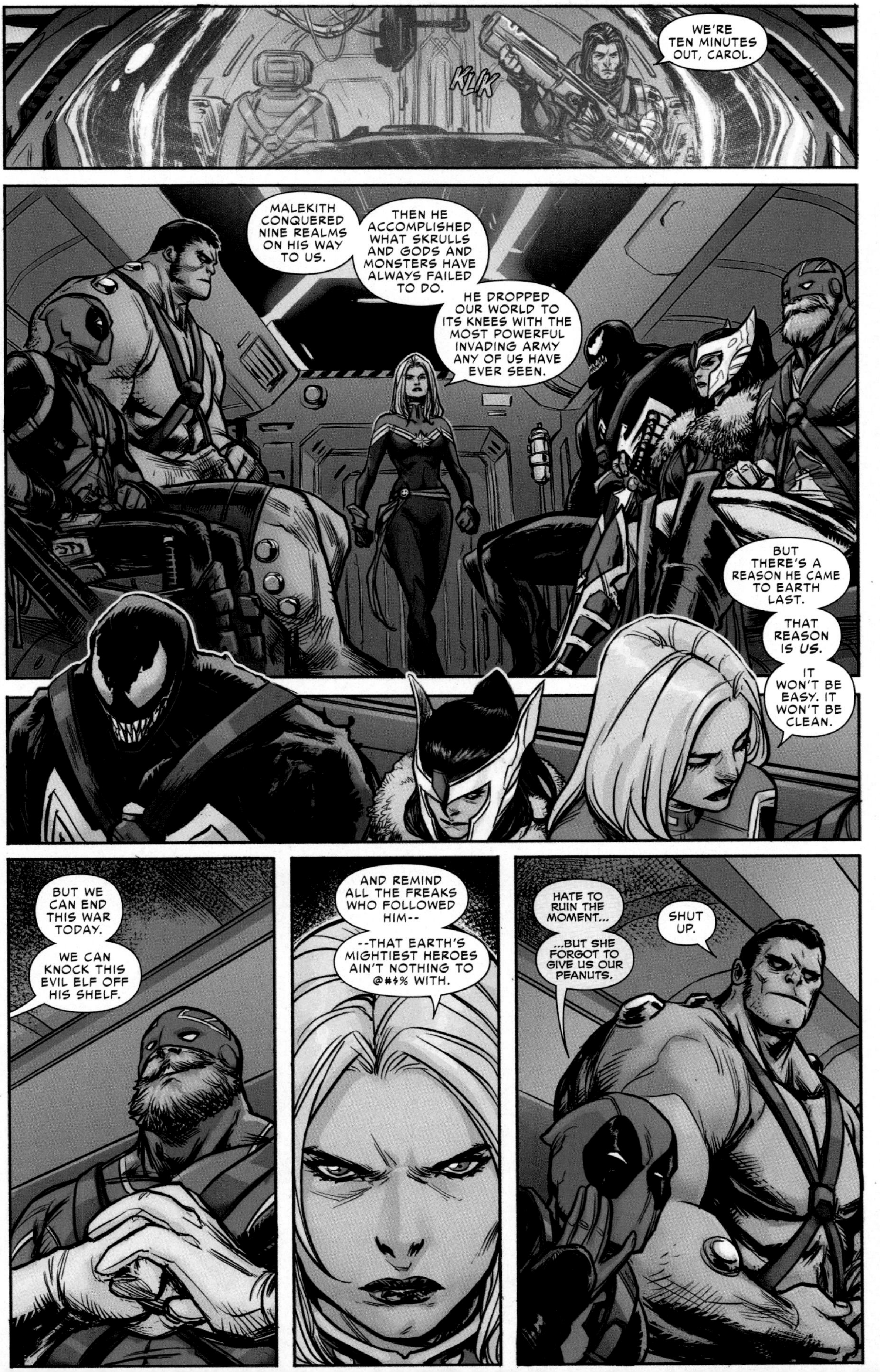
WE'RE TEN MINUTES OUT, CAROL.
KLIK
MALEKITH CONQUERED NINE REALMS ON HIS WAY TO US.
THEN HE ACCOMPLISHED WHAT SKRULLS AND GODS AND MONSTERS HAVE ALWAYS FAILED TO DO.
HE DROPPED OUR WORLD TO ITS KNEES WITH THE MOST POWERFUL INVADING ARMY ANY OF US HAVE EVER SEEN.
BUT THERE'S A REASON HE CAME TO EARTH LAST.
THAT REASON IS *US*.
IT WON'T BE EASY. IT WON'T BE CLEAN.
BUT WE CAN END THIS WAR TODAY.
WE CAN KNOCK THIS EVIL ELF OFF HIS SHELF.
AND REMIND ALL THE FREAKS WHO FOLLOWED HIM--
--THAT EARTH'S MIGHTIEST HEROES AIN'T NOTHING TO @#$% WITH.
HATE TO RUIN THE MOMENT...
...BUT SHE FORGOT TO GIVE US OUR PEANUTS.
SHUT UP.

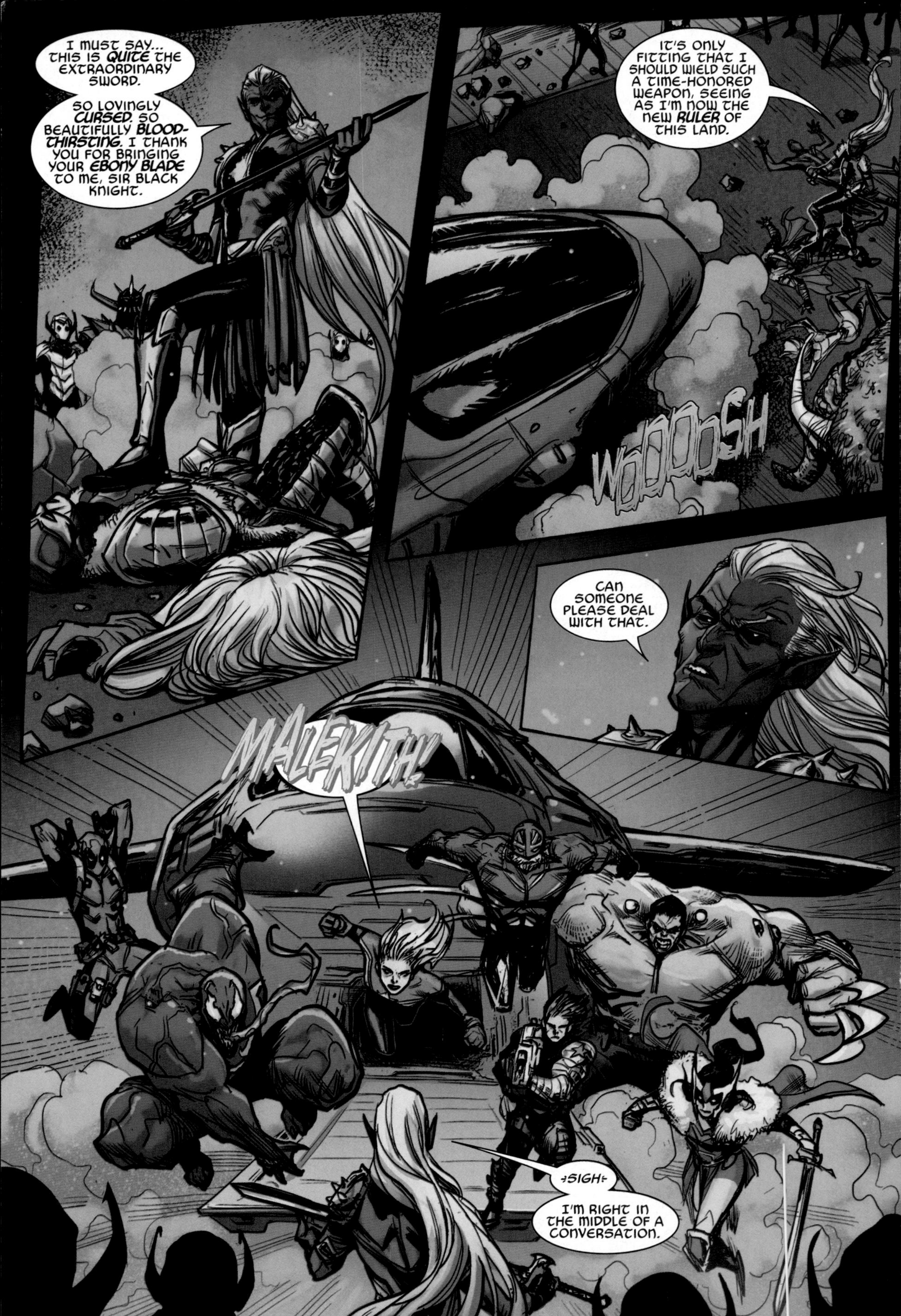
I MUST SAY... THIS IS QUITE THE EXTRAORDINARY SWORD.
SO LOVINGLY CURSED. SO BEAUTIFULLY BLOOD-THIRSTING. I THANK YOU FOR BRINGING YOUR EBONY BLADE TO ME, SIR BLACK KNIGHT.
IT'S ONLY FITTING THAT I SHOULD WIELD SUCH A TIME-HONORED WEAPON, SEEING AS I'M NOW THE NEW RULER OF THIS LAND.
WOOOOOSH
CAN SOMEONE PLEASE DEAL WITH THAT.
MALEKITH!
-SIGH-
I'M RIGHT IN THE MIDDLE OF A CONVERSATION.

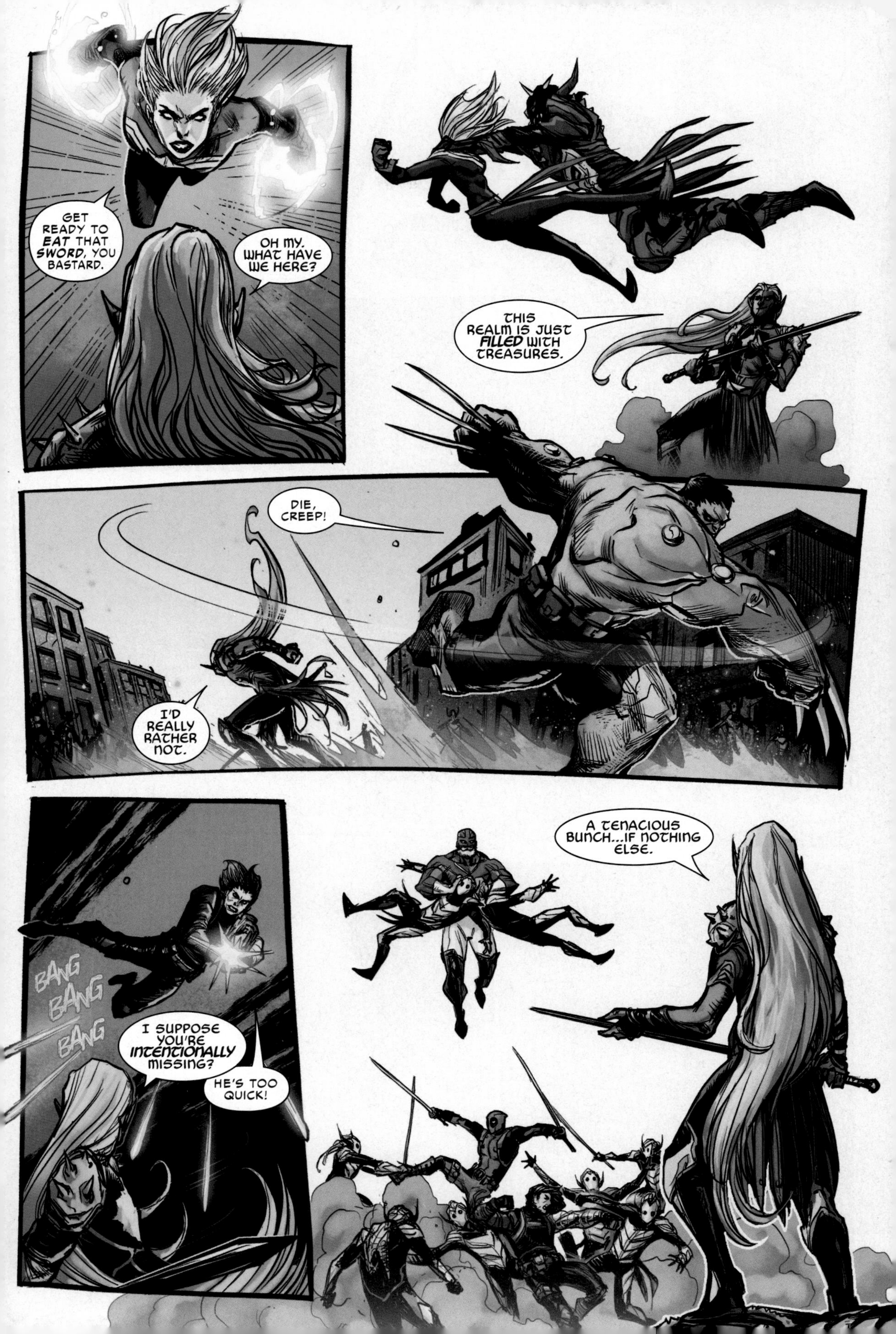
GET READY TO EAT THAT SWORD, YOU BASTARD.
OH MY. WHAT HAVE WE HERE?
THIS REALM IS JUST FILLED WITH TREASURES.
DIE, CREEP!
I'D REALLY RATHER NOT.
BANG BANG BANG
I SUPPOSE YOU'RE INTENTIONALLY MISSING?
HE'S TOO QUICK!
A TENACIOUS BUNCH...IF NOTHING ELSE.

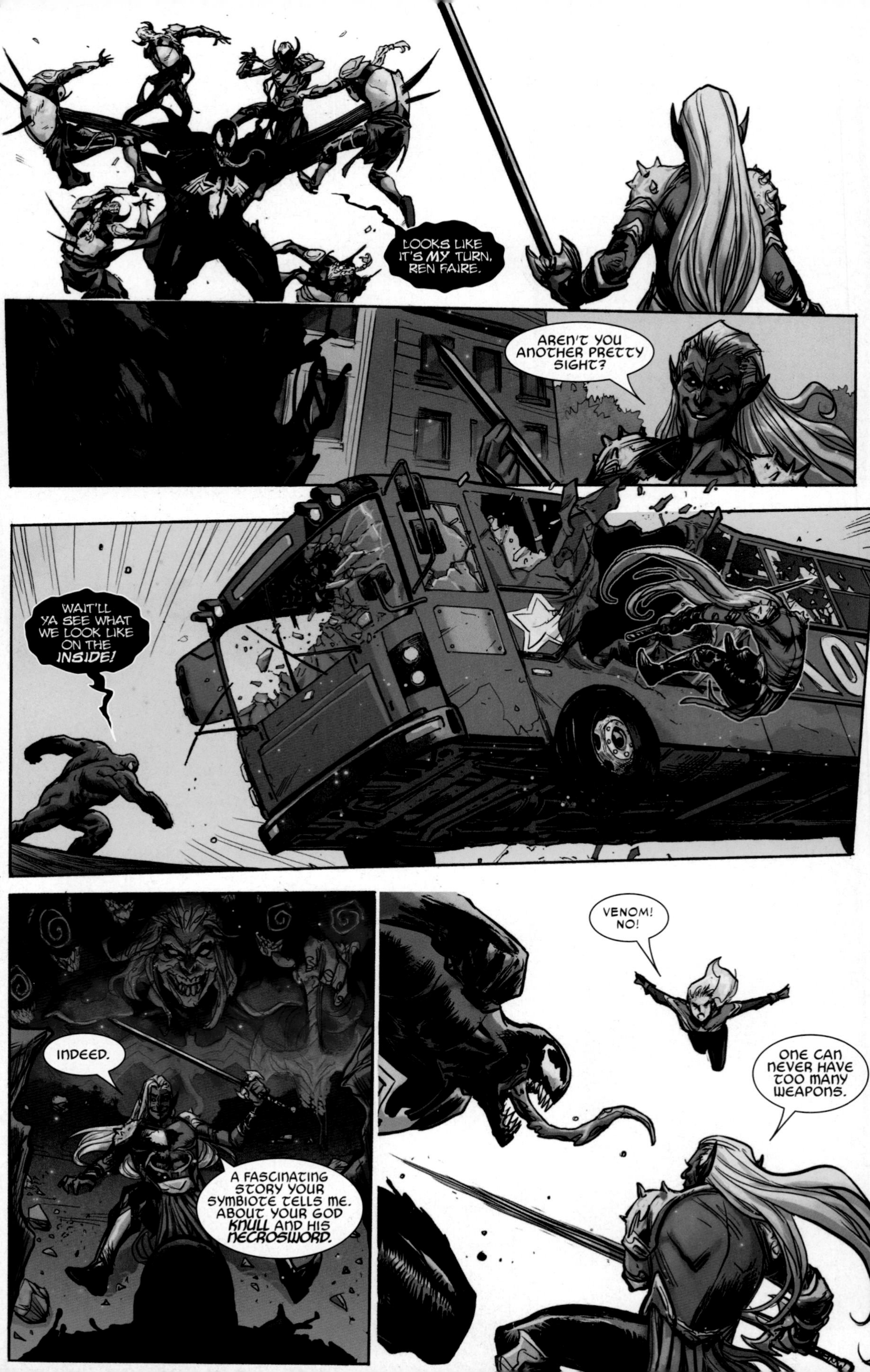
LOOKS LIKE IT'S MY TURN, REN FAIRE.
AREN'T YOU ANOTHER PRETTY SIGHT?
WAIT'LL YA SEE WHAT WE LOOK LIKE ON THE INSIDE!
INDEED.
A FASCINATING STORY YOUR SYMBIOTE TELLS ME. ABOUT YOUR GOD KNULL AND HIS NECROSWORD.
VENOM! NO!
ONE CAN NEVER HAVE TOO MANY WEAPONS.

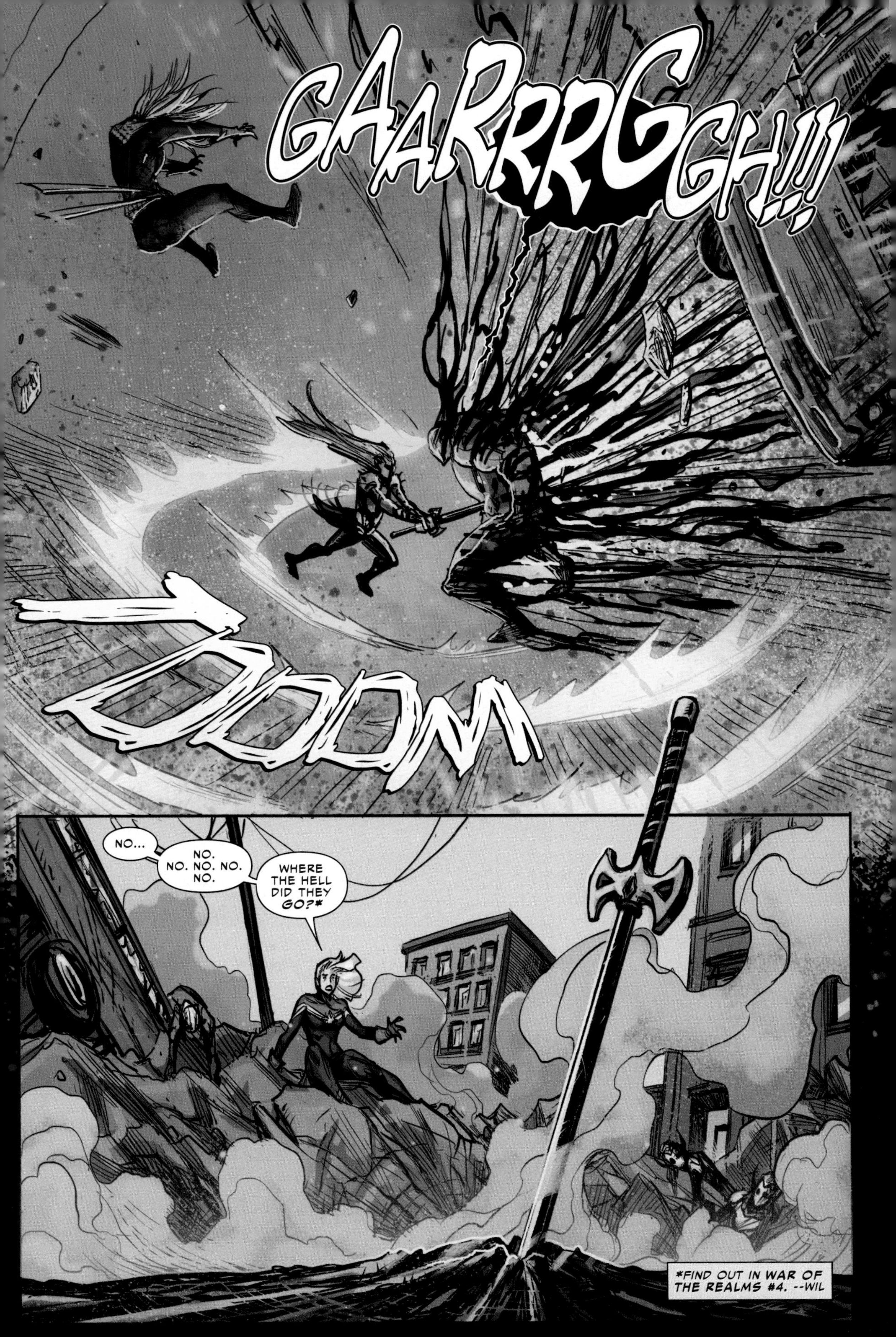

GAARRRGGH!!!
TOOOM
NO...
NO.
NO. NO. NO.
NO.
WHERE THE HELL DID THEY GO?*
*FIND OUT IN WAR OF THE REALMS #4. --WIL

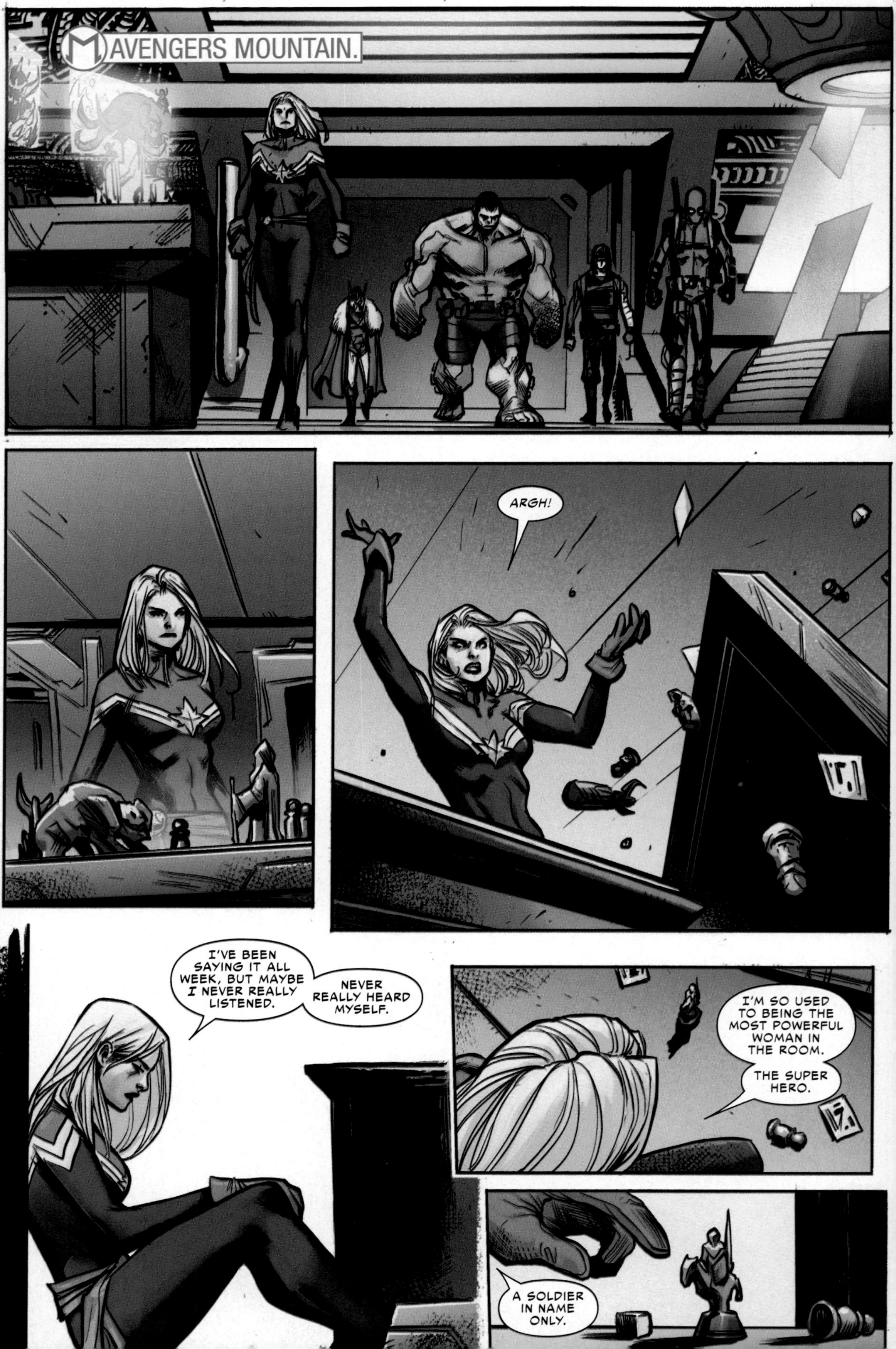
AVENGERS MOUNTAIN.
ARGH!
I'VE BEEN SAYING IT ALL WEEK, BUT MAYBE I NEVER REALLY LISTENED.
NEVER REALLY HEARD MYSELF.
I'M SO USED TO BEING THE MOST POWERFUL WOMAN IN THE ROOM.
THE SUPER HERO.
A SOLDIER IN NAME ONLY.

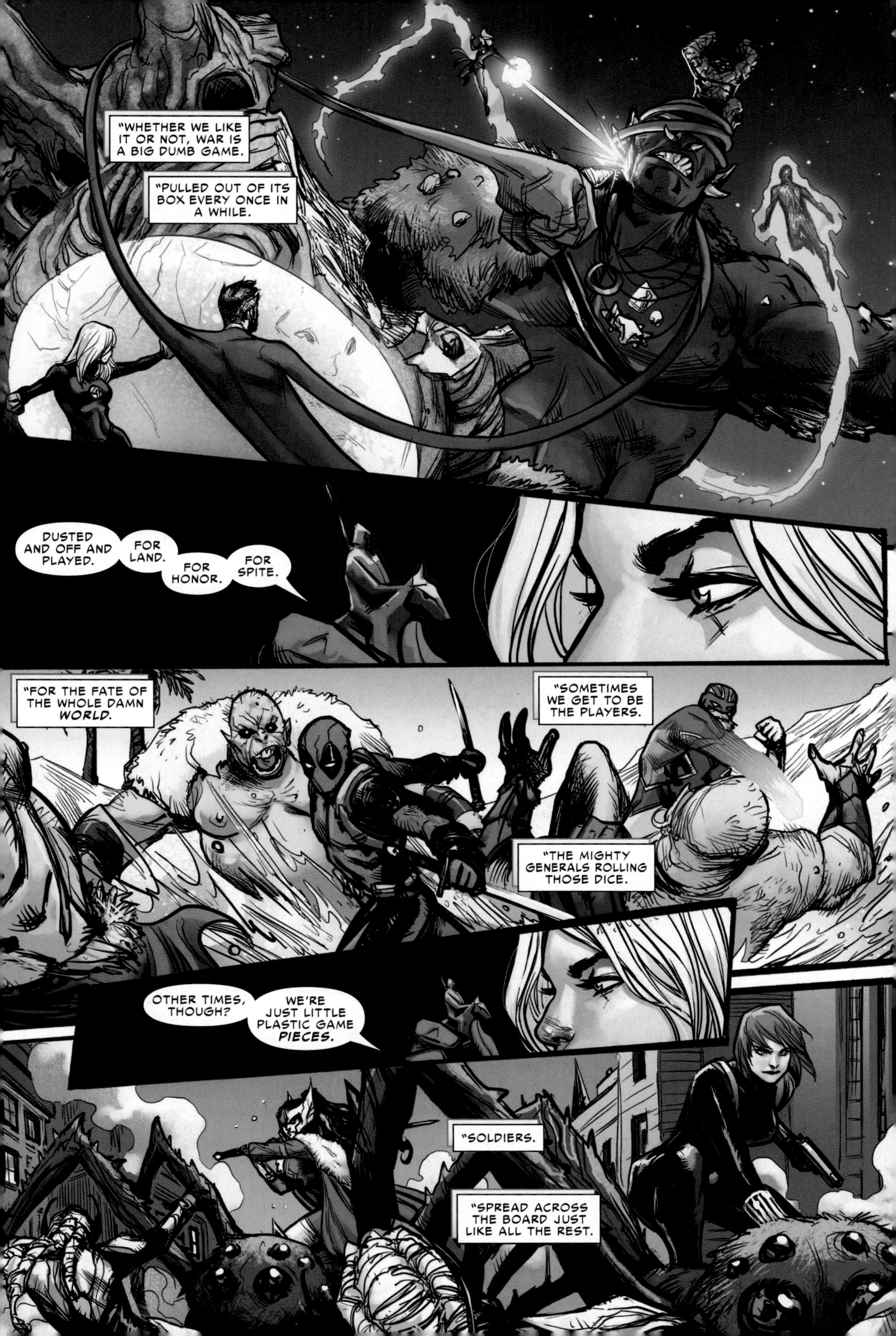
"WHETHER WE LIKE IT OR NOT, WAR IS A BIG DUMB GAME.
"PULLED OUT OF ITS BOX EVERY ONCE IN A WHILE.
DUSTED AND OFF AND PLAYED.
FOR LAND.
FOR HONOR.
FOR SPITE.
"FOR THE FATE OF THE WHOLE DAMN WORLD.
"SOMETIMES WE GET TO BE THE PLAYERS.
"THE MIGHTY GENERALS ROLLING THOSE DICE.
OTHER TIMES, THOUGH?
WE'RE JUST LITTLE PLASTIC GAME PIECES.
"SOLDIERS.
"SPREAD ACROSS THE BOARD JUST LIKE ALL THE REST.

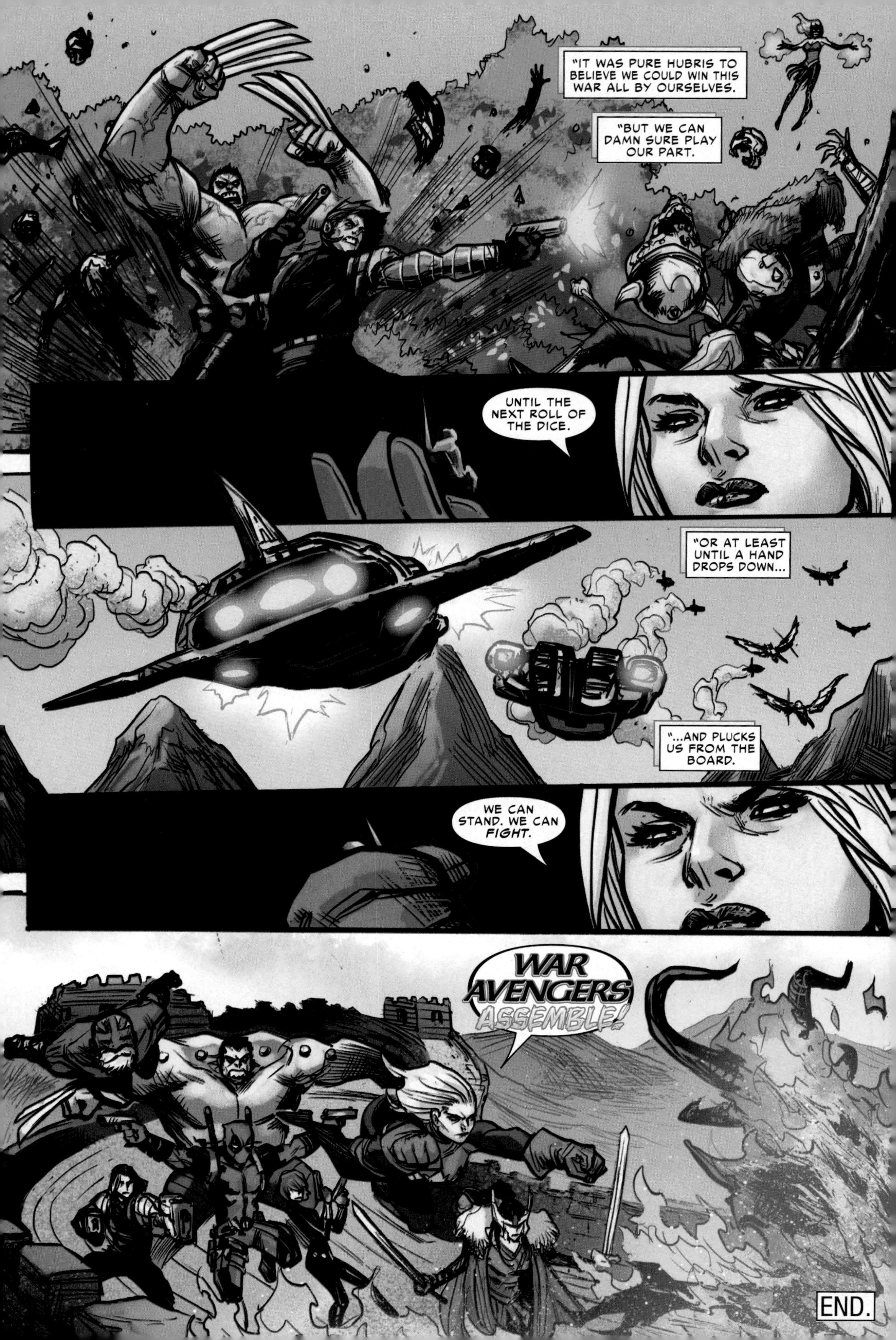
"IT WAS PURE HUBRIS TO BELIEVE WE COULD WIN THIS WAR ALL BY OURSELVES.
"BUT WE CAN DAMN SURE PLAY OUR PART.
UNTIL THE NEXT ROLL OF THE DICE.
"OR AT LEAST UNTIL A HAND DROPS DOWN...
"...AND PLUCKS US FROM THE BOARD.
WE CAN STAND. WE CAN *FIGHT*.
WAR AVENGERS ASSEMBLE!
END.

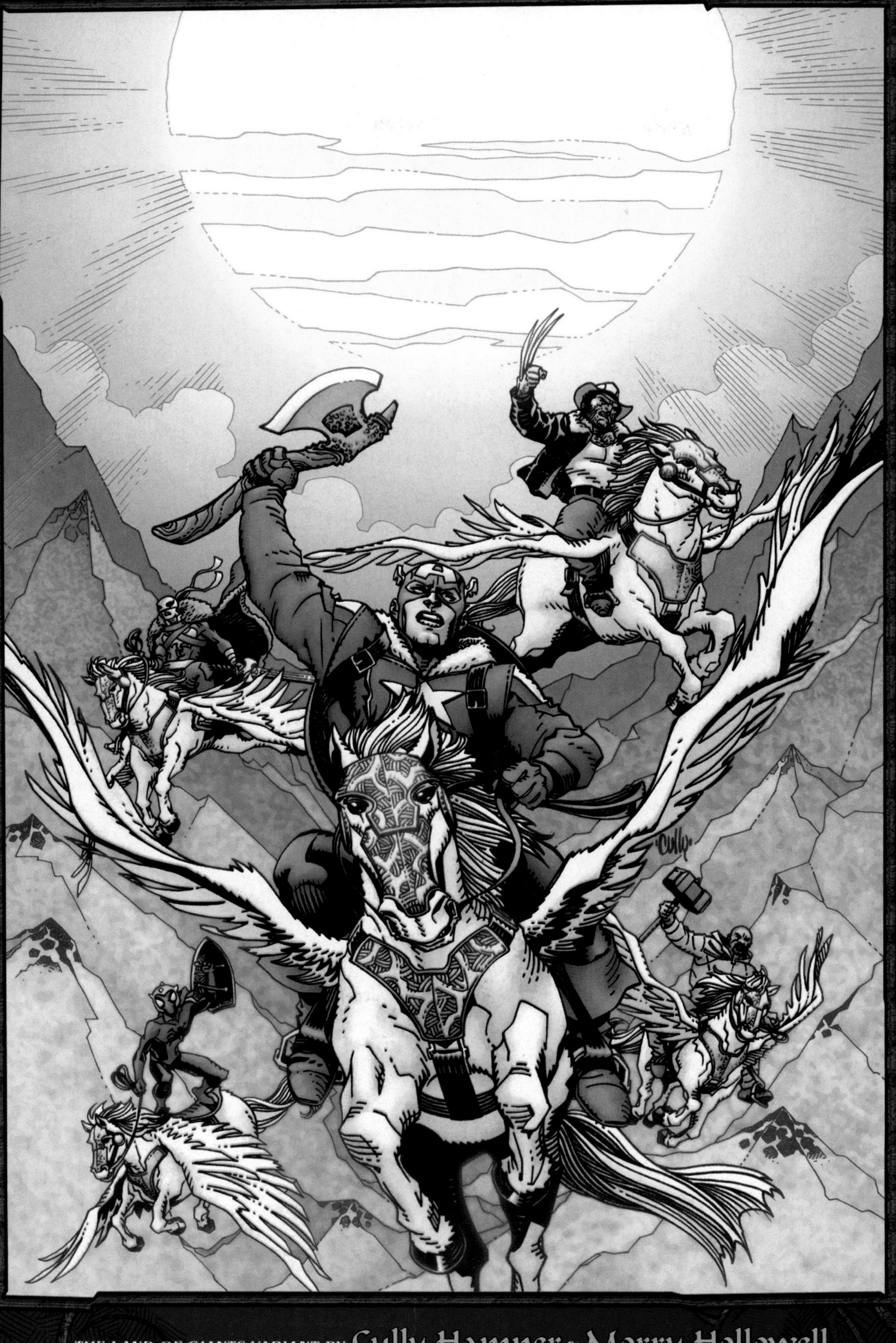

THE LAND OF GIANTS VARIANT BY Cully Hamner & Morry Hollowell

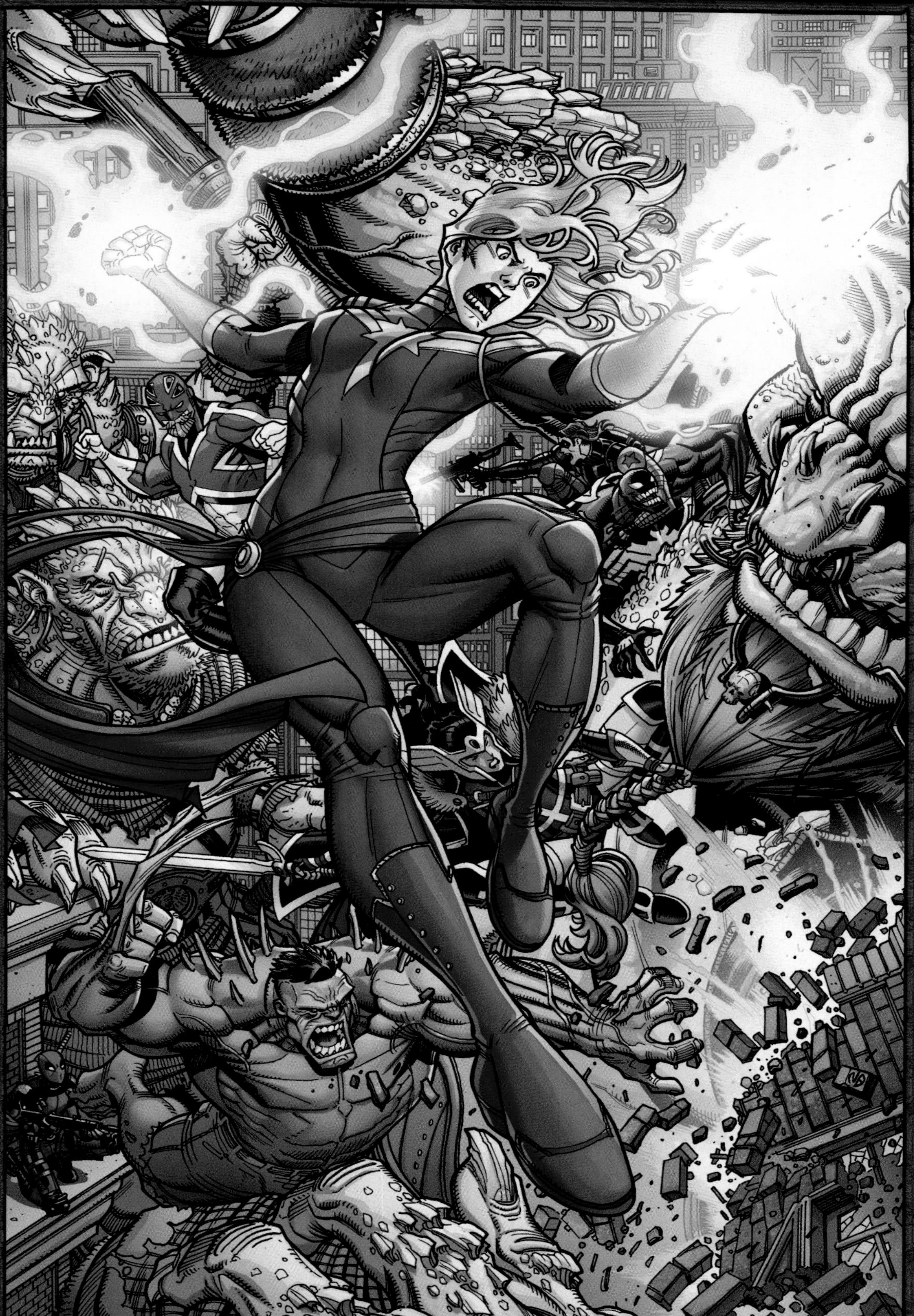

THE WAR AVENGERS VARIANT BY Nick Bradshaw & Laura Martin

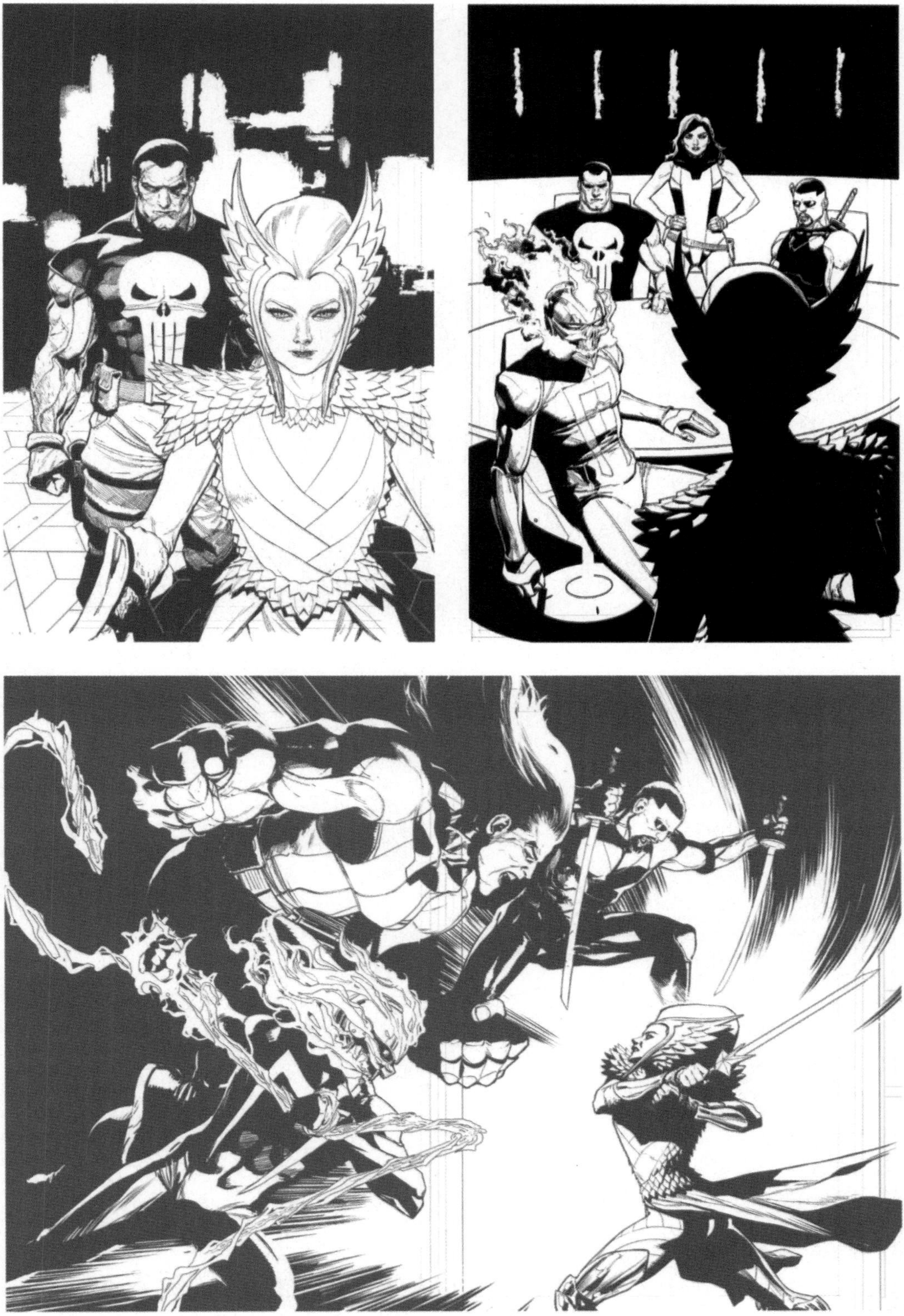

THE DARK ELF REALM PAGES 2, 5 & 18-19 PENCILS BY Leinil Francis Yu

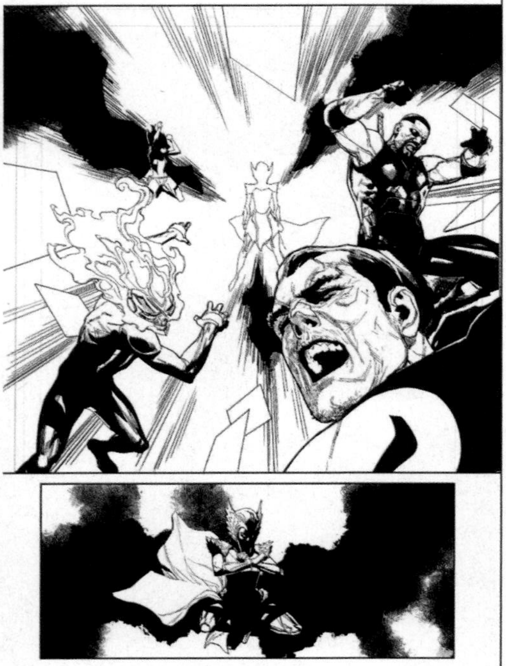

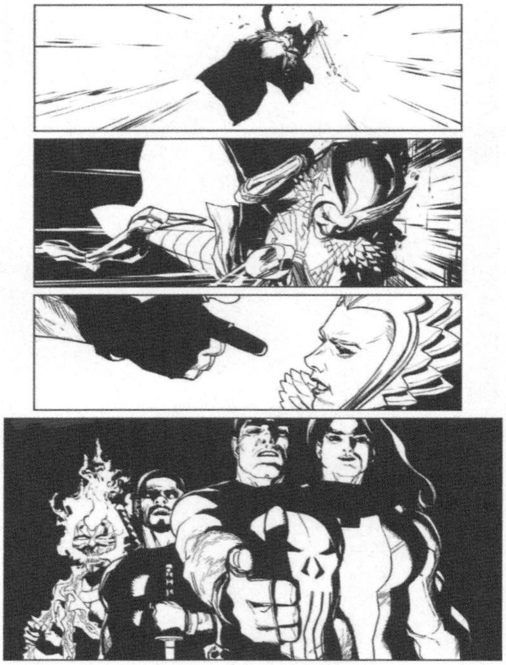

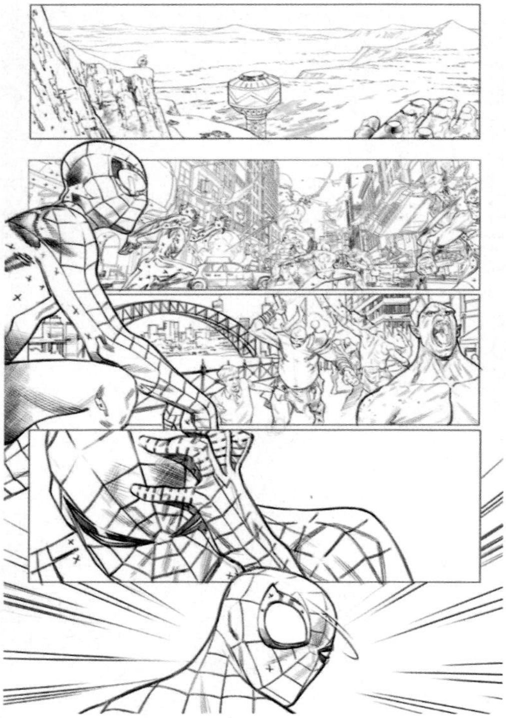

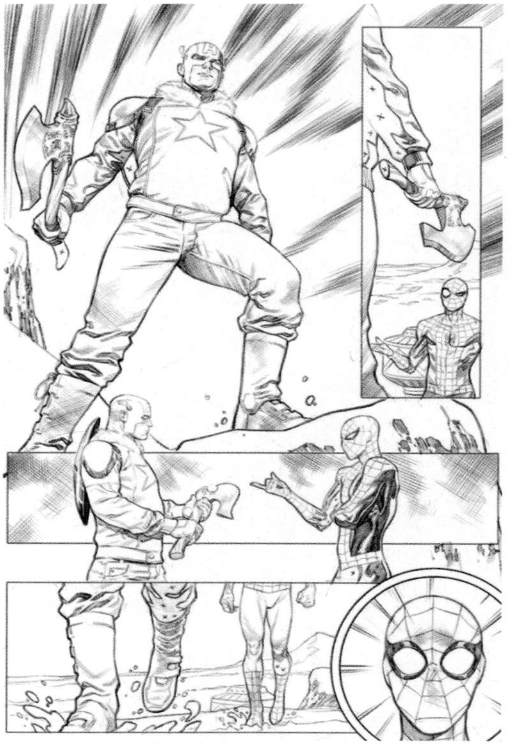

THE DARK ELF REALM PAGES 9 & 20 PENCILS BY Leinil Francis Yu
THE LAND OF GIANTS PAGES 1-2 PENCILS BY Jorge Molina

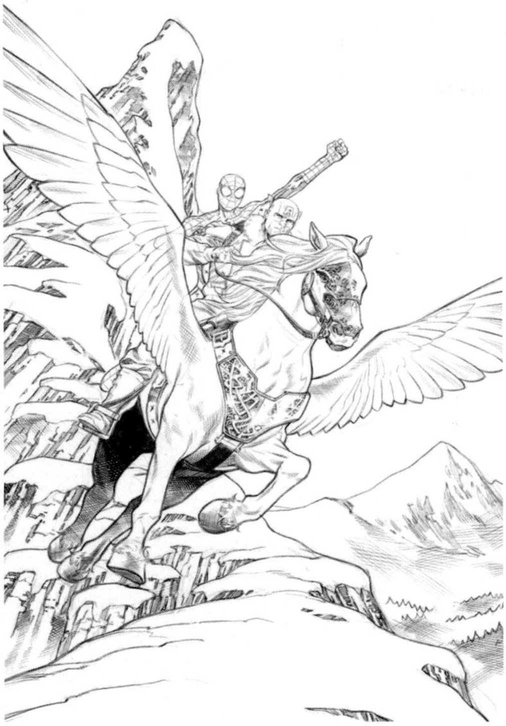

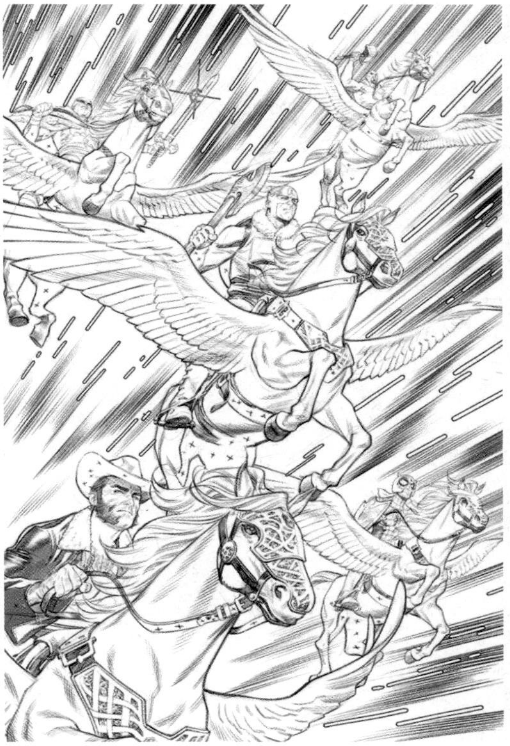

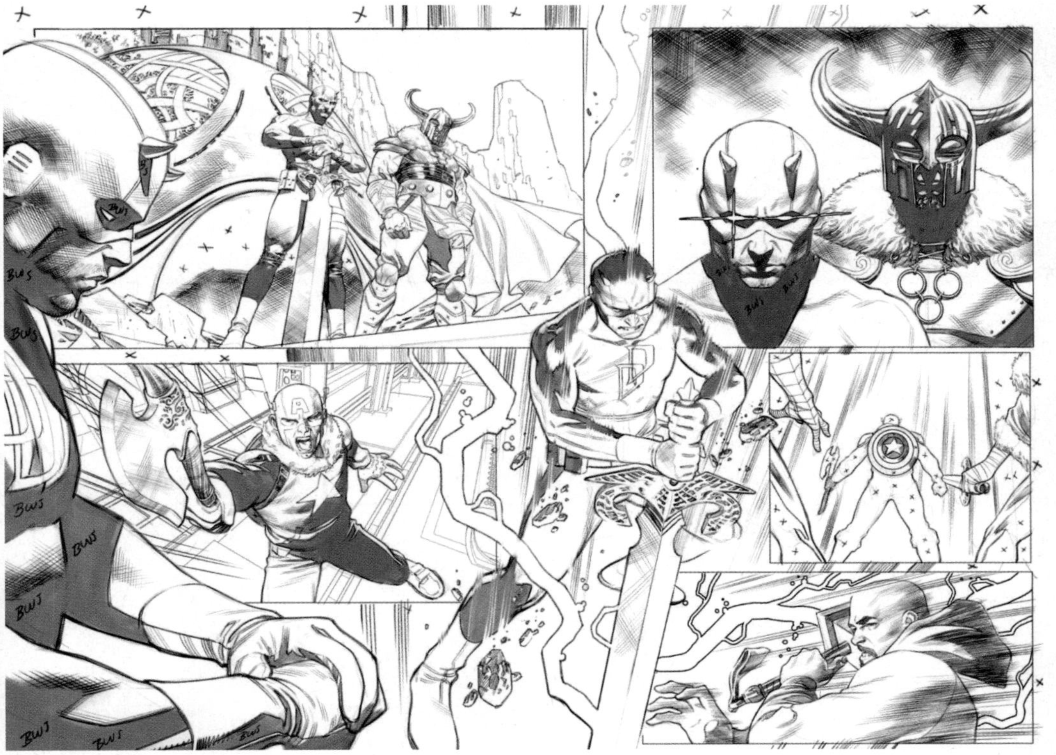

THE LAND OF GIANTS PAGES 4, 8-9 & 10 PENCILS BY Jorge Molina

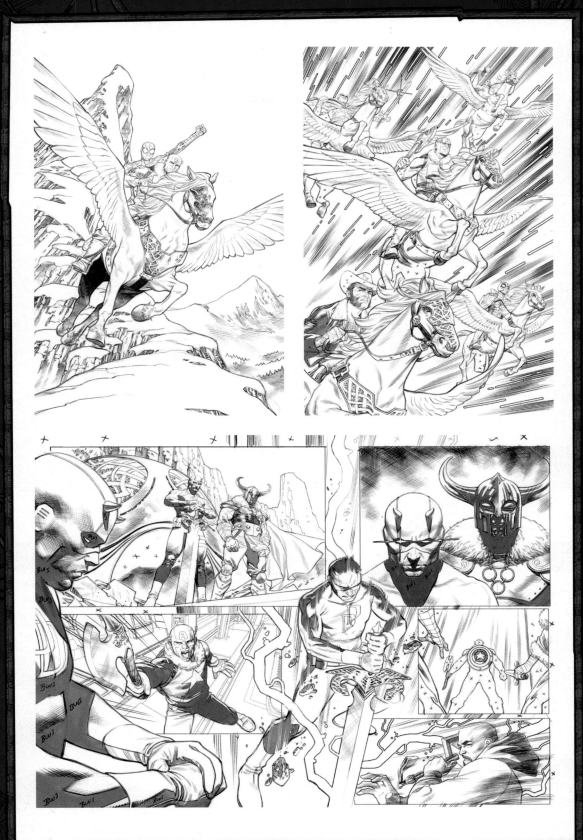

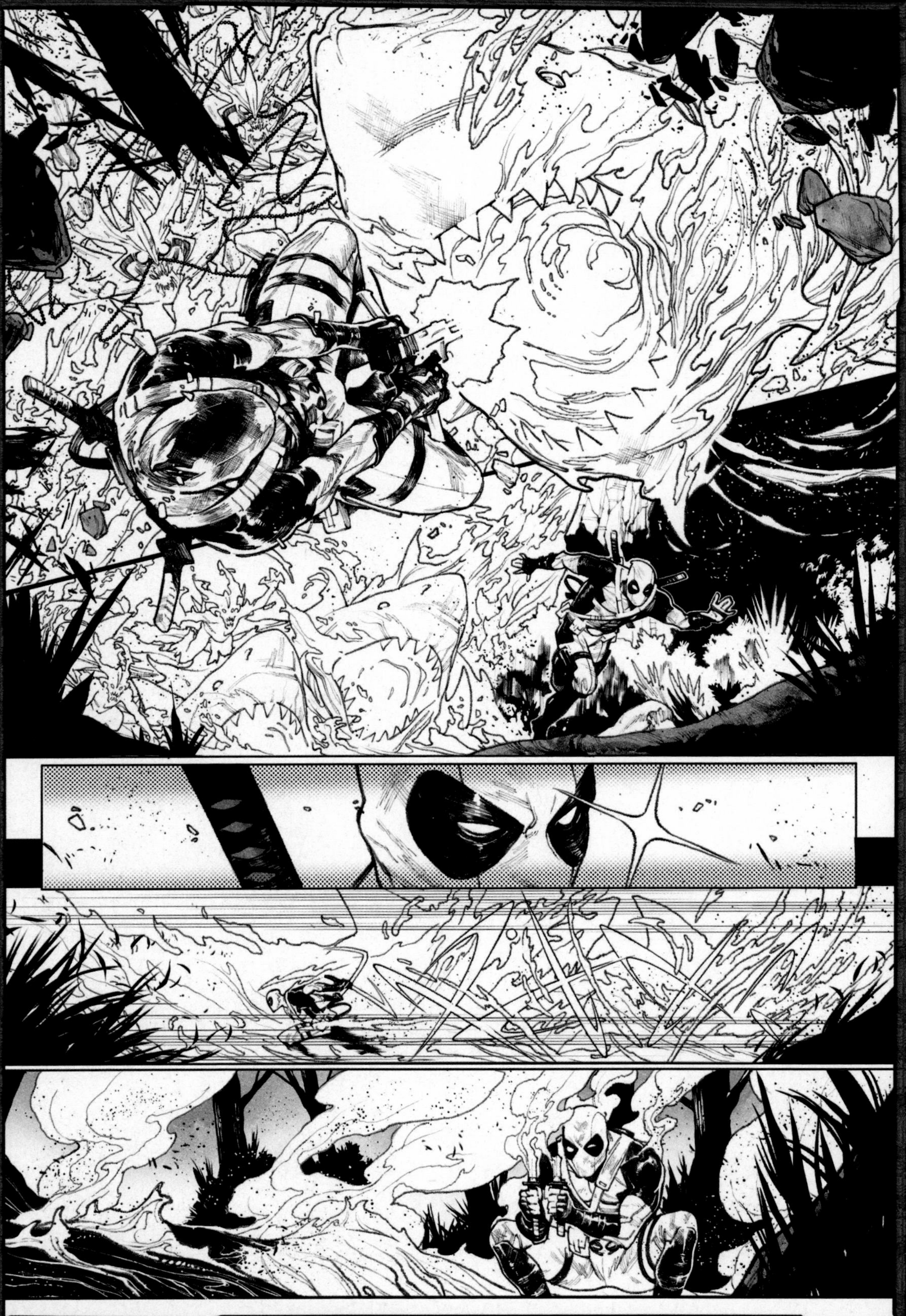

THE WAR AVENGERS PAGE 1 ART BY Kim Jacinto

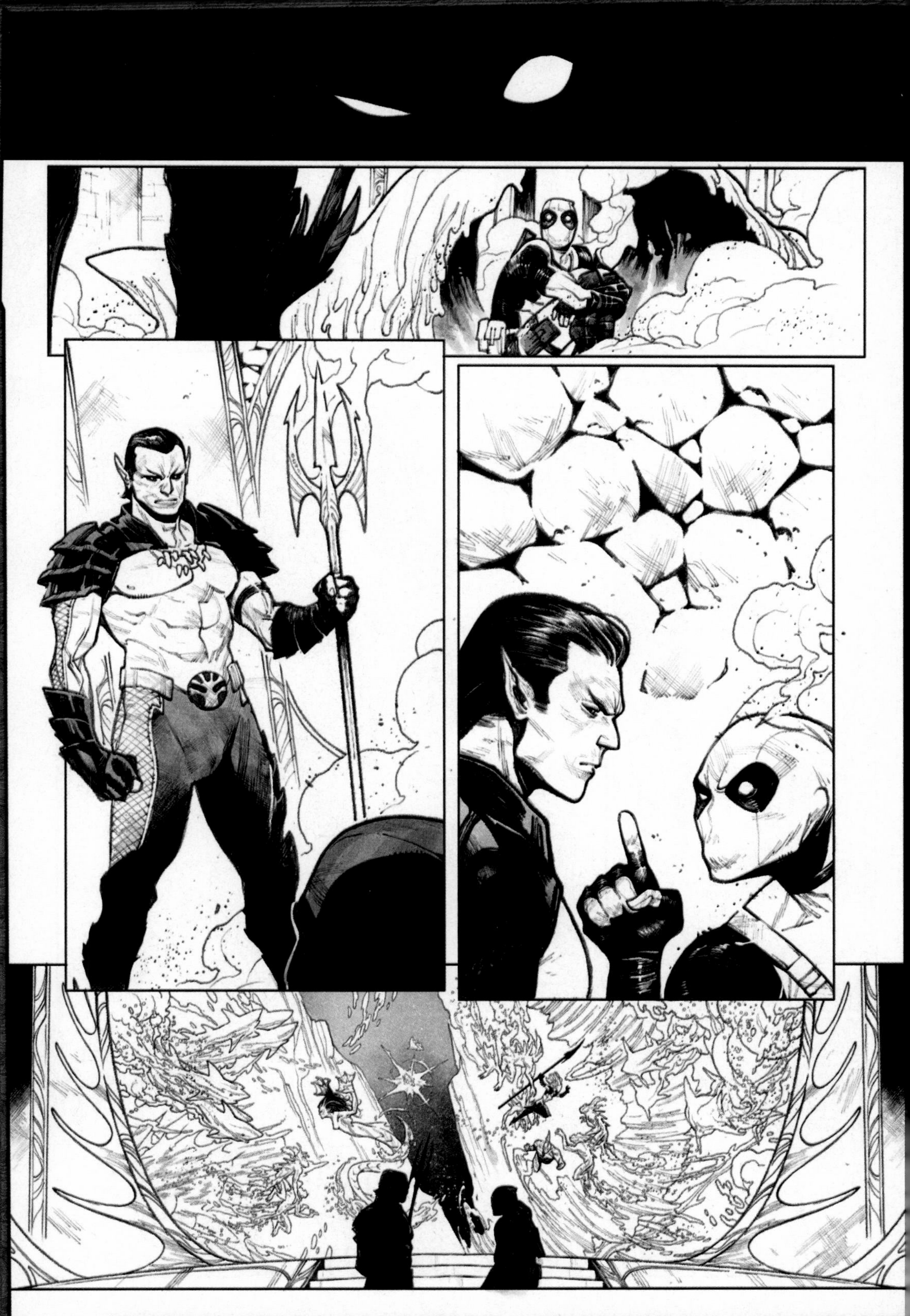

THE WAR AVENGERS PAGE 4 ART BY Kim Jacinto

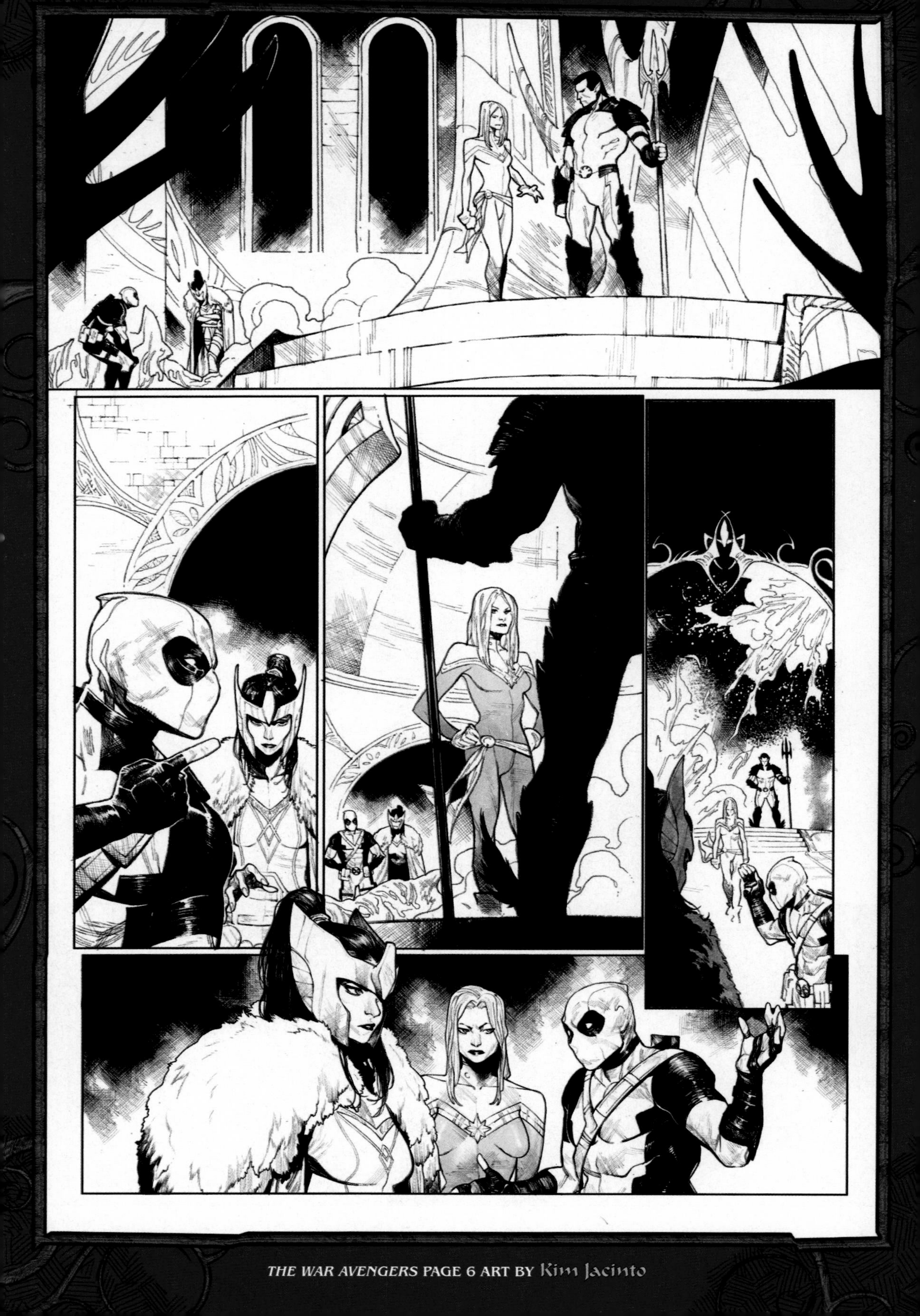

THE WAR AVENGERS PAGE 6 ART BY Kim Jacinto

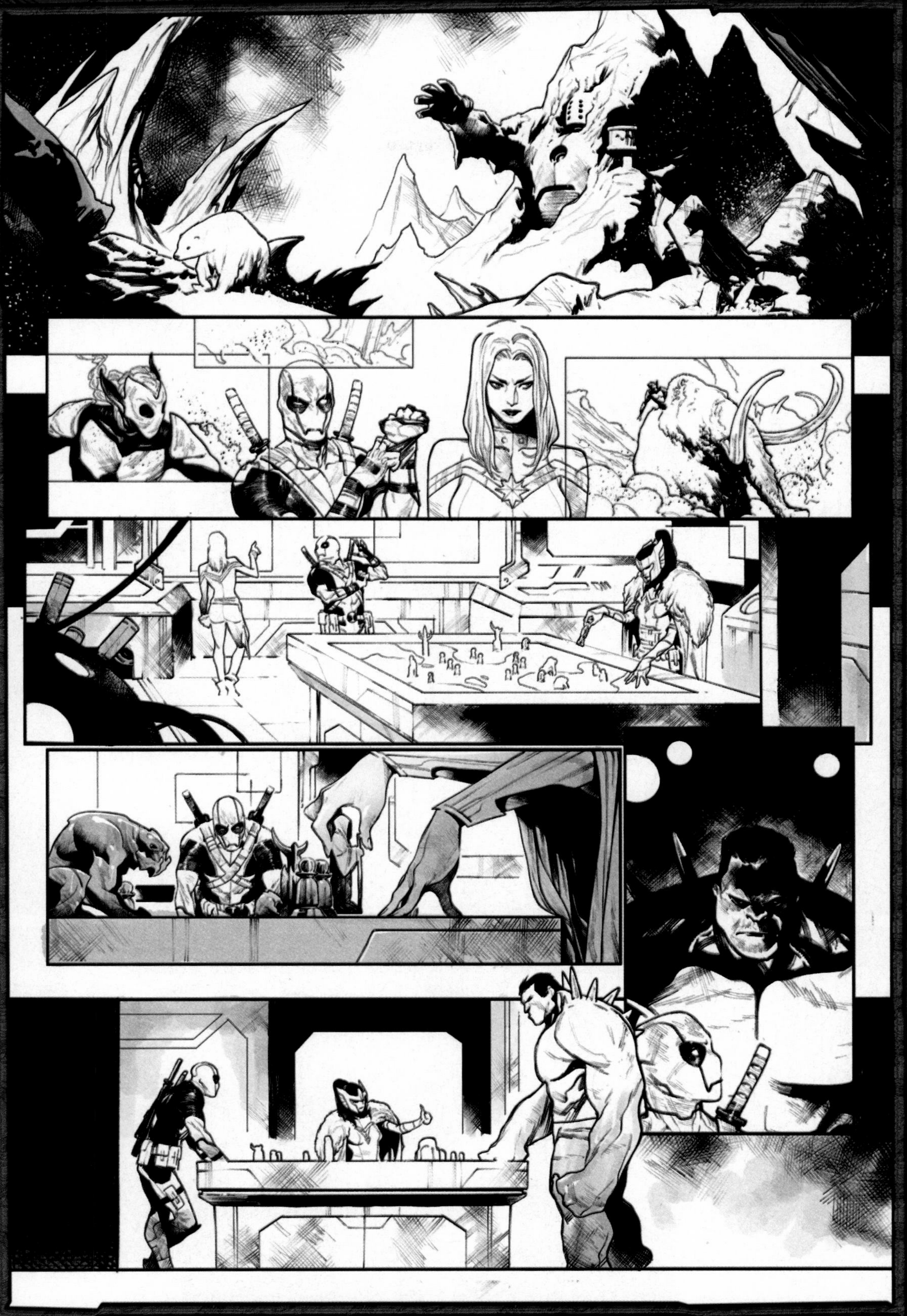

THE WAR AVENGERS PAGE 7 ART BY Kim Jacinto

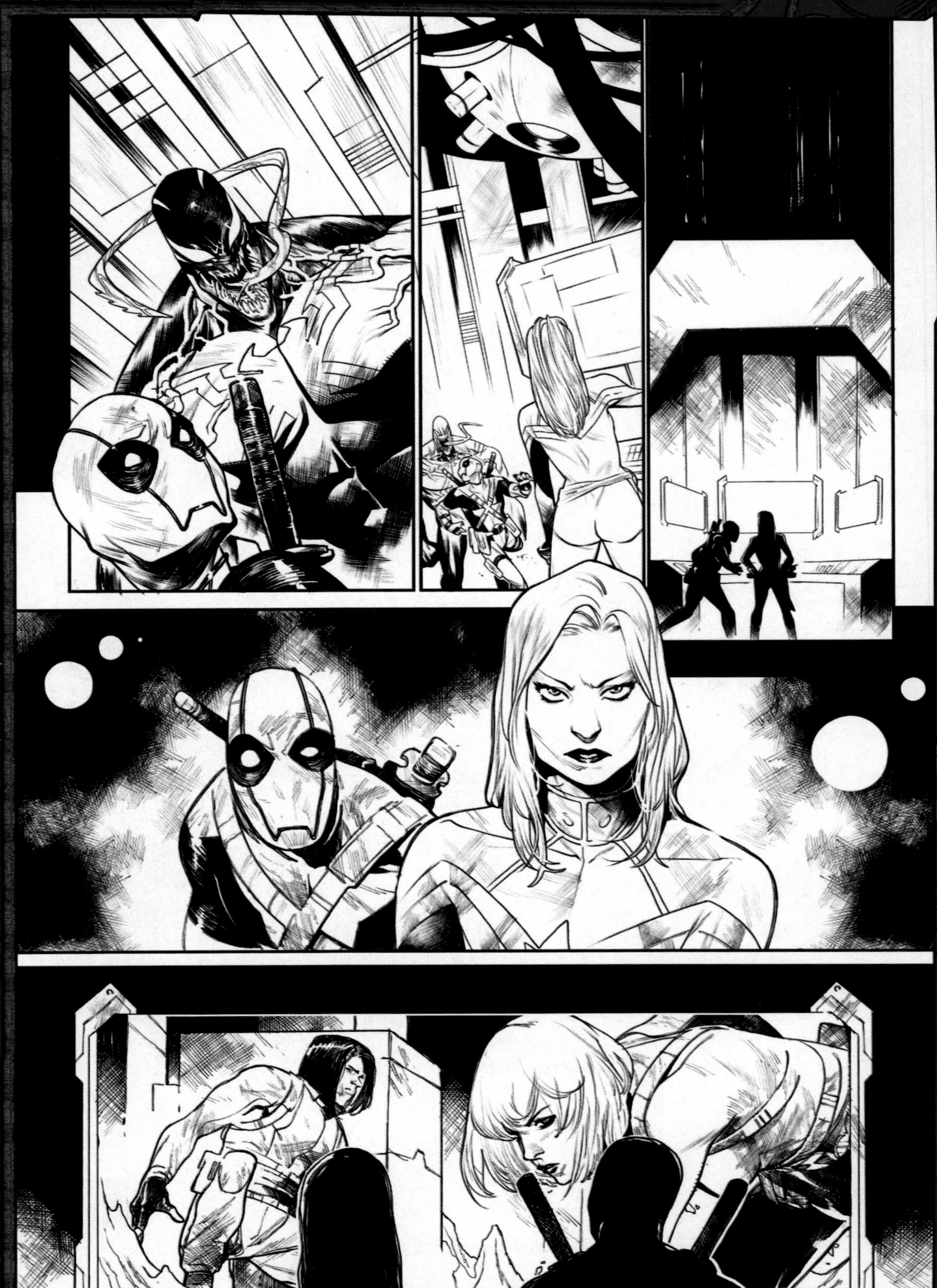

THE WAR AVENGERS PAGE 8 ART BY Kim Jacinto

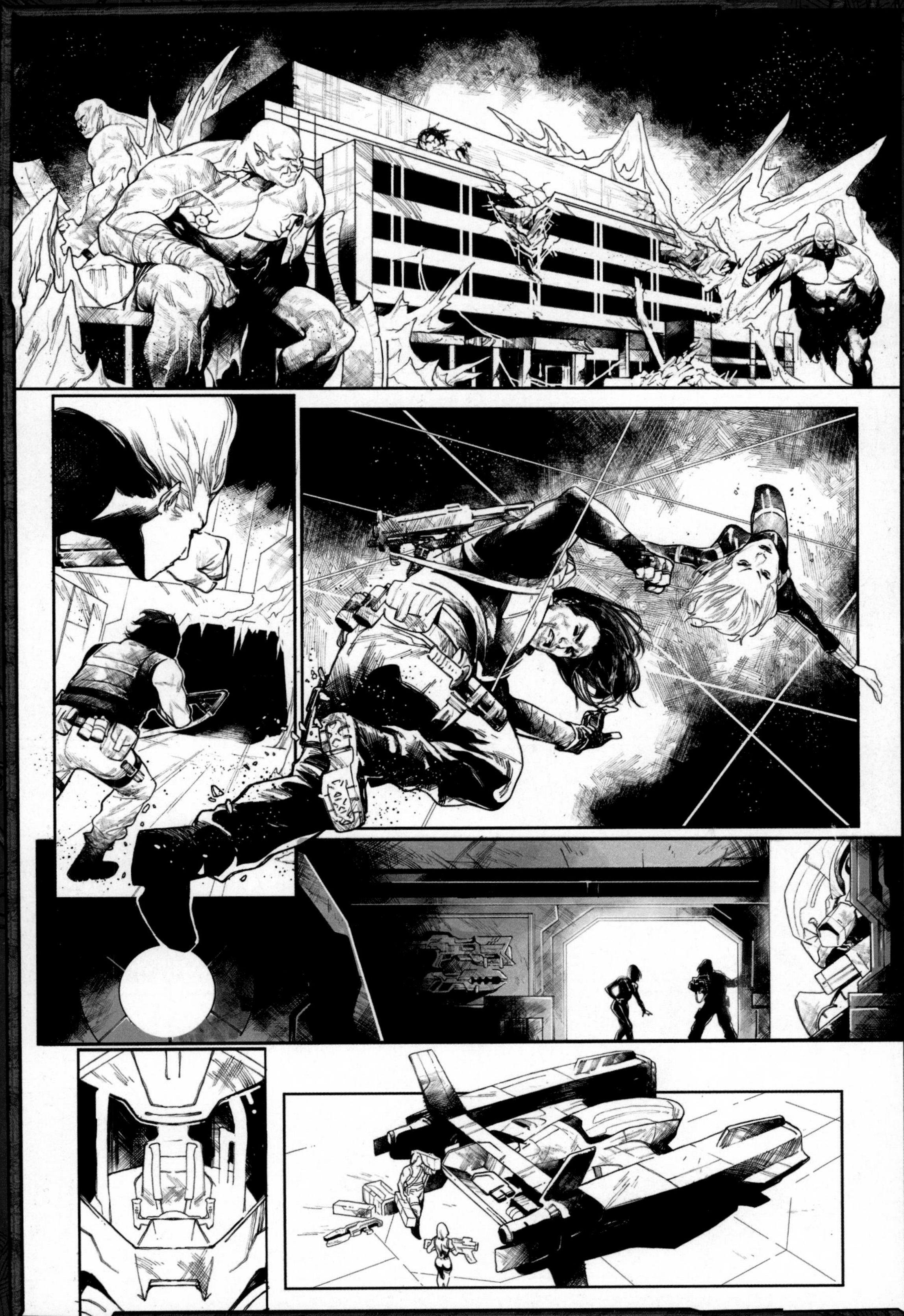

THE WAR AVENGERS PAGE 9 ART BY Kim Jacinto

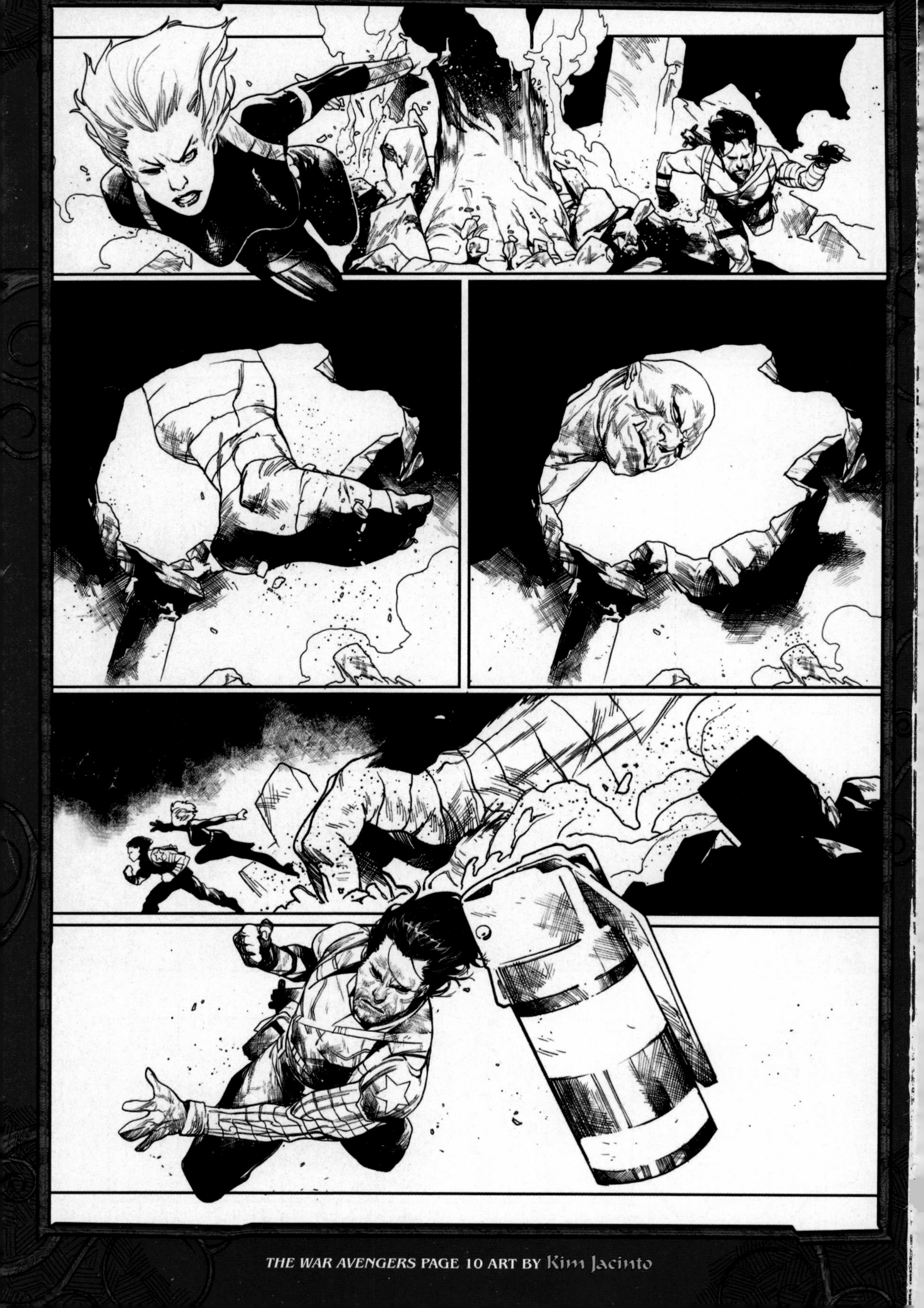

THE WAR AVENGERS PAGE 10 ART BY Kim Jacinto